White Belongings

White Belongings

Race, Land, and Property in Post-Apartheid South Africa

Scott Burnett

LEXINGTON BOOKS
Lanham • Boulder • New York • London

Published by Lexington Books
An imprint of The Rowman & Littlefield Publishing Group, Inc.
4501 Forbes Boulevard, Suite 200, Lanham, Maryland 20706
www.rowman.com

86-90 Paul Street, London EC2A 4NE

British Library Cataloguing in Publication Information Available

Library of Congress Cataloging-in-Publication Data

Names: Burnett, Scott, 1978- author.
Title: White belongings : race, land, and property in post-apartheid South Africa / Scott Burnett.
Description: Lanham : Lexington Books, 2022. | Includes bibliographical references and index. | Summary: "White Belongings critically deconstructs everyday white discourses of the land in South Africa at a time of increasing stridency and defensiveness over restitution and reform, showing how articulating environmental stewardship and belonging are interwoven with asserting ownership and control"-- Provided by publisher.
Identifiers: LCCN 2022015517 (print) | LCCN 2022015518 (ebook) | ISBN 9781793654946 (cloth) | ISBN 9781793654960 (paperback) | ISBN 9781793654953 (epub)
Subjects: LCSH: Land reform--South Africa. | White people--Land tenure--South Africa. | Land tenure--South Africa. | South Africa--Race relations.
Classification: LCC HD1333.S6 B86 2022 (print) | LCC HD1333.S6 (ebook) | DDC 333.3168--dc23/eng/20220405
LC record available at https://lccn.loc.gov/2022015517
LC ebook record available at https://lccn.loc.gov/2022015518

For Tommaso
Jag älskar dig—men orden räcker inte till

Contents

List of Figures

Acknowledgements

This book has been a long time in the making, and there are many people to whom I owe my gratitude for its completion. Getting my foot in the door of the academy in the first place was thanks to my PhD supervisor Melissa Steyn, who generously welcomed me into the Wits Centre for Diversity Studies (WiCDS) in Johannesburg, where she allocated funding from the South African National Research Foundation to make my work possible. Melissa is not only a groundbreaking scholar, but also the facilitator of a vibrant intellectual environment where young academics engage with and challenge each other. I am thankful for the conversations I have had with students and colleagues at WiCDS, among whom I would like to thank especially Haley McEwen, William Mpofu, and Nceba Ndzwayiba.

I was a late starter as an academic, after many years as a member of the loveLife HIV-prevention and youth development campaign. At loveLife I worked with people from every part of the country, and from every social background, in ways most middle-class whites never do. The grotesque unfairness of the structure of our society, and the obviousness of the fact that it really does not need to be like this, is something I learned from the outstanding loveLife groundBREAKERS and mpintshis I had the privilege of meeting. I am profoundly grateful to them for teaching me about the real South Africa.

The years it took to write this book have been some of the most momentous in South Africa's post-apartheid history, and also in mine. On my reentry into the world of the university I was inspired by the moral clarity and activist brilliance of the Rhodes Must Fall and Fees Must Fall movements, which tried (and sometimes succeeded) to rouse academics and politicians from their dogmatic slumbers. Then, in 2017, midway through my PhD, I moved from Johannesburg to Gothenburg in Sweden. This move was not because of any desire on my part to heap critique on South Africans while sitting comfortably in Scandinavia (a theme frequently taken up by white people who shout at me on Twitter) but simply to live with the man I love. This academic adventure has been made significantly more pleasant by the support and openness of critical academics who are able to see the futility of refusing to speak the "race-word" in a country that likes to avoid confrontations with its own racist and colonial history. I owe a special thanks in this regard to Malin Ideland, Rickard Jonsson, Johan Järlehed, and Lena Martinsson for inviting me to present my work for this book at research seminars. I learned a great deal from the VitKrit research network at the University of Gothenburg, headed up by Therese Svensson, who helped me to connect with a critical research community and a good yoga class. I am also thankful for the rich feedback I got on some of the arguments I make in this book at a seminar I gave in a series coordinated by the South African critical political ecologist Vasna Ramasar at Lund University's Pufendorf Centre. I would also like to thank Eusebius McKaiser back home in Johannesburg, who has been a crucial intellectual influence in my life for nearly twenty-four years, and provided insightful and useful feedback on my analysis in chapter 5. The team at Lexington Books was supportive and positive throughout the project; and I would like to thank the anonymous reviewer, whose feedback was very useful in sharpening the argument. Finally, I convey my sincere appreciation to colleagues at the department of strategic communication at Lund University, especially Jörgen Eksell, for the excellent introduction he gave me to working life as a lecturer, and also my present colleagues at the department of applied information technology at the University of Gothenburg for the time and encouragement they have given me to complete this book.

I am lucky to have had the constant support of my family throughout this process. My mom and dad, Rose and Neil, are the moral pillars around which my life is structured, and I owe them everything. My father-in-law Carlo has supported this book in many ways, including by plying me with wine and food and insisting (against much protest) that it would be a work of genius and sell a million copies. My biggest debt of gratitude however goes to my husband, Tommaso Milani, who has read and reread drafts of all parts of this book over a period of years, told me countless times to cut down on the waffle, provided comprehensive and pedagogical commentary, tirelessly debated discourse theory with me, and opened up his personal and professional networks to guide me into conferences, publication, and presentation opportunities around the world. It is no exaggeration to say that without him there would be no book, and I joyfully dedicate it to you, Tommaso, the love of my life. I have only one thing I can take all the credit for, and that is the faults, which remain mine.

Introduction

Rhodes's Soul

Until the wildfires of July 2021, the monument to Cecil John Rhodes standing high on the slopes of Devil's Peak in Cape Town was a sedate tourist attraction, with picturesque views and a popular restaurant. Designed to resemble a neoclassical temple, the memorial has an open-air sanctuary at its centre, with a bust in bronze of the mining magnate and former prime minister of the Cape Colony depicted in the pose of a daydreamer, his head resting against his hand, eyes gazing deeply into the African interior. The hallowed calm of the pillared structure, a few kilometres from the bay where European settlement gained its first foothold in southern Africa, has been broken a number of times since it was completed in 1912, a decade after Rhodes's death. Following generations of graffiti by students from the university campus below, the statue's nose was removed with an angle grinder during Rhodes Must Fall protest action in 2015. In 2020, its head was hacked off (Figure 0.1).

Still visible on the plinth below the remnants of the bust are four lines from Rudyard Kipling's elegy on the occasion of Rhodes's burial:

> The immense and brooding spirit still
> Shall quicken and control
> Living he was the land, and dead,
> His soul shall be her soul!

Though the statue no longer glares over the land, Kipling's prediction that Rhodes's soul would continue to "quicken and control" long after he was dead is borne out in the spatial and social relations the monument surveys. The rolling vineyards of Somerset West and Stellenbosch against the blue-grey mountains in the distance are in stark contrast to the lines of densely packed shacks and matchbox houses of the Cape Flats below. Rhodes was an important architect of the racial order established through these spatial

Figure 0.1: Damage to J. M. Swann's bronze bust of Cecil John Rhodes, Rhodes Memorial, July 2020

arrangements who worked passionately to extend British domination over parts of the world "inhabited by the most despicable specimens of human beings" (Rhodes 1877). Black people were valued primarily as labour to be sent down hungry mines. That such a man should be immortalised, slouched and unflinching, in numerous statues and monuments so long after the official end of colonialism and apartheid, and with so little change to the country's racial hierarchy, is a powerful symbol of how South Africa's "elite transition" has failed to dismantle racial capitalism (Bond 1998). Rhodes was no great unifier of white South Africa; he was a loose cannon and a con man whose arrogance and greed sparked a war that is still cited as a reason for tensions between English- and Afrikaans-speaking whites. And yet he is often used as an avatar of a form of whiteness that has proved persistent; a white way of thinking about and imagining the land and its riches that frustrates the emergence of a truly "post-apartheid" nation (Figure 0.2). The symbolic order nurtured in the minds of white men like Rhodes, and the material relations built on the backs of Black labour, continue to haunt the land. Nearly thirty years into the "new" South Africa, many ask how Kipling's curse—"his soul shall be her soul"—might ever truly be lifted.

Figure 0.2: Graffito on the plinth of the statue of C. J. Rhodes on the Jameson Steps, University of Cape Town, 2008

This book focuses on whiteness in South Africa at a time of heightened anxiety and challenge attending the crescendo in calls for radical land reform and economic transformation to decisively end white domination and Black marginalization. Its overarching argument is that in this historical moment, a key premise of South African non-racialism is starkly revealed: that *white belonging on the land* is articulated as dependent upon *the land belonging to white people*. While white South Africans abandoned in 1994 any recourse to the idea of the nation itself as a "white possession" (Moreton-Robinson 2015) their entitlement to the lion's share of the land and the economy has yet to face significant reversals in the new order (Mpofu-Walsh 2021). Given the depth of racial inequality, this entitlement needs to be constantly defended and repaired. Discursively, whites both mourn the "loss" of the home they knew (Steyn 2001b, 156) and work to root themselves deeper within specific territorial enclaves (van der Westhuizen 2016; Ballard 2004). The cultural work required to do this may be interpreted diachronically, against an imperial history. European colonialism was as much an imaginative as a material project, and the symbolic played a key role in sustaining, justifying, and reproducing the material asymmetries of the social order. While the advance of racial capitalism absorbed vast territories into the global economic system, the actual conquest of lives and lands was facilitated by administrators and settlers who had to take risks and suffer privations in the name of an imperial dream. As Edward Said argues, novelists and explorers played their part in stoking the ambitions and imaginations of the metropole, weaving romantic accounts of "settling on, controlling land that you do not possess, that is distant, that is lived on and owned by others" (Said [1994] 2014, 5). Storytelling was a key discursive strategy that sustained the colonial imaginary as a system of possibilities; it also conveyed a moral orientation, a justificatory logic that cleansed the settler conscience:

> The main battle in imperialism is over land, of course; but when it came to who owned the land, who had the right to settle and work on it, who kept it going, who won it back, and who now plans its future—these issues were reflected, contested, and even for a time decided in narrative. ([1994] 2014, xiii)

This book seeks to trace the afterlives of these old stories and their justificatory logics, as well as their mutation and reinvention, in everyday South African discourse, a context in which the majority of the population, descendants of colonised, enslaved, indentured, and otherwise dispossessed and historically racialised people share a minority stake in the economy. What is it that limits the national imagination to retracing the conditions for injustice, over and over again, in seeming perpetuity? Why has it proven so difficult to exorcise Rhodes's ghost? And might it be possible to identify the elements of a more egalitarian future through analysis of the discourse regimes that structure the status quo?

These questions have vexed a diverse array of scholars and commentators, whose distinct approaches offer their own insights. Sizwe Mpofu-Walsh (2021) argues for example that the officially sanctioned horizon of the country's social vision as outlined in key texts such as the Preamble to the Constitution has foreclosed radical and emancipatory alternatives, enabling apartheid to survive in privatized, denationalized, internalized forms. My approach here is to examine more mundane texts, where social groups make meaning and engage in discursive struggle through traditional and social media. I focus to a large extent on how white South Africans continue to exploit their considerable economic and cultural power to produce their belonging on the land and the land as belonging to them on a vast scale, taking in whole landscapes, and perpetuating the idea that their continued control of the countryside serves the interests of all social groups. Challenges to the established order are represented as misguided foolishness at best, or at worst part of a mendacious vendetta that will see South Africa go "to the dogs." While these discursive acts may be energised by racist intentions, the search for the ill will of prejudice is less urgent than understanding the extent to which a white imaginary delimits what can reasonably be thought, said, or done in contemporary South Africa. To put the point plainly, commonsense discourses of the land are in a constant battle to make white dispossession *unthinkable* within a stable social order, to relegate the decisive transformation of society to an indefinitely postponed fantasy time in the future, and to dismiss proposed paths to it as dangerously irrational.

WHITENESS IN SOUTH AFRICA

This book's focus on the discursive strategies of European settlers and their descendants to establish, legitimate, and defend an entitlement to the land—to root themselves in it, to take it as their property, to carve it up into farms and towns and nature reserves, and to lay claim to its future—aims to contribute to ongoing critical discursive work on race, racism and whiteness in South Africa and elsewhere. These terms are distinct but interdependent. Racism picks out how symbolic and material value is moved "up" an imagined racial hierarchy, towards the category at its apex, whiteness (Hill 2008, 158). Racism produces and exploits group-specific vulnerabilities to premature death (Gilmore 2002, 16). The particular relation between whiteness and racism was borne of the invention of race as a European power-knowledge regime, which spread globally and was institutionally fortified as a technology of control to enable slavery and imperialism. The profits of these historical processes continue to flow to white Western metropoles (Hickel 2021). Whiteness is quite simply "the category [that] race was installed to establish, defend, and maintain" (Lentin 2020, 178). Critical interrogation of whiteness has thus been an important project in anti-racist research, albeit one rife with pitfalls, some of which will be discussed in chapter 1. In the United States, what came to be known as "critical whiteness studies" has been divided into three "waves" (Twine and Gallagher 2008): the first associated with W. E. B. Du Bois in the early twentieth century, the second developing in conversation with feminist and Marxist theory in the 1980s and 1990s, and the third signaled by increasing interdisciplinarity in the pursuit of whiteness-critical research in international contexts in the first decade of the twenty-first century.

This US-centric periodization might however obscure alternative genealogies for South African whiteness studies. It is arguably in Steve Biko's Black Consciousness Movement (BCM) which in turn was inspired by the work of Frantz Fanon and other decolonial intellectuals (Ranuga 1986) that a critical sociological and psychological approach to South African whiteness has its intellectual fountainhead (Hook 2011). This is an important recognition; if whiteness studies is to address the racist world system as a whole it must start with "Black critique of how whiteness works as a form of racial privilege"

(Ahmed 2004a; see also Falkof 2015, 6). Biko's insistence in the 1970s that white liberals who opposed apartheid were part of the same "homogeneous" (Biko [1978] 2006, 19) community as committed racists by virtue of their access to a category of racial privilege they were all too comfortably wrapped up in has been taken up repeatedly by later scholars. Melissa Steyn's *"Whiteness Just Isn't What It Used To Be"* (2001b) which was based on fieldwork in early 1996, argued that while whites across the political spectrum were constructing new identity narratives in the wake of the falling apart of the "master narrative" of *baasskap* (white "boss-ship") the influential tendency of many "left-wing liberals" was to deemphasize their affiliation to the past system, and to profess the irrelevance of race in a self-serving display of "colour-blindness" (2001b, 153). These gestures of exculpation were core to carving out a post-apartheid subjectivity where whites are seen to be "good human beings, embracing values that make them decent members of a modern society" (Steyn and Foster 2008, 28). This made necessary their denial of reaping any ongoing benefits from racism, which had supposedly been decisively left in the past. Whites who had been part of progressive movements (such as the End Conscription Campaign) thus worked to "emphasize their agency in ending apartheid using discourses that are particularly brittle and hyper-vigilant to critique" (Conway 2017, 121). Because they understood themselves to be on the right side of history, and discursively produced their persecution by the apartheid state as similar to the suffering of Black South Africans, they expected to enjoy the fruits of liberation, and not find themselves the targets of calls for transformation. They combined a "disingenuous proclamation of support for the post-apartheid sociopolitical order with a simultaneous rejection of the very means by which such an order can really come to pass" (Conway 2017, 134). These discursive moves are hallmarks of the official opposition to the ruling African National Congress (ANC), the white-dominated Democratic Alliance (DA), which routinely foregrounds the role of white liberals in ending apartheid, and paints the Black government as having betrayed the ideals of liberation. They are also typical of sections of the liberal commentariat and of higher education, where many white academics who opposed apartheid played and continue to play a reactionary role in the transformation of universities (Statman and Ansell 2000; Conway 2017; Ndlovu-Gatsheni 2018).

The contribution of *White Belongings* to this ongoing critical project is its theorization of South African whiteness as a discourse regime intimately connected to the institutions of property and nature conservation, and to the subject positions of land stewards and white indigenes in intimate communion with the land, their "soul country." In the remainder of this introduction, I will sketch some of the material, historical, and conceptual context for the argument. First, I will characterize postcolonial land reform in South Africa as a problem in search of a culpable agent. I will then dig a bit deeper into the philosophical roots of liberalism, drawing attention to the congenital coloniality of modern understandings of property. Finally, I will examine how space, property, and race have been historically co-constructed, before outlining the flow of the argument in the remainder of the book.

WHOSE PROBLEM IS LAND REFORM?

While the majority of private land in South Africa is held by the white minority, very few whites own much land. The 35,000 white commercial farmers who own 72% of agricultural land, for example, account for less than 1% of the white population, which numbers some 4.7-million (AgriSA 2017; Stats SA 2020b). Agriculture, in turn, contributes only 2,3% to gross domestic product (Stats SA 2020a). Any account of the racial order in South Africa that seeks to reduce persistent white supremacy to the economics of farm ownership will thus meet with difficulties. And yet *the land* is undoubtedly the basso continuo of radical and decolonial politics, and is frequently invoked as the basis for the broader cultural dominance of white interests and norms (Chigumadzi 2016). Along nearly every dimension of difference that it is possible to measure, white people are doing dramatically better than Black people, with the two other apartheid-era "population groups" ("Coloured" and "Indian") falling somewhere in between. The median annual expenditure of white households is over ten times that of Black households (Stats SA 2019, 27). Black people account for 80% of the employment active population (EAP) and yet occupy only 16% of top management jobs, while 65% of top managers are white, though they account for only 9% of the EAP (CEE 2021, 14). Depending on the definition, 63–73% of Black South Africans live in poverty, as do 37–48% of "Coloured" people, while the same can be said of only 6.9–11% of "Indian" people and only 0.9–1.8% of whites (Wilkinson 2016). The first twenty years of ANC rule in fact saw poverty levels among white people reduced by half, a greater relative reduction than any other population group (Cronje 2013). At the statistical level, Thabo Mbeki's description of South Africa as "two nations" in his famous 1998 parliamentary address thus seems as apposite today as it was then. While one nation is "white, relatively prosperous [and] has ready access to a developed economic, physical, educational, communication and other infrastructure," a "second and larger" nation is "black and poor [. . . living] under conditions of a grossly underdeveloped economic, physical, educational, communication and other infrastructure [. . . with] virtually no possibility to exercise what in reality amounts to a theoretical right to equal opportunity" (Mbeki 1998).

As democracy entered its second and then third decade, many Black people started to feel that they "were sold a lie: that the vote would resolve our country's fundamental problems, if we only had the patience to wait" (Mpofu-Walsh 2017, 4). This patience was secured conditionally in the early years of the post-apartheid era, which focused successfully on building the social imaginary for a multiracial nation, with Nelson Mandela's conciliatory gestures to white South Africans and Archbishop Desmond Tutu's invocation of the "Rainbow Nation" internationally lauded as ushering in a politics of hope. And yet with next-to-no broad structural change in the economic fortunes of historical racial groups, and scant redress for the crimes of colonialism and apartheid, the Rainbow was from the start critiqued as a rhetorical device working to support the "denial of difference" (Gqola 2001, 98). The rainbow is a duplicitous image: as white light is constituted of other colours, so too was the prosperity of all "subsumed within the interests of the white population" (Steyn 2001a, 85). Many agree that South Africa has reached the "end of the Rainbow Nation myth" (Msimang 2015). What exactly will replace it as a social imaginary remains uncertain.

Although it may be reductive to attribute South Africa's failure to address racial inequality to the triumph of neoliberalism in the 1990s (as argued by Hart 2002; 2014) it is clear that it would have been hard for any decisive transfer of wealth to occur in the context of the "end of radical politics" (Norval 1996, 267). Though social-democratic in many of its early reforms, the ANC accepted that in order to secure long-term prosperity, South Africa would need to compete on the world stage as a market economy, foreclosing the possibility of any fundamental restructuring, and opening the door to "market fundamentalism" in economic and social policy (Bond 1998). The new constitution, signed into law in 1996, left open to interpretation the question of whether land could be forcibly expropriated in the interests of historical redress without market-based compensation. As today's political and social movements struggle for the material redistribution of the land and its fruits, a recognition of the bivalent (Fraser 1995) interdependence of symbolic and material value of land has informed the struggles of a rising tide of activism that takes aim at both racism and capitalism (Satgar 2016) and their intersections with misogyny and heterosexism (Dlakavu, Ndelu, and Matandela 2017; Ndelu, Dlakavu, and Boswell 2017). Land redistribution has been moved to the top of the agenda by activists and politicians, leading to the announcement by President Cyril Ramaphosa in his 2018 State of the Nation address of an imminent constitutional review process to allow for land expropriation without compensation. However, the resulting bill, which was tabled in 2020, included this measure only as a last resort. Land justice in South Africa remains a live wire.

With or without the necessary legal apparatus to expropriate land without compensation, attempts at land reform (including restitution, tenure reform, and redistribution) have been troubled from the start. Cherryl Walker (2008), former land claims commissioner for KwaZulu-Natal and now a professor of sociology at Stellenbosch University, points to significant underfunding and a general lack of political will as the key factors that contributed to the programme's underperformance. She argues that the "grand narrative" of colonial dispossession, while correct in its broad outlines, is a "political fable" that "simplifies, excludes, and reduces too much" (2008, 41) resulting in "opportunistic" claims without legal basis (2008, 48–50). As a prominent opponent of apartheid-era land expropriation and forced removals, Walker asserts the importance and urgency of particular claims, while problematising what she sees as the disproportionate emotive power of a mass of inchoate and unprovable demands for land, demands that pull the process in an unsustainable direction, away from the rule of law and economic growth, and into a chaotic scramble fuelled by race reductionism. She rejects the proposition that any Black person inherits colonial dispossession by virtue of their belonging to an ethnic group, pointing out that certain Black people in fact gained land under racist dispensations. Race erases "ambiguous" historical relationships between Black and white, making it unimaginable that there might have been "white investment in or identification with the land" (2008, 40–41).

This approach, which limits the scope of acceptable land restitution to the strictures of existing legal processes, and tailors reform to the iron laws of economics, is dominant in liberal accounts of land reform in South Africa (e.g. Akinola 2020; Hoops 2019; Jankielsohn and Duvenhage 2017). The "opportunistic" claims of the masses are hard to reconcile with these orderly frameworks. Though there certainly are important juridical and economic questions, couched in the practicalities of evidence, policy, and consequence, it is easy to forget that the "economy" and the "law" are social constructions no less phantasmagorical than the "political fables" of land activists. Policy discourses too often take these terms as neutral, instead of as always already interwoven with specific ideologies. Legal or economic evidence cannot speak for itself, and must be articulated around some value/s in order to be meaningful. A noted characteristic of the kind of Third Way politics practiced by the ANC is in fact the tendency to present itself as "the neutral management of public affairs" (Mouffe 2018, 4). Good governance, in this ideology, is a scientific practice altogether above the fray of partisan struggle. Appealing to "objective" evidence constructs unruly people with chaotic demands as so many spanners in works which are imagined as otherwise running smoothly. Restitution is thereby limited to legally proven title, and reform to what can be achieved while growing the economy. Thus, even as President Ramaphosa committed to "radical" change in land reform, he was careful to frame it as aiming "to bring more producers into the agricultural sector and to make more land available for cultivation [. . .] in a way that increases agricultural production" (Ramaphosa 2018).

I lay out these views here in order to contrast the very different approach this book will take. While I do not question the difficulty of the policy options facing government, I do wish to draw attention to their discursive frames. Take note, for instance, of the extent to which the land issue has become framed as a Black problem. Black people in general stand accused of an inchoate and legally baseless sense of entitlement to land. They claim to want to farm, but can they make a go of it? Do they not realise that the country's real wealth lies in the service economy? Politically, the failure of the ANC's land reform programme often looms larger than centuries of colonial land theft. At the same time, white people, at least those who are considered progressive, are represented as open to orderly and rational changes to property ownership patterns, and therefore as part of the solution. Activists for land justice by contrast become would-be Robert Mugabes, whose narrowly self-serving lust for redistribution paves the road to economic catastrophe.

The outlines of this picture should give us pause. As Clements Kadalie said in 1926, echoing W.E.B. Du Bois, "there [is] no such thing as a 'native problem'—instead, there [is] a European problem of weakness, greed, and robbery" (Ngcukaitobi 2018, 280). Steve Biko made a similar point half a century later:

> [White liberals have] the false belief that they are faced with a black problem. There is nothing the matter with blacks. The problem is WHITE RACISM and it rests squarely on the laps of the white society. (Biko [1978] 2006, 23)

While *White Belongings* does not deal with the strengths or weaknesses of land reform policies, it does address how the "problem" at the heart land reform in South Africa is discursively produced not as (white) settler colonialism, but as (Black) violation of immutable economic laws and legal principles. The discursive knot that makes land justice a Black problem ties together emotive populism, land occupations, economic collapse, and racial reductionism. It serves to rationalise and naturalise the inviolability of property rights, and in so doing subtly reinforces the idea that South Africa is by rights a white country. Untying this knot will not solve South Africa's land question, but instead do the work of critique, seeking to "comprehend the constitutive elements and dynamics of our condition" (W. Brown 2017, 28). In order to understand how it has come to pass that the beneficiaries of historical dispossession seem to have so little responsibility for solving inequality in the present, even in the discourse of anti-apartheid liberals, and how those sitting with the legacies of landlessness and poverty have come to be framed as problems, it is necessary to analyse the origins of a key nodal point of liberal ideology: private property.

PROPERTY AND LIBERALISM

While a European right to dominate other people and lands has many historical tributaries, from monarchical expansionist imperialism to the advent of "race science," various forms of liberalism, some of which invoked a utilitarian calculus that militated for the "development" and increased "prosperity" of colonised lands, played a decisive role (see Zevin 2019). The Western notion of private property extended along with the tendrils of financial markets and legal traditions to all corners of the earth, and liberals tended to argue that these processes benefited indigenous populations, offering erudite philosophies of natural law as their licence. John Locke, a central figure of both colonialism and liberalism, presented what many regard as the foundational justification for private property in his Two Treatises of Government ([1690] 1960). Locke's puzzle was how to justify an individual's "private Dominion" over that which God had given Man to share in common ([1690] 1960, 303–4). Ironically, for a man intellectually and financially invested in slavery (Mills 2008, 1382) Locke proposed that ownership of one's own body was the appropriate moral foundation for the institution of private property. Because we own our bodies, we own our labour; and so it was that when we work the land and "mix" our labour with it, that we come to justifiably exclude "the common right of other men" (Locke [1690] 1960, 306).

The process of mixing labour with land and thereby coming to own it exclusively was, he argued, morally permissible only as long as there is "enough, and as good left in common for others" (ibid.). Other aspects of his theory however work to subvert any chance of leaving common land open for others to use. His elaboration of a financialised geopolitics of property offered an explicit justification for various genocidal and colonial projects, and much of the global inequality established in their wake. He contrasted European economies, where the "Civiliz'd part of Mankind" ([1690] 1960, 307) uses money to ensure the fruits of their labour on the land do not go to waste, to America, where Native Americans supposedly neither mix their labour sufficiently with the land so that they may own it, nor prevent waste through the use of money. Surrounded by plenty, he claims that Native Americans live in a "needy and wretched" state ([1690] 1960, 312). They are "rich in Land, and poor in all the Comforts of Life [. . .] for want of improving it by labour" ([1690] 1960, 315). Native Americans, Locke argues, would not be harmed at all by the European farmer who planted "in some in-land, vacant places of America" (Locke [1690] 1960, 311) because their land is still used in common "the

Inhabitants thereof not having joined with the rest of Mankind, in the consent of the Use of their common Money" ([1690] 1960, 317). Progress, efficiency, and prosperity could only lie in making land a commodity. Taking the land out of common use and allowing the market to set its value would allow its owners to mix their labour in it, and profit from their exclusive rights to it, thereby enchaining their own interests to the growth of the collective wealth and development of the area. Thus was the expropriation of colonised land born in European liberal thought as a *favour* done to Indigenous people. If a case could be made that European ownership would increase the productivity of the land, it was morally permissible to simply take it.

Native Americans are included in "Mankind" in parts of Locke's argument, and distanced from it in others. He sees their claim to American land as demanding from Europeans a response more sophisticated than the barrel of a gun, and yet he is at pains to explain that their wretchedness, inefficiency, and laziness means that they are wasting it, and that their claims to own it might therefore be brushed aside. Perhaps they will own it in future, along with the "rest of Mankind," but only if they follow European laws, adopt settled agricultural production, and start using money. That Locke's picture of Indigenous life was a self-serving and cynical fabrication is unsurprising; Native American nations had been farming since at least 5000 B.C. (Hurt 2002, 3) and had extensive systems of trade and exchange, including money (see Sayre 1997). That only white self-ownership counts as ownership, and that only *Western* property is truly property, have consistently been implicit assumptions in liberal orders. This "racial liberalism" asserted that people are equal while at the same time "unequal treatment of [racialized people] was not seen as unequal, not flagged as an internal inconsistency, but accommodated by suitable discursive shifts and conceptual framings" (Mills 2008, 1381). Locke's argument is a prime example of how these shifts and framings work in practice. It was common for advocates of universal egalitarianism to speak about "all people" while meaning white, able-bodied, European bourgeois men. Immanuel Kant, an important contributor to liberal philosophy, did not extend full personhood to Black people, whom he considered "subpersons [. . .] by virtue of their inferior rationality and diminished capacity for autonomy" (Mills 2005). A key progenitor of English liberalism, John Stuart Mill, argued that faraway 'races' were little more than children ("in their nonage," Mill [1859] 1997) and that colonial powers might therefore justifiably override their autonomy in their own best interests, as it was appropriate to do with minors (Goldberg 1993, 18). By and large, liberalism reproduced the notion of a European "race" of people uniquely imbued with Reason, whose borders were defined by the barbarity and underdevelopment of Turks to the East, Arabs and Moors to the South, and other faraway "savages" (Goldberg 2006). Wound into the definition of the human in liberalism is a particular subjectivity, where the closer one fits the mould of a rational and culturally European man, the better one thrives in its social institutions.

The Lockean conception of property, on which much of the Western jurisprudence of ownership is built, was thus racialised from its very inception. It is unsurprising therefore to find that continuities in the reproduction of racist structure down the centuries are entangled with rights to property. In the United States, Cheryl Harris argues that whiteness can be conceptualised as a form of property, as "the set of assumptions, privileges, and benefits that accompany the status of being white have become a valuable asset that whites [have] sought to protect" (1993, 1713). In relation to African slaves, whiteness was equivalent to being a free human being; in relation to Native Americans, whiteness translated into true ownership of land grounded in the correct culture, which, unlike "Indian" title, could not be "safely ignored" (1993, 1721–22). Harris shows how the law naturalised white entitlements to the fruits of slavery and land theft, to the extent that they no longer needed to be rationalised or defended. So unmarked was the injustice of America's racial structure, that through the Civil Rights era of the 1960s and the introduction of affirmative action legislation, at no point was there the implication that "innocent" whites would ever not be entitled to a disproportionate share of property (1993, 1769). Surveying the legal history of Canada, Australia, and Israel/Palestine, Brenna Bhandar (2018) similarly concludes that property regimes in these colonial contexts are profoundly entwined with racial fictions, which protect the claims of the dominant group to unjustly acquired colonial land, while undermining or erasing the claims of its original inhabitants. W.E.B. Du Bois's definition of whiteness thus has a persistent ring of truth about it:

> "But what on earth is whiteness that one should so desire it?" Then always, somehow, some way, silently but clearly, I am given to understand that whiteness is the ownership of the earth forever and ever, Amen! (Du Bois 1920)

In South Africa, the notion of land "expropriation without compensation" could be read as largely targeted at the Du Bois's "forever and ever, Amen!." Writing at a time of exuberance about the transition to democracy, both Norval (1996) and Harris (1993) pointed to the new South African Constitution as a potential instance of a legal framework that might decisively decouple racial difference from entitlement to a disproportionate share of the country's wealth. But, as shown above, this did not happen. The hegemony of non-racialism entwined with broadly liberal economic policy has foreclosed any substantial challenge to white people's enjoyment of the fruits of colonialism and apartheid.

BLACK VAGABONDAGE, WHITE BELONGING

Present-day South Africa came to be dominated by white settlers over a process of about 300 years from the mid-1650s, through successive waves of violent conquest, dishonest conniving, coercive concessions, and legal and political interventions. The passing of the Natives' Land Act in 1913, which governed tenants' rights, is often cited as a decisive moment, a death blow after gradual encroachment and theft, which effectively cancelled Black security of tenure in 87% of the country. The words of journalist, sociologist, and founding member of the ANC Sol Plaatje have resounded ever since: "Awaking on Friday morning, June 20, 1913, the South African native found himself, not actually a slave, but a pariah in the land of his birth" ([1916] 1982, 21).

A pariah is an outcast; stripped of dignity, they no longer belong. As the attorney Richard Msimang put it at the time, Black people had been reduced "to a state of vagabondage" (Ngcukaitobi 2018, 151). With the stroke of a pen, tenants were transformed into criminals, while white farmers "acquired" their livestock, which could no longer be legally pastured (2018, 152–56). Combined with coercively designed taxation, Black farmers had no choice but to become a class of labourers, either on the land they used to farm themselves, or down the labour-hungry mine-shafts. In the country's white Parliament, the Act was lauded as an effort to protect Black tenants from economic exploitation by irresponsible landlords, giving "it a semblance of a paper restriction on European encroachment on native rights" (Plaatje [1916] 1982, 61). Plaatje's analysis of the Land Act demonstrated how "the control of land and the disruption of land tenure are central to the pattern of domination, the play of interests and the consciousness of groups" (Connell 2007, 110). While it would be inappropriate to alloy the experiences of all colonised, racialised, and dispossessed peoples into a singular universal experience, there are key similarities in the face of European might that are worth exploring. Around the world, land is a nexus point where social and economic production meet; it is the crucial 'base' for participation in a human community. Frantz Fanon observed that for "a colonized people the most essential value, because the most concrete, is first and foremost the land: the land which will bring them bread and, above all, dignity" (Fanon 1968, 44). As Australian Aboriginal and Torres Strait Islander social justice commissioner Michael Dodson explains:

> Everything about Aboriginal society is inextricably interwoven with, and connected to, the land. Culture is the land, the land and spirituality of Aboriginal people, our cultural beliefs or reason for existence is the land. You take that away and you take away our reason for existence. We have grown the land

> up. We are dancing, singing and painting for the land. We are celebrating the land. Removed from our lands, we are literally removed from ourselves. (Yunupingu 1997, 41)

Colonisation removes the pre-existing "basic structure" (Fanon [1952] 2008, 72) of a society and imposes a new one from the top down, informing people about who they are, and where they fit in. Cultural production in colonial societies (its fiction, advertisements, its children's games and stories) structures the expected subjectivities, moulding specific social spaces people are expected to occupy. The white child on the train who famously points at Fanon and cries "Look, a Negro!" ([1952] 2008, 82) batters him down into a two-dimensional "racial epidermal schema" which he experiences as a barrage of racial imagery, pushing him into a "zone of non-being," the zone of Plaatje's pariah.

Colonial cultural production turns colonised racial Others into vagabonds, but it must also produce the white coloniser as unassailably entitled to the land they dominate. Central to South African literature has been "the diastole and systole of appropriation and renunciation, aggression and resistance" over the land and its resources; an "endless drama of domicile and challenge" (van Wyk Smith 1990, 2–3). Two broad traditions in white South African writing have been identified, both bound up with the land. The first, the pastoral, is a "dream topography" of a patchwork of "thousands of farms, each a separate kingdom ruled over by a benign patriarch" (Coetzee 1988, 6). Structured around the cultural elaboration of the idealised family farm, this vision is anchored in the classical (and also Lockean) requirement that man preserves his virtue in the rural idyll through honest toil. The fact that ownership of the land is white, while the labour is mostly Black, must be "[occluded] from the scene . . . [for] how can the farm become the pastoral retreat of the black man when it was his pastoral home only a generation or two ago?" (1988, 5). A contrasting tradition is anti-pastoral: it sees land not as bountiful and parcelled off in farms, but as mysterious, silent, and blank, representing the "failure to imagine a peopled landscape" (1988, 9). Where communion with the land does happen, it brings forth monsters, "the return of what is repressed in the poetry of the silent landscape" (1988, 10). White writing about the land starts with a "puzzled 'reading' of a terrain which is both familiar and unknown, welcoming and hostile, a place where the European feels he has somehow always belonged—indeed, to which he feels he has a right—while at the same time sensing its utter strangeness" (van Wyk Smith 1990, 2). In a similar vein, white writers in pre-independence Zimbabwe "crafted a property claim and self-image around the figure of an absent native unworthy of his environment" (Hughes 2010, 7). Whites affected simply not to see Black people in their cultural production, which erasure worked as a "political technology of belonging" (2010, 24) for colonial whites.

These cultural exertions affirmed the broader system of power that secured juridical, military, and economic domination. In the colony, those who "decide what is visible and what must remain invisible are sovereign" (Mbembe 2017, 111). White ways of thinking about and managing land reproduced the logics that came to be considered natural, even eternal: white settlers were in an economically and productive symbiosis with their newly conquered lands, and may confidently take up space; Black must be off-stage, in strictly demarcated areas performing limited social roles. In Fanon's theorisation, the colonized subject "is at once sequestered and forcefully given space" (Sekyi-Otu 1996, 72) and racism is at heart "an alienating spatial relation" (Kipfer 2007, 703). Dehumanising spatial relations are also building blocks of racial capitalism. Gilmore (2002, 22) argues that understanding the imbrications of race and economic exploitation requires analysing the "territoriality of power." Racism's production, renewal, and exploitation of group-specific vulnerability to premature death (Gilmore 2002, 16; 2007, 247) works not least through the production of spatial orders. Ultimately, the desired outcome is to keep the costs of labour as low as possible. In her work on carceral capitalism in California, she shows how stories deriding Black women as an urban underclass of "welfare queens" built public support for locking up their sons in rural, peripheral, but also profitable prisons that ultimately serve as reservoirs for cheap labour. Space in these orders is one realisation of the symbolic and material hierarchies that govern vulnerabilities to premature death.

Under South African apartheid, stories about who belongs—who is at home and who is a "pariah"—were crucial to the establishment of the Black labour reservoirs called "homelands" or derided as "Bantustans." Economic and territorial domination, political rights, and the psychology of the colonised were here produced in tandem. The relationships between these dimensions were famously critiqued by Biko, who warned:

> Slowly the ground is being swept off from under our feet and soon we as blacks will believe completely that our political rights are in fact in our 'own' areas. Thereafter we shall find that we have no leg to stand on in making demands for any rights in 'mainland White South Africa' which incidentally will comprise more than three-quarters of the land of our forefathers. ([1978] 2006, 40)

His insight was what people *believe* their rights to be is a fundamental site for struggle. It is this expansion of the imagination, of Black people's righteous sense of entitlement to the land, that Biko feared was curtailed by the Bantustans. This principle was certainly grasped by Afrikaner nationalists. In the words of apartheid prime minister J.B.M. Hertzog, it was in the homelands—and certainly not in white South Africa—that the "Native ought to feel at home" (Ngcukaitobi 2018, 278).

As fundamental to the apartheid system as it was, this division of the country into home and not-home has persisted in the form of a latticework of norms, expectations, and practices that has emerged to replace statutory racism. In their case study of how on-going segregation in a small Karoo town is justified by residents, McEwen and Steyn (2013) point to the role of "racialised epistemologies" in the construction of space. Supposedly common-sense ideas about tourism and economic growth are deployed to re-mark boundaries, while protecting white consciences from complicity in racial prejudice. In the suburban gardens of Johannesburg, servant's quarters are converted into middle class "garden cottages" access to which is either denied outright to Black tenants, or policed in ways that echo the social norms of the apartheid-era "maid's room" (Falkof 2016). Along the coast the "place-images" of formerly whites-only beaches are produced through a "neo-separatist discourse of manners" that normalises white cultural codes, while problematising the presence of Black people (Durrheim and Dixon 2001). In their middle-class communities, white South Africans assert a "right" to define a "neighbourhood character" (Ballard 2005) organised as an exclusionary space for people who are not white. These discourses are often legitimized through appeals to supposedly universal, liberal, non-racial values such as protecting public health (Ballard 2010). Another supposedly laudable strategy for spatial control is environmental protection.

Mainstream environmentalism and conservation have often antagonised the struggle for liberation in South Africa (though this does not mean that conversation is merely a "white" pursuit, see Dlamini 2020). At the dawn of democracy, Azanian People's Organisation vice-president Dr Gomolemo Mokae averred that the

> green movement agitates on behalf of flora, of fauna, of the entire animal kingdom, with but one exception: black mankind . . . we have better things to do than run along with the bandwagons of ignorant white people who need an interest to fill their time. (Khan 2000, 172)

Creating the country's famed national parks and protected areas involved the forced removal from their ancestral lands of thousands of people (Carruthers 1995; McDonald 2002). Though some gains in inclusive environmental policy-making were made after apartheid, a broad-based social compact around environmental issues was undermined by "corporate-led globalisation" (Cock and Fig 2001, 25). Race has continued to be a divisive issue in nature conservation, and neither race nor class inequality has been an issue of substance for prominent green organisations (Death 2010; Kepe 2009). Similarly to elsewhere in the world, where the most visible and best-funded environmental work confirms market-oriented orthodoxy (Fletcher 2013) common-sense capitalist ideology neutralizes much of the revolutionary potential of ecological thinking. Ostensibly radical environmental movements in the United States for example reproduce the contours of racial capitalism through the "libidinal investments" in property of settler activists (Bosworth 2021, 681). In mainstream environmental movements, corporate "greenwashing" or the dictates of "green development" undermine the liberatory social potential of radical environmental visions.

Given the urgency of the ecological and climate crisis, discourses of the earth are especially important targets for critical analysis. As Baldwin (2012) has argued, the tropes of utopia, apocalypse, hope, potentiality, possibility and fear that saturate green politics are intimately involved in a politics of race and class. Bodies and bodily relations that are ecologically "good" are distinguished from those that are ecologically "Other," most significantly the "non-white" whose fecundity is an environmental threat (Gosine 2005). In the South African suburban context, ecological arguments are deployed to problematize black residential encroachment (see e.g. Dixon et al. 1994) and white neighbours invoke their "sentimental, ethical and material investment in the relationships between plants, animals and people" (Ballard 2010) in order to anathematize the slaughter of animals in Black households. At the same time as trying to keep African customs outside of a middle-class suburban cordon, some have created "eco-villages" where only indigenous gardens are allowed, producing amongst themselves "a certain kind of localism and attachment to place" (Ballard and Jones 2011). The experience of wilderness furthermore features prominently in the narratives of home and belonging present in the discourse of British migrants to South Africa (Conway and Leonard 2014), and white South African national identity more broadly was historically produced through the "imaginative appropriation" of landscapes "washed with sun" (Foster 2008). Convivial human relations with the natural world are affirmed by these dominant groups in ways that confirm white belonging, while estranging their Black neighbours. At a different scale, transnational conservation projects, represent for many whites a reason for belonging in Africa after the end of colonialism that is aligned with a "congenial postnationalist geography" (Hughes 2005) making room for them above Black-ruled nation states. Metaphorically, they stand astride national borders in ways reminiscent of the famous image of Rhodes as Colossus, straddling the continent from Cape-to-Cairo. We will return to a number of these themes in chapter 4.

OUTLINE OF THE ARGUMENT

In the preceding discussion, I have blended together different ways in which relationships between people and place have become wound up in the racial order: as differential property rights, as space one belongs in or does not, as imaginative possibilities in fiction, as peopled or empty landscapes, as a base for capitalist production, or as the canvas for contestations of social and environmental futures. In the next chapter, I will lay out an approach that ties together some of these eclectic elements into a discourse analytical toolkit suited to the task of deconstructing racial hierarchies, bringing materialist analysis of social structures into conversation with poststructuralist scepticism about the stability of semiotic systems, remaining alert to the pitfalls of both. I will also further problematise the role of 'whiteness' in critical approaches to race, as well as explain the process of data selection and analysis. I argue for the relevance of mediated communication, with a specific focus on social media, as a key site for the production, renovation, and contestation of social identity in contemporary South Africa.

Each of the four analytical chapters that follow presents a discursive formation that speaks to the ongoing articulation of white belongings. The first is the production of *white stewardship* as aligned with, and good for, the natural world. This stewardship is in many ways embodied in the figure of the white conservationist. For many white South Africans, the suffering of butchered rhinos poached for their horns weighs far more heavily than the lives of the poachers taken in the war on poaching, or the livelihoods of their families who eke out an existence along the boundaries of wilderness areas. Through analysis of various anti-poaching campaign materials, I show how over-sexed and rapacious Black male poachers surface in anti-poaching discourse alongside under-sexed and effeminate Asian rhino horn buyers, and how these representations work to normalise and centralise the masculinity of the white male conservationist in his khaki uniform, striving to save the rhino. The production of the white man as a trusted steward of the land and its enigmatic beasts is crucial both to sanctioning the extra-judicial killing of poachers, and to reproducing their continued primacy within the neoliberal conservation industry.

The second chapter analyses the production of specific South African landscapes as *white ethnoscapes* in which settler belonging is inviolate. This chapter also focuses on dynamics within middle-class, white-dominated environmentalist campaigns. Based on analysis of four years' worth of discussions on the country's largest Facebook group to prevent hydraulic fracturing ('fracking') in the arid Karoo region, I show how white campaigners produce themselves as better knowers and lovers of the land than spoiling (Black) governmental and corporate interests. Through praising the "unspoiled" beauty of agricultural land, histories of genocide and colonial encroachment are obscured, and white people invent a status for themselves as a quasi-autochthonous ethnic group whose relationship to the land is natural and eternal. The Karoo, in particular, is produced as "soul country" for white South Africans.

The next chapter moves on to discourses of injury and alienation. Given the stark contrasts between Black poverty and white prosperity described above, and ongoing calls for restitution and redistributive justice, this discourse foregrounds white *estrangement*, *uprootedness* and *victimisation* by a vengeful Black government as the distinctive tragedy of post-apartheid South Africa. While an illusory "white genocide" in the country is a popular theme of the global far right, this chapter looks instead at a mainstream story picked up by local and international media: the supposed "crisis" of white poverty. News and documentary video clips "exposing" white poverty in the new South Africa are shared on YouTube and other platforms, attracting millions of views. These texts rely on powerful visual representations of dirty and injured white skin, and on the life stories of individual whites represented as pariahs, who have been made landless, vulnerable, and powerless. Now alienated from "their" land, these whites are produced as in a metonymic relationship to white South Africa as a whole, despite all evidence to the contrary. Moral panics about "poor whites" played an important role in the ascent of the National Party in 1948, and today the white poverty discourse is fuelled by "rights" organisations such as AfriForum, which use them as cover for narrow ethnic projects.

The fourth discursive formation produces *property rights as inviolable*, attempting to fix the horizon of possibility for South African political vision. I analyse this formation not through its defenders, however, but through instances of discursive struggle, where the limits of the hegemonic order are probed and its proponents ridiculed. Analysis of a joke cycle shared on Twitter and Facebook by mostly Black contributors about what would happen when white people "give back the land" provokes reflection on how the definition of what is humorous within a particular social order may also point to what is hegemonic. As a phenomenon sparked by symbolic gestures in public spaces and on social media, laughing at "white tears" represents the attempt to think outside of current hegemonic ways of thinking about race and land. While these articulations are shown to point towards a new social imaginary with its own defining moments, their inscription on the horizon of possibility as a new hegemonic order would require extensive ideological elaboration in the future.

While stewardship and ethnoscaping constitute dimensions of a positive cultural affirmation and justification of continued white land domination, and estrangement and victimisation oppose their removal, the discursive struggle over the inviolability of property rights shows a great degree of indeterminacy about whether or not a future South African property order will be based on similar jurisprudential and ethical structures—cleansed of their connection to racial hierarchies—to those envisioned under liberalism. Rhodes's "immense and brooding spirit" might conceivably outlive extensive white prosperity. The end of "whiteness as property" in South Africa does not, after all, imply the end of all elites, nor of class-based exploitation.

In the concluding chapter, I lay out the argument not only for imagining a different landscape, a different way of thinking South Africa, but for materialising imagination in everyday practices. Often the culture/structure or idealism/materialism dichotomy empties out into a sense of futility, with the weight of material arrangements and their sedimentation in capitalist hegemony appearing to permanently anchor social relations in hellscapes of inequality. I argue that by approaching discourses as material practices, the possibility of counter-hegemonic praxis in discursive struggle is opened. It is through policing property rights, through representations of landscapes, and in the way that shared natural resources are managed, that we reproduce social hierarchies and racial orders. And there is nothing outside of these practices, no historical necessity that is going to arrive on a white horse to rescue the world from them. To end the racial order in South Africa requires both imagination and action: changing ownership patterns, developing a different relation to property, physically reconfiguring space, and pursuing material equality as an end in itself. Only then might we exorcise the soul of Rhodes from the land.

NOTES

1. The South African War (1899–1902), also known as the Second Anglo-Boer War.

Chapter 1

Deconstructing Post-Apartheid Discourse

The discourse analysis presented in this book is informed by activist and critical intellectual traditions that in some instances are in broad agreement as to the nature of the imbrication of capitalism, colonialism, and racism, and in others irreconcilable. My aim in this chapter is not to conjure up such a reconciliation, but instead to outline and defend a particular approach, addressing both its perks and its pitfalls, as a contribution to ongoing efforts in critical anti-racist and decolonial scholarship. There are a number of productive and convincing ways to theorise the cultural and structural dynamics of racism within historical materialism (see Hall 2021; C. J. Robinson [1983] 2021). And there are also good reasons to be sceptical of a "postcolonial" fixation with representation, identity, and difference that eschews revolutionary praxis (see, e.g., Turner 1996) as well as of research that claims to be "decolonial" while potentially carving out futures for whiteness and comforting subject positions for settlers (Tuck and Yang 2012). These challenges to the complacencies of discursive approaches that deal in the "merely" symbolic will be used in this chapter as spurs to a sharpened account of the interactions between culture and structure, race and class, representation and the "real."

The introduction laid out some evidence that in the South African context the "Rainbow Nation" ideology has worked to preserve white hegemony through failing to surpass the historical and colonial conceptions of property, place, and space that underpin the racial order. A discourse-historical account of how this has come about would focus on the discursive struggles of the 1990s, and key constellations of texts such as those around the Congress for a Democratic South Africa (e.g., Gqola 2001) or the Truth and Reconciliation Commission (e.g., Blommaert, Bock, and McCormick 2006). Aletta Norval's *Deconstructing Apartheid Discourse* (1996) was published in the midst of these momentous events, and offered a comprehensive discourse theoretical account of the arc of apartheid ideology, from its re-articulation of elements of segregationist discourse in the 1930s, to its triumph as a hegemonic social system by the 1950s and 1960s, through to its crisis and official end in the 1980s and 1990s. My project in this book, while similar in its theoretical precepts, is both temporally narrower and discursively more diffuse. In investigating the persistence of hegemonic whiteness after apartheid I adopt a synchronic, time-slice approach, and analyse not the official political utterances of key ideologues, as Norval did, but the everyday sense-making of ordinary and, to a large extent (except for the analysis in chapter 5) white South Africans. There are other ways, however, in which the analysis in this book picks up where Norval's account left off. For that reason, it is helpful to revisit her argument, which I will do in the next section. I will then go on to lay out some of the theoretical dynamics of the approach to discourse analysis shared between her account and my own, as well as explaining the analytical tool kit that will be applied in the remainder of this volume. In the penultimate section, I briefly unpack some of the pitfalls of "whiteness" as an object of study, before going on to explain the logic for the specific texts I have chosen to analyse in the final section.

A HISTORY OF APARTHEID IN MYTH, IMAGINARY, AND CRISIS

While apartheid had its ideological roots in the colonialist and racist systems that preceded it, its relative stability as a hegemonic social order from the 1950s to the 1980s demands analysis of its specificity as a social imaginary. Norval (1996) demonstrates that apartheid achieved dominance through distinguishing itself from racial segregationism, and not, as is sometimes claimed, through doubling down on it. Apartheid discourse arose contingently from the dynamics of white politics in the 1930s and 1940s, the background for which were the tensions that lingered from the British imperial absorption of the Boer republics, which set off the South African War (1899–1902). At stake was control of the mining economy, and policies that would keep Black labour cheap and plentiful without representing a political or cultural challenge to white supremacy (the so-called "Native Problem"). In the 1940s there was white parliamentary consensus (including from "liberals") that Black people had to be excluded from centres of political power (Norval 1996, 29). While this consensus addressed the "Native Problem" it did not address Afrikaners' "Imperial Problem." After successive years of drought, urbanisation, and proletarianization, the identity of a farming people (*Boerevolk*) had been decisively "dislocated" (Norval 1996, 13). At the 1934 People's Congress (*Volkskongres*) one Afrikaner nationalist put the point clearly:

> In the life of our people, walls are torn apart and are in ruins; they call out to be rebuilt. Thousands live in poverty, in misery, in pitiful conditions, and there is degeneration in all areas of life, social, moral and spiritual. (1996, 12)

Building these walls was crucial to the regeneration of the Afrikaner *volk* in an economy increasingly less dominated by agriculture, and ethnic nationalist organic intellectuals found innovative ways to articulate an Afrikaner identity from the available discursive elements (more on which later). Norval makes it clear that the existence of an Afrikaner people at this point should not be taken for granted:

> [The] point is not that Afrikaner nationalists found a community in place, a community that it could simply mould as it wished, but precisely that no such community ever existed, at least not in the sense in which it came to be understood after 1948, and that the task at hand was to construct the elements as if they were elements of a lost community. (1996, 13)

Urbanisation and the increasing visibility of white Afrikaans poverty in the wake of the Great Depression were compounded by the 1939 parliamentary decision to bring South Africa into the Second World War on the side of the Allies, which angered the many white Afrikaners either sympathetic to Nazism, or simply opposed to standing with Britain. Norval argues that this was the decisive moment in the failure of the segregationist project to create a homogenous white "European" community opposed to a similarly undifferentiated "Native" population (1996, 47).

This was the political moment for ethnonationalist mythmaking. The exclusive possession of a specific set of Afrikaner values, connected to a specific Afrikaner way of life, was dubbed the "*volkseie*" (literally, "people's own"). The *volkseie* "is that which is 'ours and ours alone,' inaccessible to the 'other,' and that which is threatened by 'others'" (1996, 96). It is an impossible object, the obsessional search for which becomes the driving force of discursive struggle in the evolution of apartheid. Dissenting Afrikaners were said to suffer from an "*ontwortelde menslike natuur*, an uprooted human nature" (1996, 42) because if they were rooted in the volk, they too would be committed to the *volkseie*. The myth of the *volkseie* could however not become hegemonic until it articulated the social demands of other groups in society in the form of a social imaginary. By definition, hegemony (as will be discussed in the next section) supplements domination by force with domination by consent. Building on the biblical myth of Babel, the *volkseie* grew into the apartheid imaginary by finding other "nations" and similarly linking them to territory: "each racial group had to have its own territory in which it would be able to develop its inalienable right to self-maintenance and self-determination" (1996, 118). As spatial relations were increasingly made to coincide with race relations, "reserves" for Black people started to be spoken of as "cradles of nations" guided by the "Christian national trusteeship" of the Afrikaner volk (ibid.). This was the foundation of the homeland system, and the basis for Biko's concern about Black people's supposed acquiescence in their own domination discussed in the introduction. While English-speaking South Africans were not directly interpellated by the *volkseie*, their interests were clearly served by it, and English-speaking capitulation to Afrikaner nationalism at the polls was near-total.

Once the nationalists were in power, the myth of the *volkseie* structured economic arrangements: *volkskapitalisme* (people's capitalism)—an ethnic compromise between capitalism and socialism (1996, 71–72)—asserted the central role of the Afrikaner community in directing the economy to the benefit of the *volk*. It "was hailed to be an indigenous product of Afrikanerdom: it arose out of the traditions and *Weltanschauung* of the volk; it was anti-imperialist, anti-capitalist and did away with the negative freedoms of the democratic state" (1996, p. 86). Apartheid was thus not a mere intellectual edifice for underlying economic relations of racial domination, but a structuring of social life that gave form to both economic and social relations. As a hegemonic order, it started to show signs of cracking in the 1970s when inflation and a crisis in the balance of payments put the economy under pressure (1996, 198) at the same time as political resistance articulated an increasingly unified politics that mobilized the category of "the people" to refer to all groups oppressed by the apartheid system. The result was a series of strikes, protests, and uprisings that profoundly resisted the fragmentations required by the notion of the *volkseie*, These cracks moved into a full-fledged organic crisis in the 1980s, and the end of official apartheid in the 1990s.

Norval traces shifts in the way that the National Party articulated ethnic identity during this period of crisis. From being an organic, natural category "white Afrikaner" was increasingly constructed as a voluntary, cultural category, membership of which became synonymous with belonging to a minority with its own set of rights, which would need to be protected against majoritarianism (1996, 279). Though this was the period of the eclipse of legislated white supremacy, it was clear that much of the discursive work done at this time was to have a lasting impact. In the context of the end of the Cold War, the National Party combined the protection of minority rights with advocacy for free markets, and drew strict frontiers between radical or "violent" approaches that sought to "blackmail" the parties to the negotiated settlement, and their own, supposedly nonviolent and rational, approach (1996, 280–81). They thus claimed the transition as their own victory, and a vindication of their own past "in that it showed the failure of alternative conceptions of ordering the social" (1996, p. 281).

While the ANC won the election by a landslide, and the National Party and its ideologies were absorbed by other parties in the course of the following decade (van der Westhuizen 2007) there were some early warning signs that the ideologies formed in these crucial transition years had hamstrung post-apartheid South Africa as a national project. The brand of Rainbow Nation non-racialism that became hegemonic after 1994 faced some untenable contradictions. To build a truly "non-racial" nation would mean decisively breaking with racialised distributions of property and power, and that would require extensive and ambitious forms of redistribution and various forms of affirmative action led by a strong, confident state. All of this, as described in the Freedom Charter, would require facing down the power of "whiteness" in the name of non-racialism (Norval 1996, 296). At the same time, both the waning of the ANC's commitment to a truly egalitarian socialism and the persistence of free market liberal and minority rights protectionist discourses, meant that the appetite for dealing with this contradiction head-on was largely absent from the political mainstream. And so, in retrospect, it is perhaps all too clear that Norval's two conditions for the continued hegemony of non-racialism in South Africa were never likely to be met. The first was that difference would have to be fostered that was not mere antagonism or the construction of a new "Other"; the second was that material inequalities would need to be "eliminated" (1996, 305). These failures go some way to explaining the current multiplication of South Africa's morbid symptoms.

HEGEMONY, DISCOURSE, AND ANTI-RACIST STRATEGY

The theoretical precepts adopted by Aletta Norval to deconstruct apartheid discourse arose from debates within Marxism about the relationship between ideology and social change. In rejecting the Hegelian notion that ideas drive history, the Marxist tradition asserted that the "actual life-process" (Marx and Engels [1846] 1970, 47) of human existence—or its material dimension—has primacy over consciousness. Because changes in the forces of production that impact on our everyday lives are theorised as driving historical change, decades of controversy within Marxism ensued about whether ideological interventions at the political or cultural level could play a causal role in revolutionary historical change. Chantal Mouffe (1979, 168) has argued that this controversy was "the main impediment to the development of Marxism, both as a theory and as a political movement." Althusser had already suggested that the problem lay in a simplistic misreading of Marx, arguing that "material" practices include the social and cultural dynamics of everyday life, which are always involved with each other, and that at specific points in history, complex relations and forces which have developed contradictions come together into a "conjuncture" or "ruptural unity" (Althusser 1967, 23). This approach makes possible the avoidance of overly reductive "economistic" interpretations of Marx, as conjunctures are "overdetermined" by the fusion of intertwined representational and material contradictions. The discursive field is theorised not as some sort of ephemeral symbolic web, but as materialised in rituals, institutions, rules, and artefacts.

Althusser's argument had been profoundly influenced by the recently published translations of Gramsci's *Prison Notebooks* (1971), which interpreted Marxist theory (and the subsequent successes and failures in Communist revolutions) not as demanding that politics wait on economic change, but as a call to exploit economic contradictions politically in order to unseat reigning hegemonies. Gramsci argued that the bourgeois class had captured the State not simply by imposing its class interests on the rest of society, but through a negotiated process of accommodating the interests of other groups in ways that facilitated their support, achieving a "compromise equilibrium" (1971, 161) that was far more stable than mere dictatorship and which Gramsci famously defined as "hegemony." States are weakened if they spend all of their energies dominating the masses through force. They must secure the consent of critical groups of people, or be swamped by opposition. In order to secure consent, the intellectuals of a social group must articulate their interests as if they were universal to all social groups, through the "indissoluble union of political leadership and intellectual and moral leadership" (Mouffe 1979, 179). People do not acquiesce to be dominated unless they take this domination to be part of the way the world is, and aligned with some version of common sense. Hegemony is furthermore not necessarily linked to repression; if the national-popular elements of working-class ideology articulate the interests of enough of the nation, it may secure their consent to lead stably, and no other group would have to be dominated. "Democracy" is thus not merely an element of bourgeois ideology, as some economistic Marxists had claimed. What matters instead is the articulating principle of the ideology—the set of values around which elements of an ideology are given their meaning—which in turn have their origins in the relations of production and their contradictions.

For some Marxists after the linguistic turn, Gramsci and Althusser did not go quite far enough in freeing the concept of ideology from economism and class determinism. In particular, the feminist, anti-racist, and environmentalist movements of the 1960s and onwards seemed imperfectly anticipated and analysed in this tradition (Laclau and Mouffe [1985] 2014, i). These later theorists understood the elements of ideology as arbitrary signifiers with no necessary relation to the things they were supposed to signify, their meanings arising from differences between them, with no ultimate and fixed point of reference (Culler 1982; Howarth 2013). Material reality cannot serve as the basis for what is true or false, the production of which is always laden with power (see Barrett 1991). Ernesto Laclau and Chantal Mouffe advanced from these premisses to argue that Althusser's notion of overdetermination, which still made room for "determination in the last instance by the economic" makes the mistake of distilling eventually to traditional economism, as social space is "sutured" with no phenomenal remainder after the subtraction of the economic (Laclau and Mouffe [1985] 2014, 85). A "suture" is the (vain) attempt to permanently "fix" the relation between signifier and signified (1985/2014, p. 99). Both Althusser and Gramsci's accounts were thus prevented from comprehensively explaining social and political life by what they refer to as a "naïve positivism" (1985/2014, p. 91). Of the many problems that positivism causes, a central one is the naturalist vision of the economy, which draws an ontological line between the "economic" and the "social" (1985/2014, p. 67)—and imagines an external reality accessible to knowledge unmediated by discourse. Far from implying the nonexistence of a material or economic "reality," this poststructuralist perspective explains how it is always also socially structured. While an earthquake happens independently of thought, whether it is constructed as a natural tectonic shift or "the wrath of God" depends on the structuring of the discursive field (1985/2014, p. 94). In the case of race, it should be especially clear that the existence of phenotypic differences between human groups are not denied: what is denied is that they are meaningful before their articulation with other discursive elements and values in human social life.

The practice of articulation "pierces the entire material density" of the world (Laclau and Mouffe [1985] 2014, 95) and is defined as "any practice establishing a relation among elements such that their identity is modified as a result of the articulating process" (1985/2014, p. 91). An element, once enchained in a discursive formation, becomes a "moment" of that discourse: its meaning is relative to the rest of the formation, and specifically to the guiding values or "nodal points." The identities of the moments in a particular articulation have a necessary character in relation to each other, meaning that to change one part would be to change the formation as a whole (1985/2014, p. 92). These necessary relations do not prevent change because the formation as a whole is not "sutured": there are always free-floating elements available for articulation, and the "transformation of elements into moments is never complete" (1985/2014, p. 93). The nodal points serve as partial fixations of meaning that make the flow of differences possible, serving as (temporary) still points that allow meaning to coalesce around them without being "transcendental" (1985/2014, pp. 98–99). The hegemonic status of a discourse resides in its (always provisional, always temporary) ability to determine the discursive horizon. Outside of this arc, there is no sense: the discursive horizon is also "the horizon of intelligibility" (Laclau 1990) beyond which can only lie absurdity and meaninglessness. The stability of hegemony is attained through two moments: the articulation of the myth linked to the subject positions and social demands of a specific group, and then the establishment of that myth as a social imaginary that appears to address the social demands of all groups in society. Because the material world cannot be conceived of by social actors outside of discourse, what we think of as the permanence and common sense knowability of our material reality is in fact a "sedimented discourse" (Laclau 1990, 35; Laclau and Mouffe [1985] 2014, viii) that might once again at some point become unstuck. The processes of discursive change—of the sedimentation and dislocation of articulations and identities—thus becomes central to the establishment and unseating of hegemonies, through bridging the idealist/materialist dichotomy. It is also the central focus for the discourse analyst.

This all-encompassing theory of discourse suffers from something of a "methodological deficit" (Marttila 2016, 118; see also Jørgensen and Phillips 2002, 24, 49; and Fairclough 1992, 93). What needs elaboration is how the grand narrative of hegemony and counter-hegemony might be applied in analysis of mundane text and talk. Marttila (2016) proposes starting simply, by identifying discursive identities, and then their relations to each other, looking for recurring patterns. The construction of social imaginaries is always a rhetorical achievement (see Laclau 2014) and much of the teasing out of these relations can be achieved with a basic tool kit that pays attention to image and metaphor, to the pragmatics and semantics of utterances, to the formation of chains of equivalence, or the drawing of frontiers of difference. Articulations may be interpreted across paradigmatic (the equivalences evoked by a particular identity) and/or syntagmatic (the combination of identities into sentence-like associations) planes (Marttila 2016, 129–30). A discourse in this account is never ephemeral or disembodied: it is a pattern of regularities that may be observed across a particular field of articulations. So, for example, in a patriarchal discourse we may find syntagmatic chains of signification such as "woman cares for child" as well as paradigmatic patterns such as "beautiful young woman" or "crazy old hag." It is important to remember that a relational ontology of meaning (as assumed in a poststructuralist approach) proposes that none of the signifiers in these chains have objective meanings. Meaning is fixed only temporarily by differences between signs. They do not "possess" meaning; they have "meaning-potentials" (2016, 131). These potentials are realised only in a discursive web articulated around nodal points that are either identical with or governed by some paramount value(s) or ethical ideal(s) (2016, p. 133). These ideals may be threatened or antagonised by opponent subjectivities, or championed and protected by protagonists.

In line with Althusserian models of subjectivity, discourses are theorised in this approach as material practices that produce subjects. In the unquestioned obviousness of our own daily lives we recognise ourselves as we recognise something that is true, in fact only an effect of the discourse into which we have been interpellated (Althusser 1971, 160–62). These subject positions or roles are motivated or rationalised in particular discourses (a paradigmatic example is "the entrepreneur" in neoliberal market economies) and their performance works to both validate and materialise the discourse itself (Marttila 2016, 124). Together with institutions (codified systems from laws to buildings to singing "Happy Birthday"), discourses and subjects constitute discursive regimes (see Figure 1.1) which discursive acts either work to confirm (sediment) or to challenge (reactivate). Acts or events that "reactivate" or "re-literalize" (Laclau 1990, 65) a specific articulation undermine its taken-for-grantedness, its common sense status, breaking the spell of the metaphor that had given it a natural appearance. In the context of social change, these kinds of discursive events are dislocatory in that they draw attention to the contingency of all forms of identification (Norval 1996, 13) and may work to erode existing hegemonies, but only if the articulation of the available elements into moments in a new discourse is able to "explain" social life to social actors in the form of a myth that can secure their "passionate affinity"

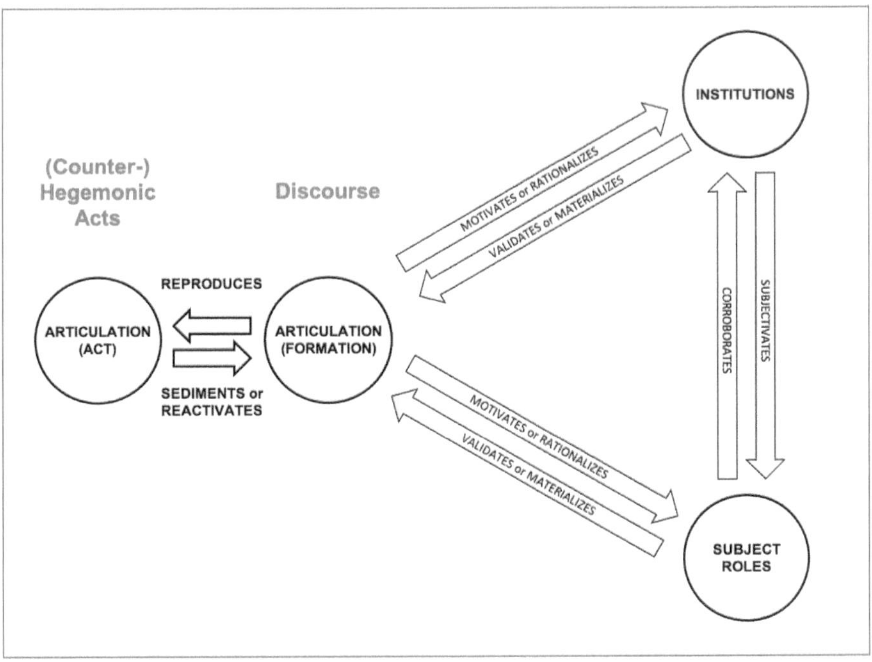

Figure 1.1: Model of a discourse regime

(Marttila 2016, 38). It is thus not the externally provable "truth" of a discourse that secures its repetition and sedimentation, but rather its rhetorical (affective and cognitive) dynamics.

The "relative regularity" of a discourse arises from constraints on the enunciative possibilities of subject roles, and these constraints or stabilising effects in turn arise from reciprocal relations with discursive materiality (Marttila 2016, 124–25). In Norval's account of the rise to hegemony of apartheid discourse, for example, the purging of "Afrikaner identity of its poor and 'coloured' elements" (Norval 1996, 36) was never "merely" symbolic, as it went hand in hand with the juridical and institutional interventions of *volkskapitalisme* that produced the Afrikaner capitalist class. The relational racial identities that gained "their specificity in their difference from other identities" (1996, p. 34) were also institutionalised in territorial homelands, and other "group areas," combined with the entire apparatus of grand apartheid. Resistance to this order involved both rejecting the social meaning of racialised and tribalized identity categories imposed by the system, and bringing its institutional framework—its pass laws, schools, mines and factories—to a standstill. The process of reactivation thus sets off its own chain of effects: eroding and dislocating established identities, sabotaging institutions, and undermining subject roles. New patterns in acts of articulation then become sedimented through repetition, in turn producing institutions and subject roles that make certain things (un)sayable or (un)thinkable, once again setting the limitations of enunciation. Hegemonic discursive regimes are thus relatively stable, but also always potentially in the process of being undermined and broken down as people develop passionate affinities for competing explanations of social life. "Articulation" is both a practice and a sedimented set of practices, and it is in the gap between these senses that opportunities for social change emerge.

DECONSTRUCTING "HEGEMONIC WHITENESS"

The work of doing discourse analysis of race and "whiteness" as a researcher who is also a white South African involves its own patterned acts of articulation, which may work to rationalise institutions that in turn make room for comfortable white anti-racist subjectivity, failing to impact materially on the racial formations that keep societies such as South Africa stratified and unjust. Decades of critique of "critical whiteness studies" have in fact pointed to the ways in which social scientists seem stuck in closed loops, reproducing "whiteness" even as they claim to deconstruct it. I consider these critiques as useful spurs to elaborating the theoretical and empirical purchase of theorising South African whiteness as a discourse regime that has (for the moment at least) retained its hegemonic status.

Sara Ahmed has pointed out that whiteness studies can easily become wound up in the recuperation of white subjectivity, reclaiming whiteness as "an object that could be loved" (Ahmed 2004a, n.p.). In a similar vein, Robyn Wiegman has argued that the field may work not to "divest whiteness of its authority and power but to rearticulate the locus of its identity claims" (Wiegman 1999, 149). Typical gestures of whiteness studies—such as showing up the vulnerability of whites to racial orders in the discourse of "white trash" (see Wray 2006) or making whiteness as an unmarked racial category visible (see Dyer 1997)—may work to create an illusory sense of "alongsidedness" (Ahmed, 2004, n.p.) where whiteness is just another racial identity in need of liberation from oppressive hierarchies. As I argued in the introduction, whiteness is not just another racial identity, but the logic of the racial hierarchy itself; it stands in a fundamentally asymmetrical relationship to other social identities, arrogating the work of structuring the world racially (Lorde [1984] 2007). Sara Ahmed argues that critical whiteness studies

> should not be about re-describing the white subject as anti-racist, or constitute itself as a form of anti-racism, or even as providing the conditions for anti-racism. Whiteness studies should instead be about attending to forms of white racism and white privilege that are not undone, and may even be repeated and intensified, through declarations of whiteness, or through the recognition of privilege as privilege. (2004, n.p.)

Heeding Ahmed's advice, and informed by a particular theory of discourse, I approach the work of deconstructing whiteness not as being limited to "white" subjectivity, but as a comprehensive critique of a way of thinking social life, sedimented in institutions that structure the social imaginary in a number of (post)colonial contexts. Whiteness in this sense is a resilient and elastic discourse regime, spread over much of the earth but always contextually specific, that works to shift symbolic and material value up an imaginary racial hierarchy, towards those who maintain themselves at its apex, and away from its broad base, to which most of humanity is relegated. To invoke whiteness is therefore to join the dots between different critiques of a world system riven with colonial and capitalist exploitation. It cannot merely be refused or abolished through an act of the will, but demands the redistribution of social goods (see P. C. Taylor 2004, 230). One analytical challenge is to unpick the ways in which the white private property owner is embedded in everyday discourse as a "mode of rationality" (Moreton-Robinson 2006, 388). Similarly, when Biko critiques the historical white "monopoly on comfort and security" (Biko [1978] 2006, 76) in apartheid South Africa it is not merely the racist laws of a particular government he has in his cross-hairs, but the internal logic of "structural oppressions resulting from capitalist modes of dominance" (Hook 2011, 24). Being white in South Africa was indeed never really an unmarked or invisible racial category (Steyn 2005). The racial system in South Africa enforced whiteness explicitly, through a system of "general harassment" that makes it "a concept that warrants being despised, hated, destroyed" (Biko [1978] 2006, 77).

What purchase does the theory of hegemony have on this problem? Whiteness is hegemonic in the extent to which it taps "into a system of ideas and images that provides a kind of commonsense background for much of Western culture" (P. C. Taylor 2004, 230). Hübinette and Lundström (2014, 426) define hegemonic whiteness in the Swedish context as "a structure, an ideology and a system that includes antiracists as well as racists and whites as well as non-whites, regardless of political views." In the United States, whiteness remained hegemonic through slavery, Jim Crow, and all the way into the era of "color-blindness" (see Lewis 2004). Patricia Hill Collins has argued that if not appropriately historicized, the very notion of hegemony can seem suffocating, making oppression seem all-powerful, and distracting from the potential for social change (P. H. Collins 2000, 51). Properly theorised, however, hegemony places political action and intellectual elaboration of social visions at the very heart of organising for change. In the accounts of a number of analysts, Steve Biko and other members of the BCM mobilized a broadly Gramscian account of apartheid South Africa (Gorlier 2002; Nteta 1987). Biko argued that because the mind of the oppressed is "the most potent weapon in the hands of the oppressor" (Biko [1978] 2006, 68) Black liberation must start with intellectual and psychological struggle: the development of Black consciousness. He saw that the apartheid state was well on its way to cowing Black people into "acquiescence in their own subjugation" (Nteta 1987, 58). And he also strained against the supposed "common sense" of white liberal resistance to apartheid in the student movement. In these contexts

> the blacks were made to fit into a pattern largely and often wholly, determined by white students . . . our originality and imagination . . . dulled to the point where it takes a supreme effort to act logically even in order to follow one's beliefs and convictions. (Biko [1978] 2006, 19)

Biko felt the vise grip of white liberalism's horizon of intelligibility, where just thinking logically (in his terms) is rendered as unreason, long before the end of apartheid when these white liberal students would claim liberation as their triumph. The analysis presented in this book attempts to think with Biko, respecting the size of the effort required and remaining attentive to the ways in which knowledge production is entangled in reproducing the status quo.

As a work of anti-racist scholarship, this discourse analysis should be judged by the extent to which it erodes and undermines entire discursive regimes, and not merely the already reviled and ridiculous figure of the white South African racist.

DISCOURSE ANALYSIS OF SOCIAL AND TRADITIONAL MEDIA DISCOURSE

Media discourses—whether online or in more traditional formats—are crucial both to the reproduction and sedimentation, or dislocation and re-literalization, of hegemonic orders. Modern social life plays out in many contexts largely on social media, which have the great virtue (from a textual research perspective) of constituting massive and often publicly searchable archives of time-and-date-stamped articulatory acts connected to specific actors. Sociality is enabled in online spaces through the affordances of social media to channel and structure information and (importantly) affect, resulting in the formation of novel groupings of people as "affective publics" (Papacharissi 2015) around shared likes/dislikes. There is massive potential in the sheer availability of discursive data, which allow for nuanced and detailed tracking of discursive formations in real time (see McCay-Peet and Quan-Haase 2017). Social media have also become an increasingly important site for the contestation of ideas and political visions in South Africa, which has high levels of online participation and internet access (Bosch 2021). Analysis of the involvement of social media articulations in processes of social change are a highly complex phenomenon with which theory is still trying to keep up. A number of dynamics are relevant in properly accounting for the interactions between social actors, discourse, and the specific affordances of digital and social media platforms (KhosraviNik and Unger 2016). What the same social actors articulate on Twitter will not be identical to what they articulate on Facebook. Facebook has specific affordances for self-presentation that are regulated through selective revelation, including through privacy settings that demarcate public social space, and censoring or removing wall posts, deleting activity, untagging, and so on (Georgalou 2016, 59). Even within the Facebook environment, Groups are different from Pages, which are different from Events or other listings. Who moderates discussions, the rules they set, and their level of active intervention result in markedly different discursive performances and effects (see van Es, van Geenen, and Boeschoten 2014). In short, social media platforms are just as complex as "real-world" social spaces. The application programming interfaces (APIs) of the platforms that are being scraped are almost always built in ways opaque to the researchers extracting data from them, and it is important to remember the extent to which social media giants are involved in the ongoing elaboration of "platform" and "surveillance" capitalism (Büscher 2020; Zuboff 2019). The world of social media is as riven by prevailing power structures as is the rest of the social sphere (Fuchs 2017, 179–209).

My identification of the four data sets I analyse here emerged from ongoing "lurking" (Bryman 2016, 450) on social media; while there are ethnographic dynamics that become relevant in sketching the context for specific posts, I did not immerse myself in the "life-worlds" of groups (2016, 461). The point was rather to identify broader patterns of articulation from specific instances of discourses of the land. Some of the anti-rhino-poaching campaign data analysed in chapter 2 was collected off-line, from billboards, posters, and bumper stickers, in addition to the online texts gathered from the Kruger National Park's "Honorary Rangers" Facebook page and other internet memes. The data that were analysed pointed to a gendered and sometimes even genital fixation in the campaign against poaching. The central themes of bodily mutilation, with special attention paid to the penises of poachers, had been noted by other researchers (Büscher and Ramutsindela 2016; Lunstrum 2017) though not before explored at length.

The data set in chapter 3 was constructed as a representative sample of the most successful anti-fracking group on Facebook, and involved the scraping of vast amounts of user-produced data and metadata over a four-year period in a purposive sample (Rieder 2013). Using the Facebook search function, I identified thirty-eight groups or pages specifically built to oppose fracking in South Africa, with a combined following of some 28,672 members. I then used a purpose-built Python script to scrape the contents of the ten largest (in terms of follower numbers) into comma-separated values files. Once accounting for the level of activity on the sites (posts as well as interactions) it was clear that the group "chase SHELL OIL out of the Karoo!" was by far the largest and most popular anti-fracking Facebook site in South Africa. Given that Facebook tracks the emotional responses of members—whether they love or like something, are enraged or saddened by it—and that affect plays a specific role in attempts to "fix" meaning within processes of discursive struggle, I opted to analyse only the posts that were significant in terms of their emotional weight. I selected the top one hundred posts (in terms of comments and reactions) for the years 2013–2016. In order not to over-sample from later years when membership numbers increased, and to get some sense of historical progression, I sampled the top twenty-five posts from each year, and included all images, emojis, videos, audio files, and text. The text component was processed both as part of the multimodal discursive ensemble, and as a corpus on its own, using the corpus linguistic software AntConc.

The online news videos (ONVs; see Kalogeropoulos, Cherubini, and Newman 2016) focused on white poverty discussed in chapter 4 were identified through a purposive search for discussions of this specific topic on Twitter. Here, the sharing of ONVs as visual proof of white victimisation under Black rule put the "spectacle" of white poverty to political use. Twenty-two ONVs, amounting to just under three hours of video footage, were gathered in this way. As will be discussed in that chapter, these ONVs were actively shared during the period of my initial data collection in 2016–2017, and have increased their view numbers dramatically since then. Many of the inserts were shot and aired (often on traditional media) long before they were posted online (see Appendix B). The jokes analysed in the final analytical chapter was gleaned mostly from Twitter and Facebook discussions about land reform. Here, jokes are analysed that were told in wake of the press furore set off by the actions of #RhodesMustFall activists Wandile Dlamini and Ntokozo Qwabe in the Obz Café in Cape Town in April 2016, and Qwabe's subsequent Facebook post describing the incident. Included in my analysis are numerous media reports, as well as Qwabe's responses.

These data sets offer a window onto South African discourses of the land in 2013–2017, I period I categorize as "after Madiba" in the Conclusion. The analysis and conclusions from each of these corpora should be understood as reconstructions of contemporary South African discourses of land, race and property within limited contexts (Marttila 2016, 145). They are not necessarily generalisable to other contexts. As a discourse analyst who is also a white, property-owning South African, I am furthermore an "implicated subject" (Rothberg 2020) whose entanglement in the materiality of this discourse is undeniable. I spent the greater part of my adolescence in a boarding school a short walk from Coronation Park, the location of the white squatter camp that will be discussed in chapter 4. I feel a profound sense of connection with the beautiful and stark vistas of the Karoo, and am implicated in ways of looking at the land that I critique in chapter 2 as continuous with a white, colonial gaze. I am personally involved and invested in environmentalist causes not entirely dissimilar to those I critique in chapters 2 and 3, and count myself as much a lover of the wild spaces and natural beauty of the land as the white conservationists whom I critique. My analysis is I hope deepened and complicated by a sense of the moral contradictions of my own position, many of which have been highlighted by the radical Black critique of the South African status quo, especially as articulated by contemporary Fallists. As Biko pointed out, the problem of white racism lies "squarely on the laps" of white people and yet instead of "involving themselves in an all-out attempt to stamp out racism from their white society [. . . they] waste lots of time trying to prove to as many blacks as they can find that they are liberal" (Biko [1978] 2006, 23–24). Taking a stance against apartheid was not a virtue to be lauded, but the moral minimum (Steyn 2001b, 156); the same should be true of thorough opposition to racist structure in the present. At the same time, a possessive investment in a whiteness that is "our" problem (and ours alone) can easily descend into narcissism. Sara Ahmed concludes her critique of whiteness studies with advice to would-be whiteness scholars:

> [Whiteness] studies should involve at least a double turn: to turn towards whiteness is to turn towards and away from those bodies who have been afforded agency and mobility by such privilege. In other words, the task for white subjects would be to stay implicated in what they critique, but in turning towards their role and responsibility in these histories of racism, as histories of this present, to turn away from themselves, and towards others. (Ahmed, 2004, n.p.)

Collins (1986) argued that the positionality of Black women in academic feminist thought brought about a unique perspective—that of the "outsider within." A white man in a not yet decolonised academy is in many ways unavoidably an "insider within"; though in making one's own insider status the object of critique, some room does open up for Ahmed's double turn. It is my hope that the work I have done mapping out the way South African whiteness is wrapped up in entitlements to own, plan, and form the land will loosen some of the discursive ties connecting white belonging to historical ownership patterns in South Africa, creating space for a future where the land and its riches truly belong equally to all who live in it.

Chapter 2

Stewards of the Land

Of the thousands of African rhinoceroses killed in the current poaching crisis,[1] the vast majority have been in South Africa, where some of the last large herds remain. In South Africa's Kruger National Park (KNP), historically home to 45 percent and 20 percent of the world's white and black rhinos respectively (Shaw and Rademeyer 2016), the white rhino population has declined by nearly 70 percent since 2008 (SANParks 2020). The illegal multimillion-dollar trade in rhino horn driving the slaughter has also had a huge human cost in clashes between armed poachers and conservation officials. Many rangers have lost their lives and, though reliable data are hard to come by, as many as seventy-seven suspected poachers were killed in Mozambique in 2014 (Büscher and Ramutsindela 2016, 4) and 150–200 in KNP in the five years to 2015 (Shaw and Rademeyer 2016, 14). This deadly conflict has enjoyed support from a conservation campaign that has pitted a "(mostly) white public in South Africa [against] (mostly) 'black poachers' from Mozambique" (Büscher and Ramutsindela 2016, 9).

The colonial underpinnings of anti-poaching discourse have received critical attention. Shoot-on-sight policies in the name of African biodiversity are supported by debasing the humanity of the poacher, while anthropomorphising the animal, and contrasting the "compassionate, sporting, and conservation-minded" white European hunter to the "cunning" violence of the Black African poacher (Neumann 2004, 826). As already discussed, the creation of conservation areas involved the removal of communities from their ancestral lands, turning indigenous people from hunters into poachers overnight (Carruthers 1995; McDonald 2002). The neoliberal conservation mode of production built around these areas is dialectically interwoven with unequal social relations (Fletcher 2013). Many poaching hot spots furthermore lie along difficult-to-manage national borders with established connections to military operations. Parallels have been drawn between the counterinsurgency methods employed by apartheid South Africa against liberation fighters crossing the borders from Mozambique or Zimbabwe, and those of the contemporary state's anti-poaching efforts, which were for a certain period coordinated by a retired apartheid-era major-general (Duffy 2014, 4; Humphreys and Smith 2014). The phenomenon of "green militarization" (Lunstrum 2014) must thus be read against histories of violent exclusions that reproduced gross material inequalities, and not as an entirely new phenomenon; and indeed, the meshing of ecological and military aims was a hallmark of the apartheid state (Lenggenhager 2015). The war on poaching is embedded in broader material, social, and discursive "green violence" (Büscher and Ramutsindela 2016) that continues to enjoy the support of prominent conservationists. State power is entreated by activists to visit extreme violence, and even torture, on rhino poachers, who are routinely represented as less-than-human (Lunstrum 2017). Concerns over whether the South African state is ready and willing to protect the rhino generate a "politics of hysteria" that is incubated on social media (Büscher 2016, 992–93). For white people especially, conservation rationalises their "being in Africa" and is a terrain in which they have "(re)asserted a continental space commensurate with a particular white history and hope for the future" (Hughes 2005, 161). The white conservationist as a subject perfectly in tune with nature is a frequent element of articulating white belonging in southern Africa (Gressier 2015; Suzuki 2017). Though concern for rhinos is to a certain extent expressed across social and racial divides, it is most intense among the white minority for whom the state's ability to protect rhinos is equated with its ability to protect broader white interests (see Büscher and Ramutsindela 2016, 9).

Overall, scholarship on the racialized aspect of green violence has focused on the deaths of marginalised Black men, historical continuities with colonialism and apartheid, and how militarisation is discursively enabled. What has not been explored in depth is how the poaching crisis has worked to valorise the subject role of the white male conservationist specifically, while anathematising the poacher whose "essential identity is . . . male, black African" (Neumann 2004, 823). Tracking down poachers is nearly always a "man-hunt" (Humphreys and Smith 2014, 813) while the online public bays for "pulling triggers and making widows" and chopping poachers' "balls off 1cm at a time" (Lunstrum 2017, 138). Plaudits for the militarised all-Black, all-woman "Black Mamba Anti-Poaching Unit" which was trained by white conservationists (see Goyanes 2017) only underscore the idea that Black men can never be fully trusted when it comes to protecting rhinos. Dynamics between race, gender and sexuality work to sustain the discursive regime of green violence, it will be argued, and are intricately involved in producing a white subjectivity positioned as uniquely suited to the stewardship of African lands.

GENDER, SEXUALITY, AND THE "TERRITORIALITY OF POWER"

Power-saturated racial-spatial orders that produce and exploit group-specific vulnerabilities to premature death are "simultaneously shaped by gender, class, and scale" (Gilmore 2002, 22). Gilmore has shown how the discursive legitimation of the expansion of "carceral Keynesianism" as a mode of production in California pitted a state constructed as white and masculine against the spectre of an "unruly African American woman" (Gilmore 1999, 177) or "welfare queen" (Gilmore 2007, 45). The welfare queen leaches off the state, while sating her sexual and other hungers, which in turn produce the criminal male children who will soon have to be jailed. New prisons must therefore be built; they demand public investment and expansion in order to accommodate a burgeoning and threatening population. Given high public expectations of state force in a country built on slavery and genocide (2002, 20) these discursive constructions feed into moral panics about criminal young Black men, authorising heavy-handed police and judicial responses, and thereby renovating what Gilmore, following Stuart Hall, has called "fatal couplings of power and difference" (2002, 16). In response to their demonisation by the state, and the locking away of their children, Black mothers organise themselves and others across the socio-spatial divides of race/gender/class/region through leveraging the "ideological power of motherhood" (2007, 246). These ebbs and flows of power across territory, where marginalised mothers in far-flung areas organise themselves to reclaim power from a state bent on imprisoning their children, are also discursive struggles that contest the hegemony of whiteness in determining hierarchical, life-or-death racial value.

That gender and sexuality are intimately interwoven in racist hierarchies has been the subject of extensive analysis across disciplines. Stuart Hall (2001, 327) for example notes a white cultural obsession with Black sexuality, and the Black man's penis, in Western media production. But it is Frantz Fanon's comprehensive psychosexual aetiology of the racial order, starting with close attention to his own body, that I will explore in more depth in this section. The Fanonian suffering body has gender, sexuality, class, and race, as well as a particular position in colonial space. The commonalities of suffering between bodies in colonial orders, Fanon argues, cannot be put down to causes arising from individual experience (to "ontogenetic" factors). Freudian psychoanalysis tended to understand ontogenetic factors as antagonising adjustment to society, the "normality" of which was seldom interrogated. This ruled out the idea that for a colonised people, society itself is the source of psychological problems. This requires "sociodiagnosis" from the analyst (Fanon [1952] 2008, 4–5). In laying out elements of Fanon's sociodiagnostic approach here, my aim is to integrate them into a discourse-theoretical tool kit for analysis of the campaign against rhino poaching that clarifies how these acts of articulation work to sediment or reactivate specific articulations within discursive regimes.

In contrast to a Jungian collective unconscious populated with universal human instincts and archetypes, Fanon invokes a context-specific *cultural unconscious*. In a description not very far from that of the hegemonic discursive regimes presented in the previous chapter, he characterises it as "a constellation of postulates, a series of propositions that slowly and subtly—with the help of books, newspapers, schools and their texts, advertisements, films, radio—work their way into one's mind and shape one's view of the world of the group to which one belongs" ([1952] 2008, 118). For white-skinned people, a black body is a dirty body, both morally and physically; blackness is to whiteness as darkness and sin are to innocence and "magical, heavenly light" ([1952] 2008, 146). The cultural unconscious thus becomes populated with what in a discourse theoretical account would be called "chains of equivalence" (see Norval 1990, 141) that inform the interpellation of subject roles in the racial-colonial state through "actor fictions" (Marttila 2016, 81–82).

The "good" white and the "bad" Black coalesce into archetypal figures called imagos. The black imago is in a relation of perfect antagonism to the white self in Fanon's account: ideally not-self and "absolutely unassimilable" (Fanon [1952] 2008, 124–26 footnote 25). This imago may appear during times of depression or anxiety as a satyr or murderer, becoming "the mainstay of [white] preoccupations and desires" (Fanon [1952] 2008, 130–31). The figure of the satyr is sexed and gendered, and arises at least in part from the white fixation with the supposed bestiality of Black men, and the size of their penises ([1952] 2008, 128). Thinking about the Black penis symbolically castrates the white man, whose sexual anxieties reduce his own penis to a "little toy" ([1952] 2008, 130). The lynching and castration of the Black man can thus be understood as a form of sexual revenge ([1952] 2008, 122–23). Belief in the superior erotic powers of Black men reveals a white male heterosexual fear of impotence, and an anxiety about giving pleasure, generated by the European aspiration towards rationalism. Fanon posits a white fear that in every intellectual gain, there is a corresponding diminution of sexual potency. Because this is experienced as a loss, there is a concomitant "irrational longing for unusual eras of sexual license, of orgiastic scenes, of unpunished rapes, of unrepressed incest" ([1952] 2008, 127). The "civilised" white man, who cannot countenance his own savage longing, must retain his virtue by projecting all vice onto the Black man. So, for example, when it comes to rape, the Black man becomes the "specialist . . . the master of this matter" (ibid.). Every reprehensible thing must be distanced from the white ego through the ascription of its origin to some other source, which role the

Black imago or satyr can conveniently play, as the icon of all that is evil (Fanon [1952] 2008, 141–47).

Fanon argues that stories (as well as games and other cultural artefacts) are particularly important because they serve as an outlet for accumulated aggression, or catharsis, which works to lodge racial imagos in the cultural unconscious during childhood. In games where "the Wolf, the Devil, the Evil Spirit, the Bad Man, the Savage are always symbolized by Negroes or Indians" ([1952] 2008, 113) the young Black child experiences identification with the white missionary being cooked, the explorer, or the pioneer who is threatened by "savages." The Black child "invests the hero, who is white, with all his own aggression" ([1952] 2008, 114) and, when the enemy is obliterated, the child experiences a catharsis (a release of psychic energy) that is anti-Black. As the catharsis is repeated, the child adopts this white explorer or missionary as a kind of paternal authority figure, or white father. All people in the colonial order are expected to revile the degeneracy of the black satyr and accept the authority of the white father. In the cultural unconscious the white father is "charged with maintaining order in it as a garrison controls a conquered city" ([1952] 2008, 112). For white children, the authority of the white father harmonises with, and is analogous to, the authority of society, to which they will be able to adjust in a "normal" way ([1952] 2008, 109). Black children however have to "ascend" from their families ([1952] 2008, 115). So while the white child matures in ways aligned with the ruling ideas, the same process for the colonised Black child is experienced as trauma grounded in alienation.

The stories of childhood are lived as real psychological, social, and material effects in the world. I noted in the introduction how Fanon feels his "corporeal schema" crumble into a "racial epidermal schema" ([1952] 2008, 84) when a French child points at him crying "Look, a Negro!" He describes his experience on the train:

> I was responsible at the same time for my body, for my race, for my ancestors. I subjected myself to an objective examination, I discovered my blackness, my ethnic characteristics; and I was battered down by tom-toms, cannibalism, intellectual deficiency, fetichism, racial defects, slave-ships, and above all else, above all: "Sho' good eatin'." ([1952] 2008, 84–85)

As Lewis Gordon (2015, 50) explains, "Sho' good eating'" is a clunky translation of the slogan for a French breakfast food called Banania, which markets itself with a smiling (and over time increasingly simian) Senegalese soldier enjoying his banana cereal, exclaiming "*Y'a bon*" in "*petit-négre*" French. Fanon is making the important point here that it is both the image of the cannibalistic satyr and the smiling Senegalese that batter him down. The smile is the "gift" of the Black man to the white (Fanon [1952] 2008, 34) as it signals his acquiescence, his acceptance of the racial order, and of the danger represented by the satyr always potentially within him. That is why "above all else" it is the Banania slogan that crumbles Fanon's "corporeal schema" and sequesters him into a zone of nonbeing. Fanon thus explains how race puts "Black bodies in place" (Kipfer 2007, 709) both materially and discursively. These discursive and material practices can work to slow down bodies in space (see Ahmed 2007) by increasing their chances of being stopped and questioned, forced to justify their presence, or, if unable to answer, to be punished in some way.

In the analysis that follows I will trace the ways in which race, gender and sexuality are co-productive in the discourse of rhino poaching, by drawing attention to the paradigmatic equivalential logics that construct the respective figures of the Black poachers, Asian consumers, and white conservationists, and the syntagmatic practices of articulation that connect them into specific relations which produce a particular approach to saving the rhino—i.e., militarised green violence and neoliberal conservation—as the only rational option. I will first analyse a representative example of how the deaths of poachers in general are discursively constructed in everyday conservationist discourse, before moving on to analysis of specific gendered and sexualised dynamics. In the concluding section I connect the subject role of the white conservationist back to the broader discourse regime that hegemonizes white control of the land.

CELEBRATING DEATH AND "FATAL WOUNDINGS"

With over 30,000 followers on Facebook, the SANParks Honorary Rangers page hosts frequent, passionate, and serious conversations about South African conservation. The page describes itself as the "preferred channel for public support towards our national parks" and is built on a network of 1,300 active volunteers nationwide who supplement the work of rangers on the SANPArks payroll. Filled with entertaining and educational content about happenings in the complex ecosystems of the country's protected areas, the page also highlights new conservation efforts, and profiles the work of the people who keep these important national assets running.

On 14 January 2016, the following press release on the actions of SANParks-employed park rangers was published on the community page:

> Two poaching suspects fatally wounded following tourist sighting
>
> A suspicious man wearing a black shirt armed with what looked like a heavy calibre hunting rifle was spotted by tourists walking in the Kruger National Park (KNP) on the 13th of January 2016, around the Napi section of the park.
>
> This according to KNP Managing Executive, Glenn Phillips, who confirmed that after at least two sets of visitors informed the authorities about this suspect, a helicopter with the assistance of the K9 Specialised dog unit was deployed to attend to the matter.
>
> He said in the subsequent search by Rangers it appeared that the man was not alone, as he was found with a second suspect in the bush. "As the Rangers ordered the men to surrender they opened fire and a shoot-out ensued with Rangers, in which both suspects were fatally wounded and a high calibre hunting rifle was recovered" [. . .]. (SANParks Honorary Rangers 2016)

A specific series of events is being related here, and close attention to the agency of the actors involved, and how exculpation and blame is distributed, reveals some interesting gestures. Stating that the poaching suspects were "fatally wounded" in the headline is a specific choice that the writers of the press release make. They could have written: "Rangers shoot and kill two poaching suspects." So why didn't they? For one thing, receiving a fatal wound is less violent an image than being shot to death; the latter might elicit compassion. For another, being wounded is something that might come about without any external agency. There are many ways one might be fatally wounded while trespassing in a wilderness area. The "Rangers" as the absent subjects of this passive construction, are thus distanced from the actual enactment of the extrajudicial killing, and responsibility for the deaths is implicitly shifted to the dead. This happens again elsewhere in the release. The reference to a "heavy calibre hunting rifle" is for example not matched by a similarly evocative description of the Rangers's guns. We don't get a strong sense of what these two suspects were up against. When the Rangers order the men to surrender, in the words of Glenn Phillips, "they opened fire and a shoot-out ensued with Rangers." That a shoot-out "ensues" is more opaque and less agentive than, say, "the Rangers returned fire." But, more importantly, how is it possible that "they" i.e., "the suspects" *opened fire* in the first place? The release makes it clear that there was only one gun between the two men, and so only one of them was able to "open fire." It might be easy to miss the implication in this press release that the Rangers have in fact killed an unarmed man. Where shooting is involved, the Rangers remain hidden or passive while it is the poachers (plural) who "opened fire." The Rangers are only active in keeping the peace: they "attend to the matter" and "ordered the men to surrender." The effect is created of an aggressive and heavily armed foe that left no course of action open other than the one that resulted in "fatal woundings."

Crucial equivalences (violent poachers, protective rangers) are thus articulated around a nodal point on which both poaching and conservation pivot, but that is not yet named: the rhino. An important third group of actors makes an appearance in the headline and twice in the text: the visitors or tourists, who work with the rangers, and who are the crucial "consumers" of conservation (Büscher and Fletcher 2015) whose sharp eyes support the work of keeping the rhinos safe. They do the work of "White surveillance" (A. Williams 2020) that establishes who is in place and who is not in the context of the racial state. The act of posting this press release to the SANParks Honorary Rangers page on Facebook effectively includes the page's 30,000 followers in this community of vigilant protectors. The release was by far the most popular post of January 2016, liked by 207 people and shared forty-three times. All comments (twenty-two in total) were supportive, with "Well done, Rangers! Stay safe" a representative comment. If the rhino was unnamed in the release itself, members of the group articulated explicitly what this discourse hinges on: "LEAVE OUR RHINO ALONE" shouted one member. Another poster commented: "Great job, take them all out." The broad licence that is thereby issued in this particular conservation group for militarised conservation personnel to "take out" suspicious men in parks, armed or unarmed, strengthens the sense of an impenetrable frontier between two antagonistic groups: protectors and poachers. The former group is the one that belongs naturally in the KNP; it is the man with his rifle, wearing a black shirt (not the green or khaki of a ranger) who is "suspicious" in ways that are not explained, and the man with him who is already a "suspect" that does not. Seen as a moral tableau, the scene resembles a public execution, with a (mostly white) group of eager and affluent protectors cheering the extrajudicial executions of guilty Black men. Race has not been invoked in any clear fashion, although its traces lurk below the surface, as a fatal power-difference coupling, exercised in the enforcement of spatial orders that separate poacher from "rightful" landowner.

The reaction to this post is fairly typical of the way that the anti-poaching campaign has historically developed in South Africa, where "vocal and mostly white people" communicate "more general feelings of rage and violence" (Büscher and Ramutsindela 2016, 19). Estimates of white participation from the moderators of pro-rhino Facebook groups, for example, range from 80 to 90 percent (Büscher 2016, 986), a proportion which is mirrored by the commenters on this specific post. On the general SANParks Facebook page, the rhino is anthropomorphically embraced by posters as a member of the national community, and violent logics structure discourse about poaching (Lunstrum 2017). Rangers are authorised by commenters to "Shoot-to-kill, Shoot-on-sight," apartheid-era border controls and military tactics are advocated for, enthusiasm is displayed for the idea of hunting the hunters, and various tropes of bodily excision with "special attention . . . paid to the removal of noses and genitals" are communicated (2017, 4–5). In order to make better sense of the why this should be, I will analyse some anti-poaching campaign artefacts that clarify the discursive salience of links between poaching and castration.

Horns, testicles, and the threat of castration

Driving behind an expensive-looking four-wheel-drive SUV in Johannesburg's infamously congested rush hour traffic one evening in 2013, I was struck by the sight of the simple black and red text of a bumper sticker (Figure 2.1).

To appropriately deconstruct a bumper sticker on a luxury vehicle driven through the streets of Johannesburg requires a bit of background on South Africa's racialised system of "automobility" (Urry 2004). In the history of this sprawling city (as in most other urban centres in South Africa) prime, white property developments have traditionally taken place in areas intentionally unconnected to the public transport network, and thus accessible primarily by motorcar, paving the way for a legacy of "neo-apartheid" (Beavon 2000) in middle-class suburbs. The car, as a commodity that "provides status to its owner/user through its sign-values (such as speed, security, safety,

Figure 2.1: Bumper sticker seen in Johannesburg rush hour traffic in 2013

sexual desire, career success, freedom, family, masculinity)" (Urry 2004, 26) could historically not be owned by, and thereby confer this status on, Black people, without challenging white supremacy. As Posel (2010) notes, the apartheid-era norm for white people to express "suspicion and distaste in the presence of . . . African people driving cars (other than as chauffeurs for white owners)" (2010, 170) partly explains why Black ownership of cars and other commodities, post-apartheid, has been "invested with the iconography of a joyous emancipation" (2010, 159). Despite economic development and a growing Black middle class, by the time of the most recent national census in 2011, only 19 percent of Black households owned cars, compared to 91 percent of white households (Stats SA 2012). Cars remain icons of economic ascendancy. Though some improvements in public transport infrastructures have changed this picture recently, the roadscape of busy city streets in contemporary South Africa is typified by poor and working-class people, mostly Black, crammed into crowded buses and taxis or walking on the streets, while most middle-class (and nearly all white) people will be driving their own cars (see Graham 2007). Bumper stickers are therefore semiotic interventions on already highly racialised and classed landscapes.

In terms of communicative functions, bumper stickers present the opportunity to "interject one's own perspectives, values and statements into the environment of mass-mediated messages" (Case 1992, 107). In the case of public support for the rhino, popular campaigns have exploited the specific sign-value of the personal car before, most strikingly in the form of red plastic rhino horns (or "rhinose") attached to grilles in the style of "Red Nose Day" charity fundraising (see Fogel 2012). People use bumper stickers to anonymously communicate public emotion (Newhagen and Ancell 1995) to engage in political protest or debate (Bloch 2000), to articulate specific social visions (Chiluwa 2008) or to negotiate complex identities in gendered, patriarchal contexts (Doyle and Tranter 2015). This identity work is performed not only for other people in other cars. Passersby and pedestrians are also interpellated by these signs. The bumper sticker is thus a kind of public billboard, not that dissimilar from an internet meme, a joke that is shared in a public context and involved in contesting norms and social visions.

Why then would a bumper sticker about rhino poaching be promoting a supposed cure for HIV? This particular text taps into a number of discourses, genres, and cultural assumptions that are worth exploring here in some detail. For reasons that include higher levels of poverty, which in turn drive so-called "transactional" sex (in return for food or other resources) as well as inferior access to healthcare, Black people bear the brunt of the HIV epidemic in South Africa. Whereas only 1.1 percent of white people are HIV-positive, 16.6 percent of Black people are (Simbayi et al. 2019, xxxi). This disparity is widely known and features in white rationalisations of the supposed sexual "undesirability" of Black people (Milani 2014). Making strong medical claims on a city street about the efficacy of a natural ingredient as a cure for a sexually transmitted infection references the genre of traditional African medicine advertising, which tends to focus, in explicit pamphlets and pasted bills, on sexual prowess, fertility, and success in life and love (Edwards and Milani 2014). By alluding to this genre, the medical practice itself (known by the isiZulu word for medicine, *umuthi*) is invoked. At the same time, because of the reference to rhino poaching, the belief in certain Southeast Asian medical traditions in the aphrodisiac properties of rhino horn, which is understood to be at the root of the poaching problem in the first place, is also being alluded to. Some Asian and African medicinal traditions share an adherence to the "Doctrine of Signatures." This is the idea that the character or appearance of a specific plant or animal part suggests its medicinal use; in "zootherapy" the utility of the medicine is ascribed to "the complete or partial resemblance of an animal or its behaviour to a specific part of the human body, organ, bodily function, bodily reaction or attribute" (V. L. Williams and Whiting 2016, 266). Under this logic, a strong rhino horn is the right substance to guarantee a sturdy erection.

Importantly, *umuthi* has specific associations in the South African cultural unconscious. Reports of "muti killings" (*sic*)—a supposed "'epidemic' of occult-related violent crimes" (Vincent 2008, 43) where people are killed for their body parts to be used as medicine, are a staple of South African tabloids as well as a preoccupation of the Western press (see Bishop 2012). That a cure for AIDS would require violent and illegal acts is also the driving idea behind the myth of the "virgin cure"—the idea that HIV-positive men were raping children who they knew could not be infected with HIV, in order to cure themselves (Epstein and Jewkes 2009). This is another instance of the Doctrine of Signatures, where the "consumption" of virginity supposedly takes the body back to the healthy state it was in before the sex act that resulted in HIV infection: consuming the purity of the virgin works to purify the body of that which was acquired through sexual excess. Though a popular urban legend, this specific motive for actual sexual violence has failed to be confirmed in research on the subject, and is furthermore "predicated on racist assumptions about the amorality of African men [and] highly stigmatising towards people with HIV" (ibid.). Given that, as we have seen, the Black man is often constructed as the "master" of rape (Fanon [1952] 2008, 127) the popularity of these myths is a predictable feature of the discourse.

This bumper sticker clearly relies on the distant and threatening presence of the black satyr to make its "joke" funny. Rhino-loving (white) middle-class car-drivers produce themselves as the protectors of the rhino by addressing what Fanon calls the "biological-sexual-sensual-genital-n—-r" ([1952] 2008, 156, alteration not in original) on the street, or in the minibus taxi, as the potential customer for a violent AIDS remedy. Situating the people on the street as in a community that stretches across geographical regions to include the poachers in the national borderlands, a racial group is clearly being sketched through mimicking the street-side traditional medicine advertisements that only “they” use. The Black man does not need to be named explicitly because everybody knows he is there. He is the one who has AIDS; he is the one who uses *umuthi*; he is the one who is killing the rhinos; and it is a terrific joke to set these violent creatures on each other.

Jokes, as will be explored in more detail in chapter 5, are very often imbricated in the disciplinary work required to reproduce a particular social order (Billig 2005). The pleasure we take from the joke may point to “what is being repressed in more serious talk” (Billig 1997, 150). The producers and users of the bumper sticker structure their joke to make it clear from its context on the bumper of a car—the unlikely juxtaposition of rhino poaching and AIDS, and the coy reference to “testicles”—that this is meant to be funny. One thing that makes the joke humorous is the unexpected use of testicles: to cure a dread disease. There is no joke in “Castrate rhino poachers!” and while “Dried rhino poacher testicles are a cure for cancer” is structured as a joke, it fails to take the “amusing” turn of joining the discursive dots between poachers and AIDS. The joke is for one audience—other middle-class car-drivers, who do not have AIDS and do not use traditional medicine—at the expense of another audience, who tend to be working class and Black, and are supposedly fooled by this parodic imitation. It is “funny,” and popular, precisely because it is shameful, precisely because white people have to repress talk of superstitious Black people with AIDS murdering each other in “normal talk.”

These kinds of jokes are not only visible in the urban streetscape, but travel through a network of online and offline spaces. Support for the rhino in a number of campaigns has included naked skydives and runs, where men wear nothing but a “rhinose” as a codpiece. Pro-rhino paraphernalia regularly involves some play on the word “horny.” The bumper sticker’s genital fixation plays on this theme not only at the level of the threatened castration, but also in its references to the sexually transmissible nature of HIV/AIDS. As was discussed above, Fanon argues that the revenge for the white man’s symbolic castration by the Black man’s ability to give pleasure is a specifically sexual revenge: castration, and then lynching. The parallels between the dehorning of the rhino, and the “horn” as synonymous with a male erection, have generated scores of online memes on the theme of “dehorning” rhino poachers, with various visual representations of severed penises, or in some cases noses (a classic penis symbol). One of these memes, widely available online, mimics a road sign warning of danger through using the internationally common road sign of a red triangle with black figures, oriented with its base downward. In capital letters, text underneath the triangle reads

"DEHORN RHINO POACHERS." This text is used to anchor the meaning of the two stick figures pictured inside the sign. The man on the left holds up a large panga or machete, which he has clearly just used to cut off the penis of the second man, who is pictured kneeling to the right of him, his arms outstretched, looking at his severed penis lying on the ground. In adopting the generic form of an official warning sign, this meme implies the creation of an imaginary space where summary penectomies would be performed on men suspected of being poachers. In invoking this real-world space, the people who share this meme also create an online space with an inside and an outside: inside is the protecting community; outside are those whose penises are fair game.

As was the case with the bumper sticker, part of the humorous effect of this text derives from a bait-and-switch tactic with the audience. The foot soldiers who might actually poach rhinos are unlikely to be warned by this sign: it is created for the amusement of the anti-poaching campaigners, to provide a specific object for their anger. The saucy pun on "dehorn" and the transgressive representation of violence and nudity also titillate the audience. Humour is achieved through the unexpected inversion of the relationship the poacher is usually in: where he dehorns the rhino, now he is being dehorned by the rhino's protector. If the rhino horn is a symbolic erection, and it is supposedly a surplus of Black sexuality that necessitates castration, then the white man's aim in both these instances (rape and poaching) can be understood as avoiding the symbolic castration caused by his failure to protect the rhino, or the woman, from the Black man. Protection against penis-destroying violence is the theme that joins the two cases, and constitutes the pretext for retaliatory violence. While the bumper sticker mimics *umuthi* advertising supposedly aimed at savage Black men, the dehorning meme incompletely mimics a road sign supposedly aimed at would-be poachers. Both signs function to police the boundary between those who love rhinos, and those who would kill them, who become castratable and killable people. This unashamed and comedic support for the mutilation and murder of poachers might be thought of as existing on the fringes of the discourse. However, there are traces of similar ideas even in more socially acceptable, public-spirited approaches to saving rhinos, one of which will be examined in the next example.

Ingesting Their Virility

The trade in rhino horn is global, and so is the campaign to stop poaching. Activists in South Africa and elsewhere have designed communication to reduce demand for rhino horn in the cash-rich markets of Vietnam and China. In these campaign artefacts, it is possible to see a specific construction of the rhino horn purchaser that is also raced and gendered, again in revealing ways.

Rhino horn buyers are generally understood to be Asian men. Fanon contrasts the production of the Black man in French colonial culture to how Indochina is constructed: as the land of "cut-rate boys and women" who have not an aggressive but a "serene" attitude towards death (Fanon [1952] 2008, 176–77). While the cheapness of Black life is rationalised by the threat posed by the savage black satyr, the Oriental life is produced as always already open to bargain, and indifferently parted with. The hyper-sexualisation of Black men, and the fixation on their large appetites and monstrous virility, is inverted in Western representations of Asian men, who are produced as asexual and feminine (Fung 1996; Hiramoto and Pua 2019). While the Black man's punishment for sexual aggression is to be castrated, the Asian man already is; he is "defined by a striking absence down there" (Fung 1996, 183; see also Eng 2001). Asian men who are taken seriously as "masculine" and as capable of sexual penetration in pornographic films are represented as assimilated into a dominant white culture, and to have left their Oriental mannerisms behind them (see Tan Hoang 2004).

A coalition of partners including TRAFFIC and Population Services International (PSI) led by the World Wildlife Fund (WWF) South Africa developed a campaign aimed at Vietnamese men, and distributed through a number of media channels (World Wildlife Federation 2014). The official campaign strategy of the 'Chi' campaign was to communicate

> the message that Viet Nam's most impressive and charismatic men have created their own good fortune with their internal drive, dedication and talent, and know that a piece of horn is no substitute for the power that lies inside of them . . . Four images (. . .) were developed to build a *new social norm* that success, masculinity and good luck, in man's life, comes from his own will and internal strength, not from a piece of horn. (World Wildlife Federation, 2014, emphasis added)

Because the social norm is "new" it is clear that the campaigners understand their thinking as not broadly accepted in Vietnam. The reigning Vietnamese norm is thus constructed as being that these good things—"success, masculinity, and good luck"—do not originate in the man himself, but in forces outside of his body, and might thus be ingested in the form of rhino horn. That "success" and "good luck" are the result of individual striving and determination alone is of course the central credo of neoliberal individualism (Salter and Adams 2013), and it is perhaps unsurprising to see it reproduced in a campaign designed in a capitalist society for implementation in a communist one. The interesting term for this analysis however is the idea that Vietnamese men are unaccustomed to looking inwards for their *masculinity*. The feeling that he currently lacks masculinity is affirmed in the text, and a solution is offered: he must work with his "own will and internal strength." Some other important equivalences are drawn: masculinity is sandwiched between success and good luck, thereby forming a key chain of signification, and a "normal" masculinity articulated around strength and determination is asserted as a valid aspiration. The campaign image[2] produced to focus on masculinity specifically elaborates on what exactly this aspiration looks like. On the poster, a beautifully coiffed and made-up Vietnamese woman wearing black lace gloves is pictured with her eyes nearly closed, gazing downwards, her neck at a forty-five-degree angle. Over the bottom left corner of the image, in bold white type, is the slogan "MASCULINITY COMES FROM WITHIN." Below the image is a payoff line in inverted commas: "A man's allure and charisma come from within, not from a piece of horn" and the Chi campaign logo. The woman who is used as a model in this image is deployed for her association with sex, as the naturalised object of heterosexual male desire. Her makeup, jewellery, hair, and lace gloves index both sexual availability and expensive taste, and the patterns of consumption that are thus also associated with "success" and "good luck." Visually, the male viewer consumes her, as she consumes these luxury goods. The angle of her neck and the tilt of her head are sexually suggestive. Her downward gaze evokes submission to the irresistible power of a masculine man, and perhaps also enjoyment of the sexual pleasure she can give him. The image does not "demand" from or challenge the man, but "offers" itself up as the object of his gaze (Kress and Van Leeuwen 2006, 148–49) while the text below sketches out new chains of equivalence: masculinity means "allure" and "charisma." This constructs a man who, importantly, is not identical with the image's intended audience, men who buy rhino horn as an aphrodisiac or treatment for erectile dysfunction. This man has masculinity that comes from his "will" and "strength" and that gives him "allure" and "charisma," facilitating sexual relations with the woman he desires. But *you* are not *him* (at least, not yet). You want her, but she wants *him*, and you therefore desire to be more like him. This "triangular structure of desire" (Coetzee 1980, 198) is ubiquitous in the design of advertisements. The existence of masculinity as an accessible essence within every man is thus asserted, along with its appropriate goal: real masculine heterosex. The problem with Vietnamese men is thus clarified in this text: they simply lack the social norm to see that the will and the strength, and therefore their masculinity, must come from within them, allowing them to be sexually successful in a way that is *real*. This endorsement of hegemonic (heterosexual) masculinity as a worthy aspiration constructs the Asian man as asexual and feminine, lacking the strength of will to be truly "charismatic" and "alluring."

THE "WHITE FATHER" WEARS KHAKI

The Black poacher with his excess aggression and virility is the agent in Africa's wild borderlands of the feminised Oriental who stage-manages the killing of the continent's rhinos with the inducements of piles of money from the markets of China and Vietnam. Who then will step in to defend these noble creatures from a gruesome end? In a similar fashion to other contexts (see D. E. Taylor 1997) a specific "actor fiction" has also been articulated around the figure of the white male conservationist in South Africa. An avatar of this figure could be seen in March 2015, when two rectangular louvered billboards were placed in parallel in the domestic terminal of OR Tambo International Airport in Johannesburg, containing the payoff line "Come Together to Protect What's Ours" and a call to donate R10 to the campaign by sending an SMS (Figure 2.2).

The billboard is branded with the familiar logo of one of South African Breweries' (SAB) flagship beers, Castle Lager, and was headed up by the famous Proteas wicket-keeper and (later, since 2019) national coach Mark Boucher, who appears in the bottom left part of the frame. When this campaign launched, SAB was the second-largest brewer in the world, with a

Figure 2.2: Boucher's Legacy billboard in OR Tambo airport

massive advertising spend. This particular billboard brings together three key pillars of white South African masculinity: cricket, the bush, and beer. As has been noted before (Mager 2005; Milani and Shaikjee 2013), SAB has articulated masculinity as central to its beer brands since at least 1960. During the transition to multiracial democracy, their advertising spend was a crucial force for articulating Rainbowism, and the togetherness of the nation (see McKaiser 2012). Extensive sports sponsorship and advertising has been central to these projects of nation- and brand-building, which leveraged South Africa's triumphant post-apartheid return to international sport as proof both of the viability of the new nation, and of the ongoing relevance and competitiveness of its white minority, who could once again see themselves celebrated as figures of global importance (Steenveld and Strelitz 1998). The extensive (and still highly racialised) emotional investment in the sporting prowess of the nation makes instant celebrities out of successful athletes, in ways that often reveal evolving sociopolitical identities and divisions (Bolsmann and Parker 2007). These celebrity figures are in turn deployed to bolster other enterprises: to support charities, drive advocacy campaigns, or to market popular brands. The phenomenon of "celebrity environmentalism" is a global one (see Abidin et al. 2020) and in this specific case Boucher's status is being leveraged as an ambassador for the rhino. But in the context of the racialised and gendered discourses of poaching sketched above, is it relevant that a white man has been chosen to lead the campaign?

Boucher is only one among many famous white men who play this ambassadorial role in the fight against poaching. The South African emigré Kevin Pietersen, whose successful international cricket career in the United Kingdom is overshadowed in the South African media by his disdain for "transforming" cricket into a multiracial sport (see Mohamed 2017) has successfully restyled himself as a conservationist, coming back to Africa in order to save it. As the leader of a charity that rescues and rehabilitates rhino affected by poaching activities, called SORAI (Save our Rhino's in Africa and India), Pietersen enjoys fawning BBC coverage:

> The rhino. An icon, all but extinct. A maverick who never backs down says he'll save them. It's raw. It's war. (Tracey 2019)

In a corpus of online news videos on the status of the poaching crisis during COVID-19 lockdowns, every single anti-poaching ranger interviewed ultimately reported to a white boss or landowner, many of whom were portrayed in terms similar to Pietersen, as quasi-heroic figures, "mavericks" who would "never back down" (Burnett 2022). The question of who leads the fight against poaching thus cannot avoid problematising the representation of these heroic white men.

The SAB billboards in OR Tambo clearly articulate links between rhino conservation, leadership, and national unity in diversity. The figure of the leader is represented by Mark Boucher, his cricket whites replaced with the standard khaki uniform of the game ranger. White men wearing khaki feature in Kenyan writer Binyavanga Wainaina's celebrated "How to Write about Africa" (2005):

> Anybody white, tanned and wearing khaki who once had a pet antelope or a farm is a conservationist, one who is preserving Africa's rich heritage. When interviewing him or her, do not ask how much funding they have; do not ask how much money they make off their game. Never ask how much they pay their employees.

The white conservationist is expected to lead, in other words, and to be celebrated, but without ever having to face a challenge on the "conservation mode of production" (Brockington and Scholfield 2010). The people that Boucher is responsible for leading are clearly shown on the billboard, and feature in close-up in other campaign artefacts. They form a diversely dressed, multiracial "human chain" of men and women of all ages, standing resolute in the wilderness to protect the family of rhinos in the centre. The inclusion of the rhino in the national community is thus made explicit on this billboard, with its iconic indexicalities: the Rainbow Nation is quite literally holding hands in order to embrace the rhino. If they form a colourful and protective border, there is also just a hint of the strength, resolve, and (defensive) violence required to perform this protection. Considered one of the national team's best ever wicket-keepers, Boucher is known for his "safe hands": i.e., that he was good at catching cricket balls, preventing the opposing side from scoring. This metaphor of the cricket match, where the other side is batting and must be stopped, is continued in the mocked-up crest on the right, which uses the motto "Our Rhinos in Safe Hands" and a drawing of a rhino, protected by two large mitts. The historical military character of the coat of arms has left its faint traces in sports, nation-branding, and countless other institutions, where the power of the shield is implicitly required to defend against violence. In the same way that Boucher wears sunglasses to protect his eyes, we are made aware as viewers that the work he is doing is tough work. The figures on the billboard are prepared for violence; one could imagine them repeating the popular white South African adage: "Africa is not for sissies" (see A. Collins 2013).

In this worldview, diverse people must unite (as the motto of the official national crest encourages them to do) but they are best advised to do so under the leadership of a white man. As was detailed in the introduction, white men are extremely overrepresented in the top management echelons of South

African companies. Given their continued predominance and power, it is clear that they regard each other as the business leaders they trust to get the job done. Within this unequal human landscape, Black people are included as having an important role to play, as long as it is in the background and broadly supportive of and collaborative with the protective goals of white bosses. They unite also to mark out the territory. The human chain becomes a fence or border, which closes the rhinos off from the bad people and from potential harm. The proprietorial assertion that the rhinos are "OURS" echoes the angry Facebook commenter on the SANParks Honorary Rangers page. The inclusion of the rhino inside the human chain, and consequently inside the national community symbolically pushes anybody who would harm them outside of it—into a zone of nonbeing, or a space of exception. Fanon's account of childhood collective catharsis resonates strongly here. In the same way that children's sympathies are with the white missionary being cooked, so our emotional support is drawn towards the white hero who steps up to save the rhino from the savages who would harm them. The poachers are phantom presences, just out of the frame, but no less real for their invocation through the imagery of the shield and the human chain. The image is in this sense "waiting for the barbarians."

CONCLUSION: DECONSTRUCTING STEWARDSHIP

The four texts examined in depth in this chapter are acts of articulation that reveal specific moments in the discursive regime of the "war" on rhino poaching. These moments represent attempts to fix the meaning-potentials of the available discursive elements, which are in turn the subject of ongoing discursive struggle between activists, academics, mainstream conservation organisations, the managers of protected areas, the South African government, the communities affected by green militarisation, and many others. What becomes visible through reading these texts in conjunction is the extent to which they draw on other discursive formations: on sedimented colonial constructions of poacher as opposed to hunter, on neoliberal conservationism, on hegemonic masculinity, on discourses of sexuality and of HIV, and of beer, sport, nation, and leadership. In the press release, the event of the extrajudicial killings of two men is articulated in such a way as to inscribe a social order as natural. It is unremarkable, and simply common sense that if you trespass, appear suspicious, or are out of place, on land you do not own, your life may be forfeit, even if you are not armed. As we saw in the comments, rather than giving the followers of the Honorary Rangers page an opportunity to reflect on the loss of human life, the press release elicited the even broader endorsement: to "take them all out." This blank and absolute antagonism is grounded both in the presence of the "black satyr" as absolutely "not-self" and unassimilable, and of the rhino which is embraced in the national family, symbolising white interests. The black satyr is invoked in the chain of equivalences presented in the bumper sticker: associated with murder, sexual violence, and disease. The rapacious Black man is always a sexual threat, and the attack on "OUR" rhinos is an emasculating attack, the revenge for which is "castration followed by lynching." The threat of the Oriental man is the fact of his "lack" of that which the black satyr has in abundance, which he will go to any lengths to acquire in order to achieve "real" heterosex, and it is in this context the only one we can trust is the white father, under whose leadership the nation can form a border around that which is ours and ours alone, and which must be protected at all costs from the Other (cf. Norval 1996, 96).

While the rhino has been an important moment in the rearticulation of post-apartheid white land control, recent events suggest that it is not a necessary one. During the ongoing human catastrophe of the COVID-19 pandemic, militarised anti-poaching squads were still being lauded in local and international media as essential conservation technologies, even in cases where desperate people were poaching antelope for meat, and where no rhino were threatened (Burnett 2022). In ongoing political contestations over making space in post-apartheid South Africa, the discursive production of the khaki-clad white conservationist as the only trusted caretaker of the nation's ecosystems is thus a highly significant and enduring one, both before and presumably after the war on rhino poaching. He becomes the embodiment of a particular kind of hope for the future which is wound up both in conservation as a mode of production, as a significant contributor to the national GDP, and of course as one of the "reasons" for white people's continued presence in Africa. Protected areas are produced as sites for the consumption of tourism; those who are not there for tourism are interlopers. Tourism spaces interlock into a broader patchwork of productive and leisure spaces that structure national imaginaries of economic development, rational progress, infrastructure, and undergird what is seen as fair-minded stewardship of the earth. As all of these good things supposedly align with the aspirations of presently poor and marginalised people, the white father has a claim to be the country's ticket to that coveted time-space of a "better future." His role is to keep people and things in place and their correct relations, against the forces of entropy. White masculinity is thus valorised as "belonging" to Africa through its positioning at the centre of the campaign as the protector of the land, while the violent Black poacher is pushed to the deviant periphery, as a threatening force. This is not just a bad thing for poachers. As is clear from Fanon's account, the phantasmagorical character of racist constructions does not narrow their effects. It did not matter that Fanon was not himself a slave or a cannibal: he was still "battered down by tom toms." The bumper sticker specifically treats every Black person in the taxi behind the car as its audience: it is not targeted specifically at poachers, but at Blackness in general. The effect of these texts is the reproduction of a racial hierarchy with whiteness at its apex.

Finally, it is important to note the extent to which this triangular structure, with Black poacher and Asian consumer at the base as threats to the land and the white father the trusted steward at its apex, is an inversion of the historical roles that these groups played. The arrival of European settlers in southern Africa four centuries ago occasioned the decimation of the region's wildlife. The historical enemy of biodiversity has been the white father. And yet, today, the descendants of indigenous people are represented as if they are the greatest threat to the land. White stewardship is constructed as trustworthy, while Black presence on the land is always suspicious, and potentially disastrous.

NOTES

1. See www.savetherhino.org/rhino-info/poaching-stats/ accessed 4 August 2021.
2. WWF South Africa, in consultation with TRAFFIC and PSI, chose to withhold permission for the reproduction of this image (Communication with the author, 17 December 2021).

Chapter 3

Protecting "Soul Country"

Beneath the stark and beautiful plains of the Karoo, South Africa's vast and sparsely populated central semidesert region, lies what might still prove to be one of the world's largest shale gas reserves. Exploiting this gas is seen by many as crucial for economic growth and the diversification of the energy sector, for job creation, and a key step in reducing South Africa's dependence on coal for the generation of electricity. The National Development Plan 2030 thus envisions "increasing exploration to find domestic gas feedstock" in the Karoo basin "to diversify the energy mix and reduce carbon emissions" (National Planning Commission 2012, 49, 171). The exploitation of shale gas as an energy resource only became economic once a process called hydraulic fracturing—"fracking" for short—showed some successes in the United States after the turn of the millennium (Zuckerman 2014). The process, which involves injecting a mixture of water, sand, and chemicals under high pressure deep into the earth at injection pads in order to release gas trapped in the rock, has stoked controversy and opposition nearly everywhere it has been proposed or implemented (Mazur 2016). South Africa is no exception. The prospect of a shale gas boom in one of the most economically depressed regions of one of the world's most unequal countries has been hyped up by advocates of fracking as a solution to unemployment and poverty, and thus also as a potential avenue to dismantling the racial hierarchy. Opposition on the basis of the potential environmental and economic harms of fracking has however been fierce, and the debate has brought to the surface deep divisions about how the government ought to make decisions about land use and control. Though mineral resources were effectively nationalised by the Mineral and Petroleum Resources Development Act of 2002, South Africa's highly consultative and deliberative democratic dispensation, and legislatively mandated environmental assessment process, mean that there are many legal and legislative avenues for members of the public to slow down the process of granting prospecting rights (see Fig 2013). So while the ruling ANC has repeatedly vowed to open up this important seam of national development, a focused and tenacious group of activists, some of whom belong to broad-based multiracial social and environmental justice organisations, but many of whom are aligned with a small but powerful group of white businesspeople, environmentalists, and landowners, have effectively challenged the process at every turn. As a result, though fracking in the Karoo has been reported as "imminent" since at least 2008, thirteen years later the first exploratory wells have yet to be drilled, and new regulations are still being drafted (de Wet 2021).

This chapter examines the role of racial identities and racialised structures in the ongoing standoff over fracking. It is clearly *not* the case that Black and "Coloured" citizens are eager for fracking to start, while a group of entrenched, racist, rich and white South Africans resolutely thwart such development in the name of landscape preservation. Rather, the ways in which rights to land and a rightful place on the landscape have been historically entangled in racial orders linger on in the various commitments of social actors, and their articulations of eco-social myths and imaginaries. While traditional media and courtrooms have been key sites of this discursive struggle, much of the energy behind opposition to fracking has been organised and popularised by activist groupings on social media. The largest and most successful of these groups, with just under 12,000 members, has been "chase SHELL OIL out of the Karoo!" which is the Facebook platform for the leading local anti-fracking campaign, the "Treasure the Karoo Action Group" headed up by charismatic CEO Jonathan Deal. In the next section, I introduce this group, and the sample of posts that I analysed, contextualising their discourse in the economic and cultural meanings of the Karoo that have profoundly influenced their specific form of activism. Through close attention to self-other distinctions, I proceed to lay out three dominant "frontiers" that are drawn between "us" and "them" in the discourse of the anti-frackers. Discussion of these frontiers lays the groundwork for a discussion of how connectedness to the land is articulated for the "us" group, where white settler autochthony is produced as a consolidating myth that rationalises the various frontiers. In the concluding section, I discuss how the myth of autochthony is developed in concert with a white ethnoscape, which is simultaneously the scene on which settlers made history and the grounds from which settler history arose.

TREASURING THE KAROO ON FACEBOOK

Representing the seemingly endless plains of the Karoo in fine art or literature has been one of the animating challenges of white cultural production, especially connected to "anti-pastoral" traditions (Coetzee 1988) and "an enduring topos for imagining South Africa and, more broadly, Africa" (Geertsema 2006, 106). Though there are a number of new solar and wind farm developments, as well as mines, the economy of the Karoo has since the wool boom of the 1840s been primarily an agricultural one, with sheep-farming playing a key role, and tourism growing in size and importance since the 1990s (Atkinson 2016). The sheer openness of the landscape, the brilliantly clear night skies, and a sense of "nothingness" (Ingle 2010) have been marketed as destinations for domestic and international tourists, as well as for "semigrants" (Ballard 2004) from urban areas who often form middle-class artistic or creative enclaves where they settle to enjoy the lifestyle, and sometimes also cater to the tourist trade. "Sleepy" and relatively undeveloped Karoo towns with their quaint architecture and steady daily rhythms are marketed as "heritage" destinations where the historical racial and social relations of apartheid and colonial orders are implicitly sanitised (McEwen and Steyn 2013, 4). In stark contrast to the relative prosperity of the creative and tourism enclaves, the Karoo in general has extremely high levels of poverty, unemployment, alcohol abuse, and sexual violence (Holtmann 2008). These contrasts, like social inequality more broadly in South Africa, cleave to the historical racial divisions that produced white prosperity and Black and "Coloured" precarity.

The Karoo-lovers who rallied behind Jonathan Deal in 2011 to form the Treasure Karoo Action Group (TKAG) to prevent the threatened issuing of fracking licences by the national Department of Minerals and Energy represented a broad range of interests (see van der Merwe 2015 for an ethnography of the TKAG). Deal himself owns the Gecko Rock Private Nature Reserve near Touwsrivier, an especially arid and quiet corner of the Karoo not slated for fracking. Many of the movement's strongest supporters live in Cape Town or other urban centres, and visit the Karoo as tourists. Others live in the Karoo and own businesses, farms, or eco-tourism operations, and fear that their livelihoods are directly impacted by fracking. Others are academics, environmentalists, or members of the public committed to preserving the region's unique ecosystems. The Facebook group "chase SHELL OIL out of the Karoo!" was initiated by Deal at the same time as TKAG in January 2011, and has been one of the main communication channels for the campaign, in addition to traditional media and a TKAG website (www.treasurethekaroo.co.za). Over a period of ten years the group has retained 11,675 members (by 7 August 2021) and has thousands of posts detailing developments in the local and global fight against fracking. This poses the challenge to discourse analysis of finding a way to give a "bird's-eye view"—discursive map, or "structural topography" (Marttila 2016, 125) of what is going on in a particular set of articulations that picks out not just individual acts of articulation, but the patterned acts that constitute the discursive articulation (cf. fig. 3). I will offer a brief discussion of how I approached this problem here.

I used a purpose-built Python script to scrape the URLs and key metadata of all individual posts from TKAG's Facebook group. I chose the twenty-five most engaging posts—where engagement was defined as the number of comments, shares, and emotional reactions (like, love, wow, sad, angry) that any given post enjoyed—per year, from 2013 to 2016, to produce a corpus of the "Top 100" posts from what was arguably the most intense period of the anti-fracking campaign. The script I used in 2018 has since ceased to function, owing to changes in the Facebook API rules in the wake of the Cambridge Analytica scandal (see Tromble 2021 for a critical account). The group was, and still is, a public group, and the text and images from the posts that I will reproduce below were thus not initially shared with an expectation of privacy. However, users have not consented to be the subject of this discourse analysis, and I therefore anonymise all of the "ordinary" members of the group. I do link specific comments to key public figures such as Jonathan Deal, but only when the identity of the commenter is relevant to the analysis. In terms of a broad social profile of the users who participated in these Top 100 discussions, my own estimation (leveraging the racial "sense" of a white South African born in 1978 and growing up in a highly racialised society) based on people's Facebook profile pictures and their family pictures, their names, and language use, is that just under 90 percent of the contributors were white. In order to refer to the specific posts, I use a simple code reference system, where the top posts are organised chronologically in 2013 (posts 1–25), 2014 (posts 26–50), 2015 (posts 51–75) and 2016 (posts 76–100). These codes are linked to individual URLs, which are all listed in Appendix A.

My approach to reading the posts was to identify what the ethical principles were behind the construction of frontiers between "us" and "them." The construction of opponents who antagonise a particular social vision, as discussed in chapter 1, are crucial figures to the stability of a discourse regime. The values that they threaten are very often also the key nodal points that give structure to the rest of the discourse as a whole, interpellating its specific subject roles and rationalising institutions. These dynamics of the discourse are also revealed in the moments when specific heroes are hailed as the protagonists who will serve as the "champions and protectors of the paramount ethical ideals" (Marttila 2016, 133). These frontiers cordoned off a specific space in which the outlines of a myth connecting people to it became visible. The Karoo is represented in photographs, poems, songs, and in evocative language. This space and the connection of the members of the TKAG group to it is produced as a "heartland" or "soul country" that must be protected against the Other. These processes of boundary maintenance (see

Yuval-Davis 2006) rely on the interplay between social identities and societal structures which produce the discourse regime.

Frontier 1: Rainbow Consumers

The anti-frackers of "chase SHELL OIL out of the Karoo!" repeatedly assert that their movement is a non-racial one, and there is often a defensive tone in articulating this. Some members talk of themselves as "liberals like us" (post 3) while some align their own campaign with the liberation movement, through (for example) honouring the "activist legacy" of the four ANC cadres abducted and murdered in Cradock in 1985 (post 80). Significantly, group members are reprimanded or excluded for racist speech, and at a number of points in the corpus there are gaps or references that suggest some comments have been deleted (e.g., posts 12 and 63). The pantheon of environmental heroes lauded by the group gives prominence to the Nigerian writer and activist Ken Saro-Wiwa, the details of whose execution in 1995 in circumstances connected to his threats to the interests of Royal Dutch Shell Oil are seen as an appropriate parable for what is going on in the Karoo (posts 11, 15, 27 and 31). White TKAG activists and administrators (such as Jonathan Deal and Jeanie le Roux) are celebrated by group members alongside TKAG vice-chairman Daantjie Japhta, traditional leader of the Khoisan[1] Inqua clan and charismatic former mayor of Graaff-Reinet (post 18). And though he is not mentioned in this corpus, it is worth noting that the chairperson of the TKAG at this time was Barry Wuganaale, a Nigerian pastor and activist from Ogoniland, who is introduced in other campaign-related texts as a relative of Ken Saro-Wiwa (Du Toit 2013). Black South African public figures are lionised, such as Advocate Thuli Madonsela, the popular former public protector praised for her integrity in standing up to creeping state corruption under Jacob Zuma (posts 86, 89 and 91), and the activists of the community at Xolobeni (post 98), who successfully protested and delayed the building of a new titanium mine by an Australian company. Building on these various indications of a campaign that transcends racial divisions, Jonathan Deal clearly states that the critique that TKAG is only "protecting their own big fat white interests" is launched by "dishonest people with vested interests" (post 15) and must therefore be dismissed with contempt.

The fact that the vast majority of the group members involved in articulating this non-racialism are in fact white South Africans occasionally seems to provoke anxiety about who is participating in the conversation. Images of public consultations on fracking, where South Africans of all races come together to grill oil companies, are shared eagerly as proof of "greater unity between the different stake holders" (post 18). Fracking in the Karoo is said to affect everyone, no matter "what colour of skin you are" (post 12). This anxiety works to sediment a particular conception of the "Rainbow Nation" as the guiding value for this particular discursive regime. This value includes the idea that the evil of racism was in singling out people for differential treatment on the basis of the colour of their skin, and that the true antiracism lies in refusing to discriminate at all between different race "groups" (see Bonilla-Silva 2006; and Steyn 2001a for critiques of "colour-blindness"). This plays out in the anti-fracking movement in a specific and revealing way.

In 2015 a group member shared a meme containing the first lines of the 1955 Freedom Charter in celebration of the anniversary of this key text of the liberation movement:

> We, the People of South Africa, declare for all our country and the world to know: that South Africa belongs to all who live in it, black and white, and that no government can justly claim authority unless it is based on the will of the people. (post 70)

The rhetorical constitution of "the people" is foundational to the articulation of social vision (see Laclau 1990). It is thus significant that this meme sets off a string of angry comments about who exactly is included in the definition of "the People." One commenter insists: "All the people - not only tenderpreneurs and their supporters" (post 70). The neologism "tenderpreneur" invokes a particular actor fiction: the supposedly inexperienced, unqualified, or corrupt companies or individuals who are awarded government contracts under a policy of preferential procurement to adjust for the racial imbalances of South African society (see Kitis, Milani, and Levon 2018). The idea that this in-crowd of the "Ruling Mafia" (post 70) should be given preference is read as evidence of the exclusion of others from the definition of "the People": poor or marginal people not connected to the ANC, but also good, liberal supporters of the anti-fracking movement who are seen to be "previously advantaged." Hostility to the practice of preferential procurement in general is however not equivalent to critique of "tenderpreneurship" per se. It is still possible to support preferential procurement within the broad-based Black economic empowerment (BBBEE, or BEE) framework while worrying about corruption, or believing that the process of awarding government tenders is flawed. This is not however a middle ground that many members of this group articulate clearly, tending instead to a blanket rejection of preferential policies.

BBBEE and Affirmative Action (AA) are repeatedly criticised as "racist." What is clearly meant by this is that they are antiwhite. The despised practice of "load-shedding" (i.e., planned service interruptions to reduce the load on the national grid) and other failures in electricity provision by Eskom are attributed to AA specifically, and the remedy prescribed is to employ "people of proven competence in the relevant field in these positions regardless of race, creed or political affiliation" (post 65). Buying your own solar panels is a way to get "off the racist Eskom failing grid" (post 90). The state of the parastatals is summed up by one member in the following terms: "but we only have idiots left—the clever ones left the country and the rest are sitting at home" (post 74).[2] This statement is meaningful in relation to implicitly shared knowledge of one popular narrative of post-apartheid history: that there was a wave of white emigration, that white employees in public service or in parastatals were retrenched or pressured into voluntary retirement, and that this left only "idiots" who happen to be mostly Black people—working at places like Eskom. In the oil and gas industry, it is speculated that "fracking companies will gladly give 33.3% to BEE's . . . who in any case will just break everything down and sell it as scrap" (post 69). Erstwhile minister of energy Tina Joemat-Pettersson is said to be "the type that will close a deal with plumbing company to build the [nuclear] plant" (post 82). Don't worry, says another "no nuclear energy will happen. The fools can't even build 2 simple coal stations" (post 53).

These chains of equivalence between Black economic empowerment, corruption, incompetence, failing parastatals, and "racism" against white people are articulated around colour-blindness and "fair" competition on open markets as their guiding values. The right way to organise activism in this context is constructed as being to withhold one's participation as a consumer. A boycott is a tactic through which white people can compensate for their relative lack of power as voters by leveraging their economic might, allowing them to be heard by government and industry. Group members construct this influence as similar to that of a persistent "mosquito" (post 27) and as a few good people kicking up a "*moerse* [hell of a] fuss" (post 65). While oil companies are reviled for a variety of reasons, one that is mentioned as justifying a boycott is its implementation of BEE policies (post 64). The boycott of Shell, in which the ANC is a stakeholder, is understandably a thoroughgoing preoccupation for members. "Shell forget that we have the money," says one member (post 64); boycotting Shell is "voting with our wallets" (post 96). TKAG however does not officially call for a boycott of Shell, leaving it up to its supporters to decide what to do. This stance becomes awkward for Jonathan Deal when he instead threatens an official boycott of the expensive and popular chain of Brazilian-style coffee shops, Vida e Caffé, which through a new franchise deal would open coffee shops at Shell petrol stations. When one of the group's members challenges him on this apparent contradiction, Deal explains that it is very difficult to get a boycott of Shell going, and that "ANC Ex politician and wealthy businessman Chris Nissen told me to my face that if we called a boycott of Shell he would make sure that every black-owned taxi in the country filled up at Shell" (post 15). This logic reveals the structure of the consumer economy in South Africa, and the way that white activists understand themselves as operating within it. Vida e Caffé—a purveyor of expensive coffee and food in upmarket neighbourhoods—is seen as being responsive to the consumer behaviour of white people, whereas Shell is not. Deal takes Nissen at his word, affirming that an ANC politician would be able to make good on his threat, and that all "black-owned" taxis in the country would follow the instructions of the ruling party. Whereas Black buying power is constructed as consisting in the vast number of consumers and (risibly) in their monolithic political solidarity, (mostly white) environmentally conscious buying power is presented as focused, ethical, and potentially felt in the fortunes of a well-known luxury brand that the majority of the population cannot afford.

If middle-class buying power is one side of the "voting with your wallets" coin, the other is the threatening demographic predominance of poor, Black, working-class and/or unemployed people at the polls. The main problem with the "poor and less-educated sector" (post 37) from an anti-fracking perspective is that they are willing to believe the lies of the oil industry. There is an awareness that the interests of unemployed people must be taken into account, but this is weighed up against the sense that poor people are unable to understand the bigger picture:

> One of the big challenges in SA is that the bulk of the people are fixated (understandably and necessarily) with improving their economic position and being treated in a socially just manner. They (again, understandably) are desperate to believe the untruths being told to them that environmental exploitation is an essential way to achieve economic growth, create jobs and build a better life for all. The links between unsustainable environmental exploitation and the erosion of socio-economic wellbeing need to become common knowledge. (post 12)

While this statement asserts some commitment to social justice, and is careful not to blame poor people for their "fixation" or "desperation" it works to foreclose the building of alliances, or the eventual sharing of "common knowledges" as the "bulk of people" has been constructed upfront as lacking the critical consciousness necessary to think strategically about development. The relationships between "socio-economic wellbeing" and "environmental exploitation" are not up for discussion, but asserted as known. There are many ways, such as those practiced by Indigenous land rights and environmental justice activists, of involving marginalised people in environmental conversations without undermining their agency or intelligence. That poor Black people's desperation is constructed as the "challenge" furthermore distracts from a critique of the structuring of South Africa's liberal market economy, setting the horizon of intelligibility at more education for these "desperate" people about the way the world really works, rather than a dismantling of its conditions of possibility.

The post above is very much on the progressive side of the anti-fracking discourse, which at the other extreme articulates elements of neo-Malthusianism. The problem with the world is that there are too "many people in the planet" (post 75) and a "growing population exacerbates the problem" (post 12); unless "human population gets under control we will lose our wild spaces" (post 92). These fears of the "barbarian hordes" (Fletcher, Breitling, and Puleo 2014) are at certain points articulated with other elements:

> What about facing the real problem? Numbers. What about using technology to stop US, the cause of all pollution, consumption, waste, of breeding untill we are say "responsible" enough? Or, as is the case, is our "rights" sacrosanct? Is it easier to chop down a forest for that townhouse complex, easier to give "grants", to hike taxes, than to face the real cause? (post 28)

This statement reveals complex interlocking ideological commitments. While the poster is concerned that "we" are irresponsibly expanding the population and killing the earth through our "breeding" the question of who pays the taxes that pay for the grants introduces an implicit us/them division. There is a thinly veiled eugenic urge here to implement "technologies" to limit population growth, which is connected both to expensive taxes and to environmental decline. The idea that social grants in South Africa encourage young Black women living in poverty to get pregnant, though thoroughly and regularly debunked (see Makiwane and Udjo 2006), is a perennially popular one, and it is the Constitutional order that secured this social net that is the tacit target of the critique of sacrosanct "rights." The provision of these grants relies on a fairly small base of businesses and individuals who pay tax, the category to which most of the white minority belongs.

Though there is clearly disagreement and discursive struggle between members, repeated acts of articulation work to sediment something approaching a consensus, which includes various affirmations of colour-blindness, the corroboration of the fairness and efficiency of the market, and a focus on the strategic importance of consumer power for an embattled minority. A frontier is thus drawn between those who hold firm to these principles, and those who threaten them. The latter group includes tenderpreneurs in league with their "mafia" enablers in the government, public employees who keep their jobs despite being "idiots," the enforcers of "racist" BEE and AA policies, and, as was shown in the claims about taxi-drivers and the "problematic" masses, in the legions of helpers that are willing to keep them in power. The poor majority is not necessarily an active antagonist, but rather a blank presence stuck in a particular mode of thinking, and sometimes also a burden to the environment and the taxpayer with their unsustainable fecundity. This bad form of (state-funded) consumption and (re)production is implicitly contrasted to the good forms of production and consumption displayed by the anti-frackers: economic productivity on sustainable economic principles, and ethical consumption that boycotts the businesses that threaten environmental or social harm.

It is worth restating here that non-racialism gained hegemony in South Africa in the mid-1990s in a time of triumph for economic liberalism at the end of the Cold War. The "Rainbow Nation" imaginary was thus from its very inception constituted by multi-coloured members of a global consumer society (Hart 2002). This meant different things to different people. For many middle-class white South Africans, the end of economic sanctions and international opprobrium inaugurated a new era of economic growth and prosperity. Key events such as the Truth and Reconciliation Commission and the awarding of the joint Nobel to Nelson Mandela and F. W. de Klerk signalled that far from being held directly responsible for historical crimes, or being made to pay reparations, their participation in a peaceful transfer of political power would be rewarded with forgiveness and high social status. The anti-frackers on Facebook retrace the outlines of these founding myths of the New South Africa, while attempting to rearticulate the dislocation experienced because of AA and BBBEE, which policies in their understanding contradict the principle of non-racialism, and are thus both "racist" and "corrupt." These discursive moves are thus attempts to renovate and repair the Rainbow Nation imaginary without the loss of any of the relative advantage inherited from the apartheid order, reaffirming and legitimating their existing entitlements to property and prosperity.

Frontier 2: Rooted in the Karoo

Being affectively linked in some way to the Karoo was another major frontier between "us" and "them." Group members think of themselves as "Karooists" (post 52) and give encouragement to specific small towns to continue the battle against fracking. Honest, earthy work such as farming is contrasted to the shady and suspect work of elites. One commenter complains that "we have to survive in the Karoo on our farms and when it goes wrong they [the government] will pull up their shoulders and carry on living like kings" (post 10). When an oil company bigwig is taken to task at a community meeting in Aberdeen (post 51), townspeople are constructed as having a particular fighting spirit, they "stand together," you can't "mess with them" and they have shown the world that "we are no sissies." Karoo people have long-standing ties of blood and friendship (e.g., posts 24 and 30) that make them a tough and close-knit clan. The Indigenous Khoisan people appear within

Figure 3.1: Daantjie Japhta, former mayor of Graaff-Reinet, deputy chairman of TKAG

the definition of this clan in the figure of Daantjie Japhta (Figure 3.1) who is presented on Facebook as representing the "people of the Karoo" (post 18).

Japhta is however not mentioned again in the corpus after this point (in November, 2013) and is not himself a member of the Facebook group who makes any contributions to the conversation. By 2015, members are wondering where Indigenous people stand on the fracking debate. One group member asks: "I'm wondering where the voices are of the people who are the original karoo dwellers?" (post 55). This member seems reticent to name the "original dwellers," is not clear where they are geographically, and has no clear sense of how to make contact with them. Not knowing exactly where the Khoi or San people are is an important admission in a discourse so concerned with rootedness, with place-names, and honest work on farms. The inability to place a Khoisan community or individual other than through the representation of Japhta speaks to a role in the discourse that turns the "original dwellers" into symbols of connection to land that are unthreatening to present-day white land occupation built on histories of dispossession and exclusion. In this vein, a revealing articulation is made by another member:

> Ultimately, the Karroo belongs to the "people of origin." As their artwork found throughout the Karroo testifies to the copyright of the land. They have final say, don't they? (post 45)

It is interesting that what the Khoisan are said to own is the "copyright" of the land (and not the land itself) and that their exercise of this right is, like the rock-art they created over thousands of years, implied to be an aesthetic one related to the Karoo landscape. This particular reaction, which also clearly assumes that Khoisan people would support the anti-fracking movement, turns the Khoisan into ghostly historical presences that have always actually held "copyright" control over the land, but have somehow hovered above the processes of white settler colonial agricultural expansion with depoliticised benevolence, as their descendants are recruited as manual labourers, their livelihoods destroyed, and their cultures decimated. These processes must be elided in order for such benevolence to be asserted. It also works to articulate into the self-definition of the anti-fracker the noble autochthonic artist, whose ancient inscriptions on the land are transmuted into legitimation of their entitlement to direct its future development. Where existing landowners might have much to be ashamed of in the stories of how Khoisan land was historically taken, here their rock-art becomes marks of pride on the land. This shame is only suppressed through not asking questions about why it is that their art is "found" throughout the Karoo, by whom, where it lands up, who now "owns" it, etc. The Khoisan are thus used to sanctify historical dispossession by associating them with contemporary environmental protection, even as their original presence on the land is given discursive form. This is a good example of how "good feeling" (Ahmed 2004a, n.p.) may be retrieved from colonial shame.

Corporations, on the other hand, and the government officials that enable them, are represented as being foreign to the Karoo: as not being rooted. The devastation of the land that is envisaged by the anti-frackers is linked in a comment to an argument by an environmentalist called Jerry Mander:

> Corporations exist beyond time and space . . . they are legal creations that only exist on paper. They do not die a natural death; they outlive their own creators. And they have no commitment to locale, employees, or neighbors. This makes the modern corporation entirely different from the baker or grocer of previous years who survived by cultivating intimacy with the neighbors. Having no morality, no commitment to place, and no physical nature (a factory someplace, while being a physical entity, is not the corporation), a corporation can relocate all of its operations to another place at the first sign of inconvenience: demanding employees, too high taxes, restrictive environmental laws. (post 1)

Commitment to place and rootedness in physical location—having to look a community of people in the eye—pits the kinds of economic activity many of the group's members are involved in to the ephemeral, unnatural, and immoral character of the corporation. For the "Karooists" of the anti-fracking movement, this is the very essence of the problem. They understand themselves as guarding the land against the devil (posts 40 and 41) who would turn "*ons arme Karoo* [our poor Karoo]" into "Mordor"; (post 20). This does not however imply a critique of capitalism, only of the global corporation. This frontier is drawn in a Manichean fashion as a relation of perfect negation: the rootless corporation is a satanic force. The Karooists, who are rooted in the land, take care of the Karoo and its economy in a rugged, masculine, capitalist, and practical way, whereas forces of evil from outside of the area can only result in despoliation. As helpers for their role as the key protagonists of a healthy and functioning Karoo they enlist the ghostly figure of the indigenous Khoisan, who remain silent, excluded from exercising their subjectivity within the anti-fracking movement.

Frontier 3: Logical People

The third and final frontier I will present here is drawn around in-group rationality. The ruling ANC government is consistently represented as lacking reason. This manifests itself in many ways. Firstly, there is a thoroughgoing preoccupation with the education of ANC ministers who are said to have "bought" their qualifications (post 93). The minister of mineral resources Susan Shabangu "needs to be educated and then held accountable" (post 11) while the minister of energy Tina Joemat-Pettersson "only got the job as Energy Minister, because she knew how to switch a light on and off" (post 53). When Joemat-Pettersson proposes procuring nuclear energy she is said to know "NOTHING about the technicalities about nuclear and SQUAT about the cost [of] money" (post 82). Secondly, government officials are routinely represented as more similar in intelligence to animals than people. When Minister Joemat-Petterson was caught in an unguarded moment in parliament licking her teacup she is called "the missing link" (post 82). At another point she is referred to as "that thing" (post 88). In a discussion of former president Jacob Zuma, one member remarks that to "run a banana republic you need a baboon in charge" (post 23). Thirdly, ANC politicians are repeatedly said to be incapable of logical thought. "Logic and the ANC do not go together" (post 57) says one member; "The ANC are an ecological disaster, but without the logical" (post 65) says another. One member makes the point succinctly: "Our primitive government can not use logic" (post 43). The most popular post in the corpus, with 744 interactions, was a meme of animated comedy character Homer Simpson (post 74). Famously a very stupid man, whose catchphrase is "Doh!" while hitting himself on the head, he is shown with his head in his hands at the realisation that South Africa is an excellent location for solar energy, and yet the government is considering building a nuclear plant. A later comment posits stupidity as necessary for career advancement in the national government: "The dumber, the more senior the position"[3] (post 82).

These discourses have a tendency to make the ANC government seem so incompetent as to be harmless. The apartheid government managed to build actual nuclear power stations and weapons facilities (at Koeberg and Pelindaba) but the ANC government "cannot do it, they are incapable, don't worry, it won't happen" (post 53). The ANC is a "kindergarten" (post 10) whose key decision-makers are frequently infantilised. One commenter argues for more concerted campaigns for renewable energy so that "by offering Government a viable alternative to shale gas - a bit like distracting a naughty toddler with a new toy - we ought to be able to wean them off this disgusting technology" (post 17). The problem is that renewable energy "technology is mature. . . . our decisionmakers are not!" (post 32). This discounting of the full agency of not only the South African government but those of other "developing" countries is also articulated more subtly:

> I fear it is also ignorance and inexperience that make some of our leaders so easy to hoodwink. These corporate gluttons count on the inexperience of so many of the leaders in governments in "developing" countries, especially when it comes to their understanding of global business, environmental issues, etc. (post 11)

The picture of government as impressionable, inexperienced, and not quite in control of their own policy decisions also emerges in a controversy over WWF South Africa's wish list for Jacob Zuma's 2013 State of the Nation address, the first point of which was: "No fracking without environmental safeguards." This wording infuriated Jonathan Deal, who observes that the "South African government . . . needs little encouragement to make the wrong choice" (post 1). Only unequivocal language that allows no nuance can be countenanced.

The clearly racist tropes directed at Zuma and Joemat-Pettersson also appear in attacks on the CEO of Shell South Africa—Bonang Mohale—who is said to be typical "of the kind of monkeys we have running most of the big corporate gangs" (post 26). In one meme, a photo of Mohale sitting in a radio studio during an interview is reproduced, catching him in an unfortunately comical pose: hand scratching his head, lips parted in a smile, brows wrinkled, looking quizzically at the host. One of the comments below picked up on the visual cues of this particular shot:

> I ALMOST described the face I saw. And the gesture. And the animal it reminded me of. Archetypal image. Goodness luckily overcame me before I spoke out of turn. (post 62)

As discussed above, overtly racist speech is generally, though not always, policed in the group. By drawing attention to the fact that they are censoring themselves, this commenter both performs their moral "goodness" and manages to call Mohale a monkey. Another commenter picks up on the racist associations of African traditional medicine or *umuthi* discussed in the previous chapter, and comments "if i rub this muti on my head no one can see me" (post 62).

Mohale is likened to Jacob Zuma. They have the "same hairstyle" (post 62) though Mohale is the "bigger bullshitter" (post 26). In a reference to Zuma's representation by the satirical cartoonist Zapiro as having a shower-head[4] protruding from his forehead, Mohale is called "another showerhead" (post 45). These persistent equivalences shade into confusion: some members are clearly not sure whether Mohale is a businessman or a politician. He is "obviously bribed" (post 62) and needs to be voted out of power; another speculates that he is getting a "massive kickback" (post 62). When these members see a black face, they apply the discursive repertoire usually reserved for politicians. Another element of the repertoire usually used against politicians on a corporate payroll, but uniquely targeted at Mohale among other business leaders, is the idea that he is a "puppet." Commenters on post 62 claim that Mohale is a "corporate puppet," a paid-up "stooge," the "spin puppet bonehead Bonang." For these commenters, it is unthinkable that Mohale has the agency to actually be the one pulling the strings.

A not uncommon practice when talking about Black people in the corpus was to use orthography that imitated Black South African English (BSAE) pronunciation, a type of "Mock BSAE" with ideological underpinnings not dissimilar to those explored by Jane Hill in the United States in the context of Mock Spanish, which associates Spanish-speakers with "the non-serious, the casual, the laid-back, the humorous, the vulgar" (Hill 2008, 142). In the South African context, white use of mock-BSAE seems to associate Black people with a lack of education, intellectual deficiency, and the bafflement implied by the ejaculation "Eish!" Responses to memes showing up Bonang Mohale's supposed stupidity included "Eish!" (post 26) and "Seriaasly!" (post 26). Some members heap derision on poor people's environmental reasoning using mock-BSAE: "ish Charles, I've only got a honorary standard 5 we don't need clean drinking water we need short term jooobs!!" (post 11). When speaking of the impact of environmental damage on workers, one member says "the only people left carrying the can are the 'wekers'" (post 38). Politicians in the ANC are described as "pee-pull" with no morals (post 65); and one of the first responses to the Homer Simpson meme discussed above is a loud (i.e., capitalised) "EISH" (post 74). In a related attempt to debase African languages and accents, one member pretended, repeatedly, that the names of Bonang Mohale and Susan Shabangu were expletives: Mohale's "marketing rhetoric" for example, was a "load of Bonang" (post 8).

While Black business and government leaders shade into one another, and are dealt with using similar tropes and registers, white business leaders are treated very differently. White oil and gas executives are certainly reviled, but they get called things like "sulky" (post 52). Other white businesspeople are celebrated positively. Elon Musk, in particular, becomes an avatar for all that is good and heroic. He is a "genius" (post 78), an ally against fracking and nuclear power (post 78), "a very smart and generous guy" (post 78), and his way of thinking is the "future" (post 81). Musk's popularity is easily understandable. On the one hand he offers commenters the story of a white South African capitalist who has risen to international prominence and success. On the other, he offers them a future for a cherished car culture and high levels of energy consumption that is perceived as guilt-free and "sustainable." His life story is also seen as legitimising white flight from South Africa. He would never have accomplished what he has "in the backyard of the falling rand" claims one commenter, adding sarcastically: "Banana republics lead the way" (post 78).

Another white hero figure is Angela Merkel. Germany's (limited) fracking ban is repeatedly celebrated by members (posts 35, 50 and 71) and a smiling Angela Merkel is pictured as the face of the ban, leading "the number one sensible country" on earth (page 97). The situation in South Africa on the other hand is articulated as: "Only problem, we don't have a German goverment (or mentality) in SA!" (page 35). This "German mentality" is also typified in the form of Dr Stefan Cramer, the German hydrogeologist (post 43) whose arrival in the Karoo is greatly anticipated (post 24); he explains why the shale gas reserves in the Karoo are unlikely to be as great or as cheap to extract as was thought (post 57). These positive representations of Europeans and their scientific mentalities are in turn contrasted to wholesale rejections of Africa:

> Who do you think sold out the millions of African masses and their minerals to speculators, but their very own people? The ruthless few chiefs and greedy politicians were not able to manage themselves by putting something back into their economy or even creating one, but rather they bought up wall street and real-estate in London, so is that our fault as well now!! The undeveloped people have always been primitive and this cannot be blamed on Europeans. (post 65)

Africans are at one point described as obsessed "with clinging to superstition, dangerous and bizarre beliefs" (post 39); they "stream in by millions to create slums" (post 65); they kill each other when they should be farming (post

69), and the "only legacy that Africa leaves is deserts, genocide, and ruin"[5] (post 62).

This frontier is thus clearly drawn to separate Europe from Africa, reason from unreason, and (effectively) white from Black. Even the Black environmental heroes discussed above are lauded for their bravery and leadership in the face of oppression, but not for their scientific rigour or intelligence. While these figures appear as helpers and supporters in other articulations, the main protagonists of a social vision grounded in reason, science, and business acumen are all white people, and its opponents are all Black people, who are often described in vile and racist language.

MYTHS OF SETTLER AUTOCHTHONY

The anti-frackers situate themselves on the right side of three frontiers: they are the true protectors of the non-racial, free-market Rainbow Nation; they are the people authentically rooted in the Karoo; and they are on the side of reason, truth, and progress. These frontiers mark off the discursive territory that they understand themselves to inhabit, as well as delimiting a specific mythic vision of the Karoo which warrants detailed investigation. At first glance, this Facebook group is all about protecting territorial boundaries. Its name, after all, is "chase SHELL OIL out of the Karoo!" The Karoo is constructed both as a physical and an imaginative, affective terrain. It is "a place that touches every Afrikaner"[6] (post 8) and "our heartland"[7] (post 32). The Karoo is "soul country and it makes better human beings out of people" (post 62). One member says they will "never forget the stars" (post 72) and another agrees: "it never leaves you" (post 72). The ineffability of the Karoo makes the idea of exploiting it for shale gas a "clash/confrontation/war between head and heart, tangible and the intangible, measurable and the immeasurable" (post 67). It is easy to forget in these articulations of the sublime that the landscape is already parcelled out, much of it in commercial farms that certainly have "tangible" and "measurable" modes of production. The "sublime" may thus work to abstract from the messiness of individual and group histories of oppression and dispossession (see Geertsema 2006).

Fracking is thus on occasion articulated as supported by an exploitative scientific rationality which seeks to dispel the mysteries of the Karoo, while protecting it is grounded in affective and spiritual attachments that reject these simplistic reductions. Articulating this dichotomy opens an internal rift, however, along which members struggle to rearticulate the guiding values of the campaign. Opponents of this view do not dispute the importance of strong affective connections, but strive to balance these with a "scientific" approach. When a member dismisses scientific studies as informed by greed, they are sharply rebuked: "Let us forget about science and studies and, I suppose sing Kumbayaa? . . . You will lose the Karoo and you will lose it because of this attitude" (post 32). Not "losing" the Karoo is strongly articulated in a number of examples with scientifically knowing it: the claim that dolerite intrusions "cooked" the gas out of the shale (posts 3 and 24) is cited as one of six "reasons why fracking will never happen in the Karoo" (post 43). Members engage in their own reviews of what they understand the evidence to be for the size of shale gas reserves (post 6), and conclude that oil and gas companies are on a fool's errand. This assertion of the importance of scientifically knowing, while loving, the Karoo come together in a number of places in the corpus. A key articulation is the anti-fracking video by the progressive white South African folk singer David Kramer (post 67). In the video, he starts by singing a song in Afrikaans, which starts with the question: "Do you know the Karoo? The home of snake and lizard . . . ." Kramer then continues to sketch the evolutionary history of these animals: that the lizard used to be a fish, and that today you find shells in the rocks and fossils in the Karoo clay because the whole area used to be underwater. The song ends with him crooning: "Underwater, underwater: This whole dry expanse was underwater, believe me!"[8] (post 67). Kramer then speaks directly to the camera, and says, in English: "There's a place, a vast and beautiful place, an ancient place. It's a place I come from, and it's a place I write about, it's a place that's inspired me and my music. It's called the Karoo" (post 67).

To know the Karoo in Kramer's song is to know it on an evolutionary or geological timescale. He is both referring to the paleontological importance of the area, which was a prehistoric inland sea that became a rich fossil field, and to the awe and musical inspiration this knowledge gives him. In this context, it is this "ancient" prehistory that makes the Karoo worth saving—both for the head and for the heart. The implied audience of his song are people who don't know, or perhaps have heard but don't believe, this paleontological reading of the land. Kramer thus places himself and his own personal connection to and belonging in the Karoo on a timescale that stretches back millions of years. It is not a matter of recent history: it is ancient, and it is known through science.

These connections serve both to anchor Kramer's claim to belonging in geological time, and more subtly and unintentionally work to brush over the details of intervening, historical time and the social and political relations grounded in more recent human actions. Dealing with similar discursive strategies, David McDermott Hughes noted how white Rhodesians mythologised Lake Kariba—a dam that was opened in 1959 at the height of colonial influence—by representing it in geological time, even at one point imagining it surrounded by dinosaurs (Hughes 2010, 36–37). This representation allows the changes to the land wrought by white colonialists to be represented as ancient, and to naturalise and normalise their presence on the land. It was as if they had always been there; as if their presence was what nature intended. Similar gestures are made by the "Karooists." Kramer is produced as the sage-like white man connected both to the science and the mystery of this "ancient" history, while pushing into the background other histories and knowledges that might compete with his. Obvious alternatives include the colonial era genocide of the Khoisan, and the ensuing treatment of Black landholders in the region. The "you" that Kramer's song addresses might be aware of some of these histories, but Kramer draws their attention to the broader picture, which is a more accommodating and expansive timescale in which human actions seem relatively insignificant.

The naturalisation of white settlement in the Karoo and elision of histories of violent dispossession are also achieved in the way that landscapes are described by the anti-frackers. The Karoo is repeatedly called "perfect." Bonang Mohale's biggest sin when interviewed on the radio (posts 45 and 62) was to assert that Shell's investment might "improve" the Karoo. The Karoo is "already perfect, it cannot be made better" (post 45) and there is "no tampering needed!" (post 62). This perfection was ordained by God, making interference sacrilegious: "I'd like to know what both the Soul of The Karoo, and Creator, think about the improvements that Shell has in mind" (post 45). "Anyone who thinks they can leave it (the Karoo) better than they found it is actually saying that they can do a better job than He who created it!" (post 62). Articulations of the Karoo's perfection attach to typical Karoo scenes such as Figure 3.2 in response to which a commenter states that the "purity and awesome beauty of the Karoo is so worth fighting for" (post 36).

When group members use the language of "purity" to describe an image that has a windpump, a concrete farm dam, and a wire fence at its focal point, the presence on the land of the trappings of extensive agricultural activity originally established through European colonial incursion is effectively naturalised. The Karoo is elsewhere said to be "pristine" (post 32), "untouched for millions of years" (post 45), "unspoiled" (post 62), and a "wide open space of unspoilt beauty" (post 72). The typical "Karoo scene" is natural, God-ordained, peaceful, perfect, and beautiful, filled with the "'quiet' of memories and history" (post 72).

What's wrong with this picture? The establishment of agriculture in the Karoo in the eighteenth and nineteenth centuries was a catastrophe for Khoe, San, and Xhosa people. Many were killed in battles over territory as the frontier moved eastwards, pushed by administrators and settlers covetous of the abundant herds and verdant grazing lands of indigenes (Laband 2020). Entire bands of San were hunted down and massacred by mounted commandos in calculated acts of genocide (Adhikari 2011). Many people died of sickness and starvation, while the people who were left found themselves with little

Figure 3.2: A typical Karoo scene

option other than to serve as agricultural labour. All were eventually displaced and uprooted. Many of their descendants are low-paid and precarious agricultural workers to this day, or have been remaindered to urban townships to swell the legions of the unemployed. To invoke a "quiet" history in this context is an act of erasure that works to sanitise colonial history and cleanse the settler conscience, speaking to the ongoing contracting of "epistemologies of ignorance" (Steyn 2012; Mills 2007) in the formation of white subjectivities. For most other South Africans alive today, there was nothing "quiet" about this history.

Certainty of the Karoo's perfection is one of the guiding values that informs the construction of Manichean us/them frontiers, making the government's granting of exploration licences to frackers a potential "deal with the devil" (see Figure 3.3, post 40). The appropriate institutional bulwark against this advancing threat is articulated as the rights of the landowners to prevent access to their properties. The anti-frackers invoke a very strong sense of property rights: they say they would defend their land with "locked

Figure 3.3: Satirical cartoon shared by Jonathan Deal on 30 October 2014 (post 40)

gates and loaded shotguns" (post 51) and Jonathan Deal tells a farmer that nobody else can make plans for "YOUR farm" (post 61). Statements of possession are very common, sometimes with great emphasis: "OUR country, OUR Karoo, OUR livelihoods and OUR frigging environment" (post 68) or simply: "LEAVE OUR KAROO ALONE!!!!!!!" (post 45).

While they clearly assert that the Karoo is their possession, there is a contending claim that is not articulated as a contradiction or disagreement by the anti-frackers. This is the idea that the Karoo is not reducible to the property of any one person, and cannot be reduced to a monetary value. "How can you put a price tag on the Karoo?" asks one member (post 11); it is "not for sale" because it "belongs to everyone" (post 45). These vague assertions that the Karoo belongs to everyone are at odds with talk of "locked gates and loaded shotguns." As has already been noted, it is also often convenient to assert that "the original dwellers" have some claim to determine what becomes of the Karoo. This claim may be upheld as long as nobody can quite place them. The assertion that the Karoo "belongs to everyone" is similar in its vagueness about what this "belongingness" entails or how "everyone" will decide to exercise their ownership.

When articulated as elements of a discursive regime, these ideas form a potent myth. Instead of grounding their claims to possess the land in a specific narrative of historical ancestry and inheritance, close attention to which might disturb the conscience, a claim to being "of the land" is rooted on a much longer timescale. Scientific knowledge of evolution and geology, safe and ostensibly "Western" pursuits that make colonial histories seem fleeting and inconsequential by contrast, are invoked as the correct understanding of the Karoo. Other ways of thinking the current economic and social arrangement are foreclosed through an appeal to the land's sacred perfection, which includes all the marks on it of colonial agriculture. Because these marks are produced as natural, their own identities become inseparable from the land. Their culture is the soil, and they thus have a claim to autochthony uncontested by the ghostly presences of Khoisan that are invoked as fellow anti-frackers. They play the subject role of land protectors, while the institution of private property is corroborated as the appropriate way to save the landscape from antagonistic spoilers, and in so doing serve the best interests of "everyone" to whom the Karoo, after all, "belongs."

CONCLUSION: WHITENING THE ETHNOSCAPE

The occupation of lands not previously possessed, and over which threatening Others still make claims of ownership, to paraphrase Said ([1994] 2014, 5), demands the elaboration of systems of meaning that justify settler presence on the land, helping whites to develop a sense that they really belong in Africa, and that their possession of the land is justified. The frontier drawn by white environmentalists between rational, scientific ways of knowing and making decisions about the land, and the "idiotic" policies of a mentally deficient, childish Black government wilfully enabling the spoiling of the land, can be read as a legacy both of hardcore biological racism and its more subtle liberal version, which articulates complex economic and political decisions as best taken by people who have reached their full intellectual and cultural maturity. Though parts of the Rainbow Nation frontier were developed more recently, the liberal commitment to the utility of free trade and liberal markets has been around for a long time. The prosperity supposedly brought to the Cape frontier by open trade was the argument made by Grahamstown merchants in the nineteenth century to get military support for the expansion of the border into the territory of the amaXhosa (Keegan 1997, 71–73). And the frontier articulated around "rootedness" in the Karoo, as we have seen, is enabled by concerted work to erase the historical conditions of its own possibility, installing benevolent and absent Khoisan artists as legitimisers of strong property rights defended with "locked gates and loaded shotguns." I have argued that, when combined in a discursive regime where the land is symbolically produced in particular ways, these frontiers combine into a myth of settler autochthony that legitimate its ongoing occupation and ownership.

There is a parallel between the form of this myth, and ethnonationalist myths in general. Anthony Smith (1999) identified six myths central to the formation of nation-states: myths of temporal origins, location and migration, ancestry, of a heroic age, of decline, and of regeneration (1999, pp. 63–67). Smith argued that

> Ethnic myths are vital "evidence" for territorial "title-deeds"; association of the people with historic events and persons resident within a particular terrain is a sine qua non of the quest for a recognized "homeland" . . . But, equally, the title-deeds which derive their meaning from ethnic myths are charters for collective aspirations and actions; they validate, even direct, the struggle for land and recognition. (1999, p. 69)

The territorial connections thus adumbrated articulate the land historically and poetically as an "ethnoscape"[9] imprinted with and steeped in the culture of the group, which provides "the unique and indispensable setting for the events that shaped the community" (1999, p. 150). This process is dialogical: as the landscape becomes associated with the history of a people, their history becomes inscribed on the landscape. Their memory is *territorialised* in sacred sites and monuments, while their history itself comes to be seen as necessarily connected to the terrain, and is thus *naturalised.* Ethnoscapes are cultural people-place entanglements that legitimise territorial rights. In settler colonial contexts where indigenous people have been subjugated and uprooted in order for settlement to take place, the elaboration of the ethnoscape requires some sort of space-clearing gesture—the assertion of terra nullius, the organised forgetting of acts of dispossession and genocide, or (as we have seen in the case of "knowing" the Karoo) the avoidance of the topic of dispossession entirely, in favour of knowledge of prehistoric worlds.

The Karoo as "heartland" or "soul country" is a white ethnoscape informed by doctored versions of colonial history and liberal ideas about property ownership, while affirming both knowledge of and love of the land. It dovetails neatly with the production of white men as the appropriate "stewards" of the land in the campaign against rhino poaching. In the next chapter, I will present analysis that shows how white stewardship of and communion with the land is further entrenched and defended through articulations of white alienation, Black revenge, and the retreat of white domination from large parts of the South African countryside. I will show how representations of whites as "estranged" from the land work to legitimate what Christi van der Westhuizen (2016) has defined as "enclave nationalism."

NOTES

1. The term "Khoisan" is an etic and colonial portmanteau term that conflates Khoe and San people, cultures, and languages. It has however widely been appropriated as an emic term in Khoisan revivalism and in the Afrikaaps language movement (Alim et al. 2021; J. Brown and Deumert 2017).

2. Translations from the original Afrikaans are by the author. Afrikaans: "maar by ons is net idiote. . . . slimmes is landuit en die res sit by die huis . . ."

3. Original Afrikaans: "Hoe dommer hoe hoer [sic] die poste."

4. A reference to Zuma stating on the stand at his trial for rape that he believed having a shower after sex would prevent him from contracting HIV from the complainant.

5. Original Afrikaans: "Al nalatingskap wat Afrika gee is woestyne, volksmoorde en gebrokenheid."

6. Original Afrikaans: "Die Karoo . . . [is] 'n plek wat elke Afrikaner raak." This quote appears in the YouTube clip embedded at this point in the discussion.

7. Original Afrikaans: "ons hartland."

8. The original video in Afrikaans can be viewed at vimeo.com/22701774, last accessed 24 January 2022.

9. Although developed in roughly the same period, this use of the term "ethnoscape" is conceptually distinct from that proposed by Arjun Appadurai (1990, 296) who deploys the concept to pick out the cultural semiotics of particular ethnic groups visible in the context of "global cultural flow."

Chapter 4

"Strangers in Their Own Country"

In June 2018, the *Mail & Guardian* newspaper reported on a strange phenomenon. If you googled the phrase "squatter camps in South Africa" and viewed the image results, you might end up believing that it is mostly white South Africans who experience grinding poverty (Ritchie 2018). Given the disproportionate trust that people around the world tend to place in Google search (see MacKenzie and Bhatt 2020) these results presented a grotesquely misleading racial picture of who actually lives in South African informal settlements. According to official statistics, over 1.8 million Black households are classified as "informal," while the number for white households is under 8,000 (Rademeyer 2013). In other words, for every white family living in a shack, there are 225 Black households living in similar conditions. Being confronted by a sea of white faces in a search for shack-dwellers was not because of any "malice" on Google's part, the journalist averred, but a peculiarity of the search algorithm that prioritised those results that had received the highest numbers of clicks (Ritchie 2018). The combined effect of a society that commodifies "spectacle" (Debord [1967] 2014) and the workings of the online "attention economy" (see Goldhaber 2006) meant that whites in squatter camps were just being shared more; they were remarkable and strange enough to grab the attention of local and international audiences. The strangeness of these images to a large extent arises from, and as I will argue in this chapter, corroborates, the idea that white South Africans are not *supposed* to be landless and poor, and that if they are, then something has gone badly wrong with the society in which they live. Far from being a story about a search algorithm that bears no objective "malice," I will offer some evidence here that the production and distribution of these images is part of a well-coordinated communications campaign that exploits both spectacle and attention in evolving platform ecologies to portray white South Africans after apartheid as the victims of a vengeful Black government.

Representations of poor whites tend to "cluster in the archives" (Wray 2006, 134) at historical junctures where race and class hierarchies are being contested or entrenched. Far from weakening notions of innate racial superiority, these clusters are often associated with repairs to the racial formation and the reproduction of white supremacy (Willoughby-Herard 2007; 2015; Wray 2006). These repairs have been described both as *boundary work* and as *sutures* to the racial order, and I lay out these contrasting approaches in the following section. I then go on to describe the specific corpus of video texts I analyse here (summarised in Appendix B) and how it was collected. The seven analytical subsections that follow tackle the six main types of articulation, and one set of rarer alternatives. In the conclusion, I trace some of the similarities between the articulations in this corpus, and the historical deployment of the '*volkseie*' in the context of Afrikaner nationalism.

POOR WHITES: BOUNDARIES AND SUTURES

Critical race scholarship on "poor whites" in the context of the United States points to the ostensibly unsettling and destabilising effect they have on whiteness. Discussing the stigmatisation of "white trash," Wray (2006, 2) remarks that their "very existence seems to threaten the symbolic and social order." Hartigan (2005, 24) argues that poor whites expose the brittleness of the racial order through transgressing the class norms that maintain whiteness as an unmarked identity. For whiteness to remain hegemonic, the potential discursive ruptures represented by the existence of white poverty must be neutralised through its being given a meaning that stabilises whiteness as a bounded cultural entity. This stabilisation requires the rearticulation of a border that separates "true" whiteness from non-whiteness. Representations of poor whites can thus work to reproduce racial identification, and police colour lines, through constituting "intraracial contests over belonging and difference that are a crucial dimension of racial identification" (Hartigan 2005, 24). The white trash "stigmatype" (Wray 2006, 33) reproduces whiteness as a cultural entity by marking the "limits and edges of the category" (2006, 143). The logic underlying this "boundary theory," which entails the close examination of the formation, maintenance, and transformation of various social boundaries, is encapsulated in Pierre Bourdieu's maxim that "[social] identity lies in difference, and the difference is asserted against what is closest, which represents the greatest threat" ("Distinction" (1979) quoted in Wray 2006, 133).

The notion of a threatening liminal space has also been reproduced in ethnographies of poor white communities in the South African context. Poor whites in the Western Cape are a "socially constructed category between the racial categories White and Coloured . . . reflecting concerns regarding the margins of this category" (Teppo 2004, 244). A study in the Eastern Cape problematizes the poor white as existing in a racial border-zone, asking "[if] Whites had been allowed to fall into this abhorrent category . . . what then would have differentiated them from poor Blacks?" (Sibanda 2014, iii). Inhabiting this space is associated with "social pain and social death" (Sibanda 2012). At the same time, paying analytical attention to white pain is not without its problems. As Robyn Wiegman (1999) has pointed out, critical whiteness scholarship on "white trash" can paradoxically situate whiteness "as an identity object in need of the same resignification that has accompanied the civil rights and black power struggle over and in the name of blackness" (1999, 144). As poor white or "white trash" is never merely a class identity, but a *racial* identity (see Newitz and Wray 1997), the problematic idea that whites are racially oppressed *as whites*, and that they thus need to be "liberated" must be avoided. When downtrodden whites acquire a racial "alongsidedness" (Ahmed 2004a) with other oppressed groups, the asymmetrical and hierarchical structure of the concept of race is analytically obscured.

Far from demanding liberatory attention, then, the vulnerability of whiteness is properly understood as intrinsic to its historical production in South Africa as a "sacred and protected political category" (Willoughby-Herard 2007, 479). The value of whiteness in this definition is wound up in its fragility. The idea that whites can "fall" and "lose" their whiteness (see Kruger 2016, 49) exerts manipulative and disciplinary power on social actors supposedly striving to be white, and protective of the status it brings. As Tiffany Willoughby-Herard (2007; 2015) argues in her analysis of the Carnegie Commission's South African "Poor White Study" (1927–1935), the control of white bodies and their moral worlds lies at the heart of racism. Racism must first and foremost ensure that whites are in formation, exacting "compliance with the administrative, ideological, and material annihilation of whites and non-whites" (2007, 485–87). If the "misery" of the racial order is a misery shared by and at the same time oriented around whiteness, disciplined and controlled by a measure of self-hatred, it must always be remembered that this self-hatred serves as a crucial spur to anti-blackness (2015, xiv).

As was discussed in detail in chapter 1, the apartheid social imaginary was built on the myth of an Afrikaner *volkseie*. The poor whites of the 1920s and 1930s played leading roles in the articulation of this myth. They were the key evidence presented by Nationalist organic intellectuals to prove that in the life of the volk "walls are torn apart and are in ruins" (Norval 1996, 12). The walls had been broken because of English imperialism and capitalism, and its unholy (supposed) alliance with Black labour. Urbanisation and participation in an increasingly cosmopolitan capitalist economy had "uprooted" Afrikaners, promoting (in the words of one ideologue) "worldliness, immorality, sensual enjoyment and the loss of religious bonds" (1996, 75). Capitalism was personified in satirical cartoons as the cigar-smoking,

Jewish and English-speaking "Hoggenheimer" (1996, 38) who truly relishes his exploitation of the Afrikaans working classes. The only workable solution for this was that Afrikaners band together economically and socially. The myth of a *volkseie* which was "that which is 'ours and ours alone,' inaccessible to the 'other,' and that which is threatened by 'others'" (1996, p. 96) attempted to suture an Afrikaans *Boerevolk* identity that had been dislocated by urbanisation and imperial defeat. The *volkseie* is an impossible object, and the obsessional search for it becomes the driving force of discursive struggle in the evolution of the apartheid imaginary. This programme involved resolving the "Poor White Problem" through addressing the "Native Question": implementing job reservation, segregating unions, creating group areas and influx controls, and so on (1996, pp. 20–24). The aim of these policies was to allow the people who had become "uprooted" to once again be rooted as a *Boerevolk* in their land—albeit in an increasingly industrialised and urbanised landscape. In the historical development of white supremacy in South Africa, therefore, an uptick in concern about a poor white "problem" has had less to do with the kinds of boundary maintenance work analysed in the US context than with attempting to unite a group with an impossible suture between signifier and signified, i.e., between actual existing 'Afrikaners' and an essential and unchanging ethnic Afrikaans identity.

THE RETURN OF THE "POOR WHITE PROBLEM"

This corpus of video texts was built from an initial Twitter search for discussions of white poverty in South Africa that embedded video clips, and then broadened to film clips suggested by the YouTube algorithm. The corpus includes both "online news videos" (ONVs) and promotional footage for campaigns to act on the "problem" of white poverty. It contains twenty-two separate video clips (see Appendix B, Table 1) produced between (approximately) 1999 and 2018 and broadcast by traditional news and documentary channels on five continents, as well as being uploaded to YouTube for a global audience from 2007 onwards. ONVs are an increasingly popular global trend in the production and consumption of news (see Kalogeropoulos, Cherubini, and Newman 2016). While some networks produce segments that are posted directly to their digital platforms, in most of the cases of the videos in this corpus online posting happened some time after a traditional broadcast, or to supplement reporting in another medium. Clips not posted to YouTube and found on other online dissemination channels did not always include metadata about the number of times they had been played. Among those that did include data on views, tallies ranged from a few thousand (eleven clips; see Appendix B, Table 2) to over 500,000 (clips 10, 18, 20 and 22), and well over a million (clips 1, 2 and 3). Clip 2 is currently the most watched clip, with just under 1.8 million views. Two things are worth noting here. The first is that the clips that did not give public metadata on views are available on some of the world's most popular websites (bbc.co.uk and dailymail.co.uk) and thus are quite likely to have been watched many times. The second is that a number of these view counts experienced huge growth between the initial corpus construction in November 2017 and the time of writing in August 2021. Clip 2, for example, was uploaded to YouTube in February 2009 and had been watched 520,970 times in the eight years to November 2017; in the four years since then it has been viewed a further 1,277,306 times, suggesting a significant uptick in interest. It is clear that these clips have been extensively shared on social media and/or suggested by YouTube's "up next" algorithm. Most of the ONVs were produced by reputable news organisations (the BBC, ITV, Associated Press, the South African Broadcasting Corporation (SABC)), one was produced by the South African nongovernmental organisation (NGO) Solidarity Helping Hand (clip 4), and three are documentary films or clips from films (clips 8, 17 and 21). The clips are between one and fifty-seven minutes long, and together add up to about three hours of footage.

To watch these three hours of footage is to immediately notice key patterns, including a recurring cast of characters, specific locations for shooting, and patterns in the ways that these stories are framed and the narrative of the "poor white" constructed. I discuss six articulatory clusters in the sections below, which I have titled white pain, reversal/revenge, crisis, concealment, dislocation, and in/dependence. I also group counternarratives and exceptions under a seventh section, before concluding with a discussion of how the new "poor white" discourse fits into the broader discursive regime of white hegemony and land control with which this book is concerned.

White Pain

A standard part of the repertoire of white South African talk has been a narrative of victimization, injury, and disability that Melissa Steyn (2001b, 78) has dubbed "This Shouldn't Happen to a White." She observes that whereas English-speaking white South Africans draw on a shared colonial and imperial mythology with a global scope, Afrikaans-speaking white South Africans "came to regard themselves as a perpetually persecuted ethnic group in a land that was promised to them" (2001b, 80). The spectacle of suffering whites is most strongly associated in the global mediascape with the overblown phenomenon of "farm murders" and related conspiracy theories about "white genocide" which serve as "sensational signs" that secure funding for Afrikaner "rights" organisations (see Brodie 2013; Deumert 2019; Holmes 2020). Representations of white poverty follow a similar pattern. Almost all of the poor whites included in the videos speak Afrikaans, and a picture of Afrikaner suffering is painted multimodally, using mournful music played on a mouth organ (clips 8 and 21), slowly plucked guitar strings (clip 18), or Beethoven's Moonlight Sonata (clip 6). Scarred or dirty white skin features prominently, and people frequently break down in tears. In a typical scene, the camera lingers on the burn scars on the arms of a young girl living in the Coronation Park informal settlement (clips 9 and 21). Other clips show living spaces gutted by fire (e.g., clip 11), and there are a number of scenes at funerals and in graveyards (e.g., clips 8, 9 and 21). One man says he drinks because "it eases the pain" (clip 11). A woman selling newspapers at a busy intersection shows a journalist the marks on her legs where she was hit by a car, and says that she is sorry that the truck that narrowly missed her did not kill her: "I would have been freed from this life, from this living hell"[1] (clip 20).

These affecting scenes of human devastation are presented as a unique or exceptional form of suffering. White poverty, according to SABC journalist Hanti Schrader, has "its own culture, its own dialect, its own norms, its own questions, and its own appearance"[2] (clip 6). In another SABC production, we are told that the "face of poverty is different here" (clip 20). A white charity worker says that going to white homeless shelters is "a different situation"[3] (clip 4). When an unnamed Black woman is interviewed on the street about how she feels after being shown footage of whites living in poverty, she says: "I felt uncomfortable because I couldn't believe it . . . you know it's OK with blacks because we're used to it but with whites it's unbelievable" (clip 2). Reggie Yates, the Black British host of the BBC's "Extreme South Africa" programme, admits that he is used to seeing poor Black kids, but that seeing white people in poverty is "blowing [his] mind" (clip 11).

The normality of Black poverty is thus sedimented at the same time as white poverty is produced as abnormal or even unnatural. Fanon's characterisation of colonial culture as associating the Black body with moral and physical dirt, while the white body is associated with innocence and "magical, heavenly light" (Fanon, 1952/2008, p. 146) is salient. Visually, this white skin was historically produced as a bulwark against filth and disease as it "shows the dirt with unique clarity and certainty" (Dyer 1997, 76). When the camera lingers on the face of a little boy (Figure 4.1, clip 21) radiating curiosity and innocence, it is a moment that at the same time causes unease: we see him putting his dirty thumb in his mouth, as his mother says that "my little boy gets very sick here."[4]

As Sara Ahmed has pointed out, the performance of harm to the "vulnerable and damaged bodies" of white women and children has historically had a metonymic relation to the "invasion of the body of the [white] nation" (Ahmed 2004b, 119). Many of the clips retrace this metonymy. It is frequently asserted that the individual suffering bodies represent Afrikanerdom as a whole.

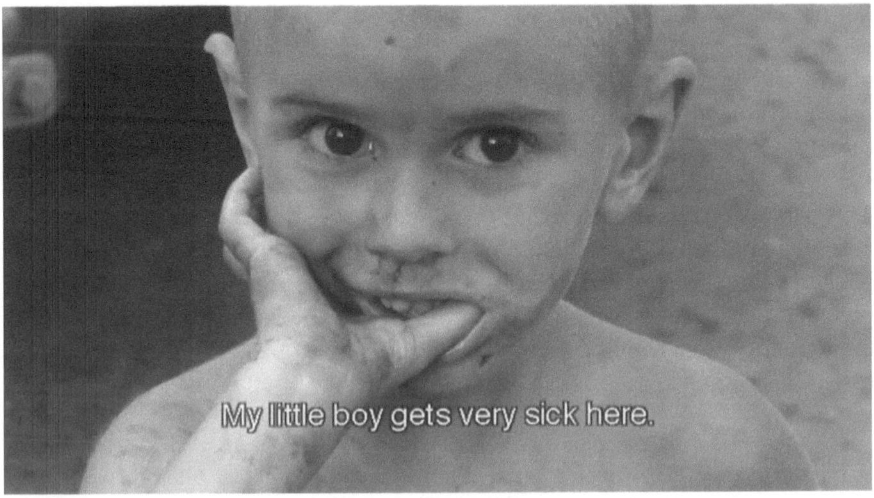

Figure 4.1: "My little boy gets very sick here" (clip 21)

Afrikaners are said by an SABC journalist to be a *volk* "again" (in reference to the early 20th century Afrikaner poverty) "forced . . . onto its knees"[5] (clip 6). White poverty is an example of how the Afrikaner is "fighting for our language . . . fighting all the time, to survive" (clip 1). The sense of a *volk* in pain is most acute in the BBC correspondent John Simpson's reportage, "Do White People Have a Future in South Africa?" (clip 8). Over the strains of a lonely harmonica, he opens his insert with footage from the Voortrekker Monument in Pretoria, "a very 1930s tribute to the Dutch-speaking pioneers who carved out the Boer Republics." These plucky pioneers "suffered terribly" in British concentration camps during the Boer War but, in what is presented as a brief and unfortunate interlude, "victims turned oppressors" in implementing apartheid. Then, in the 1990s, they realise their mistake and now "voluntarily have given up political power altogether." The character of the *volk* is thus drawn very economically in the first thirty seconds of the clip: suffering, noble, and open to admitting their mistakes. He goes on to link past suffering and the wisdom gained therefrom to present injustice: "At least 200,000 whites live in squatter camps" he asserts. But "there's worse . . . Here, outside Pretoria, the killing ground begins." He interviews an utterly distraught woman whose father and brother were murdered during a robbery at their general dealer. Over images of her in the graveyard, Simpson adds a sinister detail: "two other white farmers recently murdered are buried here too" suggesting that this is a common, and accelerating phenomenon.

Thus are individual criminal acts and instances of white poverty formed into a consistent pattern of abuse that attaches to the body of the *volk* as a whole. As one of the people interviewed by Reggie Yates observes: "we're not the chosen people anymore" (clip 11). Yates (a Black British journalist) endorses white anger against affirmative action, and sympathises with an unemployed young man, saying that "there are so many hurdles for you to get back to where you were . . . that just makes me angry." Anger at the fallen status of whites mingles with pity. When a social worker breaks down in tears, she apologises: "I'm sorry, I just feel so terribly sorry for them"[6] (clip 20). This sympathy coalesces around these white communities not only for their current state, but also for the future harm that might come to them. Irene van Niekerk, the charismatic leader of the Coronation Park informal settlement, breaks down in tears as she appeals directly to the camera to stop the local municipality from moving them from the park to Munsieville, a large historically Black township:

> It's dangerous! The people don't understand how dangerous it is over there for our people! They won't get sworn at, they won't get insulted there, they won't . . . [be called] "white trash" . . . They are going to burn us out—they're waiting for us to come—they're going to kill us![7] (clip 12)

Another resident refuses to go and "live with blacks, I'm not going to go and get raped there"[8] (clip 13). While the suffering of poor whites is thus represented as an exceptional and unnatural kind of pain that has been caused at a group level by the end of apartheid and the introduction of affirmative action, their vulnerability to even further victimization articulates a familiar figure: the Black perpetrator, the "master" of rape, who conspires now to make them pay for their historical privilege.

Reversal and revenge

In contrast to sad and suffering white folk, Black people are constructed as callous, vengeful, and engaged in an orgy of conspicuous consumption. When Reggie Yates meets a group of inebriated young Black people enjoying themselves in Coronation Park, they refuse to believe that poor white people are living in squalid conditions just a few metres away (clip 11). Their drunken frolicking on the bonnets of expensive cars is juxtaposed to the reaction of a dejected white man who used to have his "own house, with a pool." Alcohol, dancing, and vibrant South African pop music feature prominently in other representations of Black people. Compared with the mournful soundtracks of the poor white settlements, Soweto, where people "are getting rich" (clip 1) is typically introduced over a jaunty guitar riff. Black people are filmed drinking, talking on expensive cell phones, and parking their Porsches, a scene that Simpson asserts is "in many ways . . . the dominant face of the new South Africa today" (clip 8). The man he is there to interview, Mandla Nyakela, contradicts this claim, saying that white people still have the same economic power "they have possessed since they imposed brutalism against us and stole from us our land." For the duration of this quote, instead of focusing on Nyakela's face, the camera focuses on the tip of his beer bottle, leaving his face blurred and indistinct (Figure 4.2). Being in focus confers salience (Machin and Mayr 2012, 55); a shot of an authoritative interviewee would draw the viewer's attention towards their face. This shot however clearly undermines that authority: not only by leaving his face out of focus, but by focusing on an intoxicant, and thus calling into question his interpretation of reality.

In another video (clip 3) footage of shoe designers Phindi and Tshepo are interlaced with shots of the poor white Grobbelaar family. While Phindi talks about having been inspired by the style of "Louis the Fifteenth" and lights candles around a bubble bath to "relax after a long day's work," a stark antonymy is visually drawn to the dismally broken bathroom that Johan Grobbelaar is trying to fix. "One South Africa," intones the narrator, "two realities." Reducing the complexity of the whole of South Africa to these two realities is how the whole clip is framed; its title is "Poor Whites/Rich Blacks" and the construction of Phindi and Tshepo as ancien régime aristocrats and the Grobbelaars as starving peasants is deployed as a synecdoche for the society as a whole.

The implied callousness of these levels of consumption in the context of white poverty is made explicit in the way that the governmental attitude to the problem is constructed. Former president Thabo Mbeki is accused of having "created an intellectual space in South Africa that made no provision

Figure 4.2: A dissident view, out of focus (clip 8)

for something like white poverty"[9] (clip 4) in his "Two Nations" speech (discussed in the introduction). It is claimed that officials sent a sick old woman who eventually died to look for work (clip 6); that poor whites are denied social grants (clip 8); and that the government is trying to shut squatter camps down with no alternative accommodation (clip 11). Municipal officials are said to become "furious"[10] (clip 6) when asked by white people for assistance with basic services. This response to their plight is articulated as being because they are white. One man interviewed by Simpson claims that when he goes to the welfare office "99% they don't help you because you're talking to a Black person" (clip 8). The idea that the Black government denies poor whites social services is uncritically repeated by NGO workers and journalists themselves. Leigh Oxleigh of the South African Family Relief Project (SAFRP) asserts that

> [the] government refuses to assist these people. They feel that because of the apartheid era they do not deserve any assistance. . . . [But] most of these children in these camps were born post-1994 apartheid and I feel that the discrimination against these children are unfair. They were born in a supposedly free and fair South Africa, but yet they are denied assistance. It's reverse apartheid in my opinion. It's a direct reverse of apartheid. (clip 18)

Claims of "reverse apartheid" (clips 3, 10 and 22); "reverse racism" (clip 11); and antiwhite "discrimination" (clips 1 and 4) are common. Policies to change the structure of the economy, affirmative action, and BEE have supposedly turned "white people [into] second-class citizens" (clip 10). Most of the journalists merely reproduce these views, locating their analysis at the level of whether this kind of discrimination is *justified*. Thus, in pursuing a conversation about the *morality* of the current system, these highly tendentious premises become sedimented parts of a discourse of reversal and revenge.

A repeated assertion is that the Black government is intent on making whites "pay back" for the sins of apartheid. The voices here are generally those of the poor whites themselves, who face their fate with stoicism: "it's our turn—the Blacks always had to struggle" (clip 1); "the white people put them down and now . . . it's their time to put us down" (clip 2); "my generation is paying a price for our forefathers . . . South Africa's past is still haunting it" (clip 11). When journalists comment on this narrative they also frame it in terms of historical debt: "[if] getting a rough deal now [is the] price to pay for decades of oppression, perhaps this is the least worst option" (clip 11) opines Reggie Yates. John Simpson claims that poor white people are denied social services by government because "after all, white people never provided Blacks with a social security safety net when they ran the country" (clip 8).

This (patently false, on both counts) claim is repeated at other points in the corpus (e.g., clips 6 and 18). When journalists do mention state assistance, it tends to be minimised: people get "tiny" (clip 1) or "meagre" (clip 2) pensions. When one journalist asks the owner of a private whites-only care home about the extent of state support she states categorically: "Nothing, nothing, nothing. What we get from the State is people's pensions" (clip 6).

In Fanon's interpretation of the Hegelian Master-Slave relation, he observes the importance of the reciprocity of recognition, that it "is in the degree to which I go beyond my own immediate being that I apprehend the existence of the other as a natural and more than natural reality" (Fanon [1952] 2008, 169). Human relations surpass the Master/Slave duality when they "recognize themselves as mutually recognizing each other" (ibid.). If the Master does not desire the recognition of the Slave, they cannot recognise their assistance: they can only recognise their anger. This interpretation suggests a logic for why poor white people who get state support to exactly the same extent as poor Black people but are unable to *recognise* the State *recognising* them. Because the Master can only understand the anger of the Slave, even state assistance is interpreted by some of these poor whites (and their media and civil society enablers) as an act of aggression.

Antiwhite aggression is constructed as imminently worsening. The Economic Freedom Fighters (EFF) Commander-in-Chief Julius Malema's performance of "Kiss the Boer" (a menacing substitution for "Kill the Boer") played a prominent role in Reggie Yates's reportage (Figure 4.3, clip 11). After Yates interviews an EFF supporter who describes his own frustration and disillusionment with the lack of economic advancement for Black people,

Figure 4.3: Julius Malema sings "Kiss the Boer" (clip 11)

Yates comments: "I don't want to believe that everyone here wants to take violent revenge on white people, but chanting a hate song isn't building any bridges."

While the idea that Black people are taking revenge for apartheid paints them in a particular moral light, the discourse of reversal is no less insidious. The loss of white socioeconomic privilege is represented as a fait accompli in the most of the clips. We are told that whites have "lost their competitive edge" (clip 15) and their "privileged position" (clip 11); that "Blacks and whites are now competing for jobs on equal terms" (clip 2); that preferential treatment for whites has "naturally all disappeared"[11] (clip 6); and that "if you are Black, you're better off, right now" (clip 11). It is asserted that "Blacks take precedence over whites on the job market" (clip 9) and that government policies are working to "give Black people priority in employment, set Black quotas, and favour Black-owned companies" (clip 1). The (false) notion that white privilege has already been lost clearly undermines any moral argument for further structural change in South Africa.

Articulating Crisis

Together, the clips assert that white poverty is a crisis that has developed at a specific historical moment. It is variously asserted, without citing official sources, that unemployment among whites rose 200 percent in five years (clip 1), 150 percent in ten years (clip 4), or indeed by 300 over sixteen years, supposedly a worse rate than any other population group (clip 6). The white poverty rate is said to be 25 percent (clips 18 and 20). The number of poor whites in squatter camps is given as 200,000 (clip 8), 400,000 (clip 11), 430,000 (clip 4), 600,000 (clip 6), or even one million (clip 18). This is the "latest poverty crisis [which] must be addressed quickly" (clip 6) where the word "latest" is an explicit reference to the 1930s, images of which appear on the screen. White poverty in the intervening, apartheid period is erased; it was "unheard of" (clip 16) and homelessness "was confined to Black people only" (clip 15). The supposed absence of white poverty under apartheid works to prove a particular thesis: the end of apartheid caused a white poverty crisis. There is near-unanimity in the reporting that this is the case. Journalists variously assert that in "the nineteen years since the fall of apartheid more and more whites are coming face-to-face with poverty and social meltdown" (clip 10); that the "impoverishment of whites is on the increase since the disappearance of apartheid laws that artificially held them in privileged positions" (clip 16); that for "many whites, the 1994 elections changed their lives for the worse" (clip 15); that "white poverty in South Africa has doubled since the non-racial election in 1994" (clip 2); and that squatter camps "started popping up '96-'97" (clip 18).

This time line is a significant discursive accomplishment in two key respects. Firstly, as was made clear in the statistical picture presented in the introduction, it is a risible fabrication, and thorough and ethical journalism would have ruled out making most of the claims that are made in these clips. Even the scions of the white liberal order at the South African Institute of Race Relations (SAIRR) agree that white poverty decreased from 2 percent to 1 percent between 1994 and 2011 (Cronje 2013). At the very upper end of the estimate, which includes people living in sheds in the backyards of formal houses, 31,000 white people lived in informal dwellings at the time many of these clips were being made (Rademeyer 2013). The claims about the number of white squatters are thus ridiculously overblown. The second notable discursive effect is to naturalise Black poverty is naturalised, while white poverty is made to appear the work of some malicious design. Discussions about the extremely high levels of poverty and unemployment among other Black and "Coloured" people in South Africa typically invoke the global financial crisis, privatisation, deindustrialization, or sluggish economic growth. None of these factors are raised to explain the predicament of poor whites. Apartheid "solved" white poverty; but then the end of apartheid created a white poverty "crisis." But if white poverty is a crisis, what is Black poverty, which is many orders of magnitudes worse? Black poverty is not fixed to a time line; it is trending neither up nor down. It is timeless, even mysterious: it has no beginning, and no end. It is just the way things are.

Concealment

Some of the journalists produce their own role in this crisis as bravely exposing what the government is trying to conceal in official narratives and statistics. John Simpson calls white poverty an "ugly secret in the new South Africa" (clip 8). The head of the NGO Solidarity Helping Hand, Dirk Herrmann, says that

> White poverty in South Africa is a quiet poverty—nobody says anything about it. It's almost politically incorrect to say anything about it. It's actually ironic because I think it's the only type of poverty on earth it's not politically correct to talk about.[12] (clip 4)

In a remarkable reversal, overwhelming Black poverty is constructed as a problem for white people because they are less of a focus for policy making (e.g., clips 2, 11 and 20). In this vein, an Australian journalist intones that white people will be ignored by government "as long as the overwhelming majority of people are poor and Black" (clip 1). This notion that it is politically incorrect to draw attention to white poverty is co-constructed by journalists and white interviewees:

> [*Journalist voice-over*] They don't talk openly, but ask a few questions and the bitterness rises.
>
> [*Unnamed white woman*] I'm sorry but it's the truth, the Blacks—[*softly*] sorry, it's the truth—is getting the job—and the white people is staying behind. (clip 2)

The woman whispers "sorry, it's the truth" as if to repair the full volume with which she said "the Blacks." Even naming "them" might cause accusations of racism. The supposed difficulty of talking about white poverty arises because poverty is overwhelmingly Black, and yet the underlying cause of white poverty is articulated as "the Blacks is getting the job." The "difficulty" of talking about it in a politically *correct* way, then, is that one has to simultaneous claim not to be racist and that no white person should be unemployed if a Black person is employed ahead of them. This is quite clearly a "politically incorrect" thing to propose.

Some journalists are quite happy to violate the supposed strictures of political correctness, which are seen as antithetical to good reporting. In a rare comment from a government official, the minister in the presidency in the Mbeki administration (1999–2008) Essop Pahad becomes frustrated with an Australian journalist's unwillingness to talk about the broader context of poverty, saying he does not "find it acceptable" (clip 1) that she wants to only talk about white poverty and not the broader structural dynamics of poverty. The journalist then blankly states in their voice-over:

> Being told that you ask politically incorrect questions goes with the territory here. The South African media rarely challenges the government. It's clear that a group of people who were protected by the system no longer are in the so-called Rainbow Nation. (clip 1)

Pahad's refusal to allow poor whites to be centred in a conversation about poverty is taken as proof that the Rainbow Nation is a ruse, and a cover for Black domination. The journalist makes it clear that, from her Australian perspective at least, the promise of a non-racial South Africa was always premised on the perpetuation of white comfort. In revealing that not every white person has continued to enjoy a life of privilege after the start of Black rule, the journalist is positioned as a brave truth-teller.

Certain of the journalists have doubled down on their "truths" even when faced with complaints pointing to the robustness of the evidence that proves their version of the story to be wrong. When the BBC was flooded with complaints from South Africa about clip 8, John Simpson wrote a response that was published on the BBC website. In it, he dismisses the official picture of white poverty as produced by the Statistician-General as an "estimate" and stuck to his bizarrely inflated figures (Simpson 2013). The intransigence of the high-profile Australian, Canadian, British, and Belgian journalists involved in producing these clips speaks eloquently to how entangled the narrative of white poverty in South Africa is in the affective investments of "global whiteness" (Willoughby-Herard 2015).

Dislocation

South Africa is represented as inhospitable to white Afrikaners in the video clips in ways that are explicitly compared to the sense of alienation that Black people experienced under apartheid. John Simpson points to the fact that the only white faces in the centre of Pretoria are those of the Boer Republican statues, saying that because of this "many whites feel like strangers in their own country, precisely as Blacks did under apartheid" (clip 8). Black people are pictured taking photos of each other against the statues, and enjoying the green space of the public park. The use of the word "precisely" in the journalist's voice-over discursively affirms an exact equivalence, with a (perhaps deliberate?) echo of Sol Plaatje's famous description of the dispossessed African as having been made a "pariah in the land of his birth" (Plaatje [1916] 1982) by the Land Act of 1913. It is worth pausing at this point to remember that the legislated dehumanisation of Black people under apartheid and colonialism severely curtailed their entitlements, leaving them landless and without rights, considered socially valuable only as cheap labour in mines. Now, in Simpson's view, "precisely" the same feeling is experienced by white people when Black people are visibly occupying public space in Pretoria, and having fun on Boer ethnonationalist monuments. This is a truly remarkable claim. As a cheerful song sung in isiZulu plays in the background, Simpson goes on to explain: "Now there's a move to change the names, like Pretoria itself: that'll be called Tshwane" (clip 8). In another documentary, the narrator repeatedly points out that the place-names used by local white people no longer map onto the official ones: they live in a place she calls the west of Tshwane but that is "still known to the locals as Pretoria West" or "Wessies, as the community still calls it" (clip 20). She goes on to describe the white community here as "struggling to understand why it lost its privileges, trying to make sense of the political changes that have swept through the rest of the country."

The loss of the right of the *volk* to control the landscape—to name it and to determine which colour of person could occupy it—is articulated as a trauma on a similar scale to that of apartheid itself. In conjunctural crises, as was discussed in chapter 1, "dislocation" which reveals the contingency of all forms of identification may be experienced (Norval 1996, 96). In the specific case of poor white Afrikaners in contemporary South Africa, this is quite clearly constructed also as a "dislocation" which I use in the sense of finding oneself out of place, your identity held in place by an impossible suture: what is it to be Afrikaans, if our capital is no longer called Pretoria? Or if there are no white people on Church Square? The title of the SABC documentary on poor whites—"*Gebroke land*" (clip 6)—is very revealing in this respect: it translates roughly as "Ruined country."[13] In an extension of the body-*volk* metonymy articulated around white pain, the ruination of individual poor whites comes to represent the ruined state of the nation as a whole. Even the lush African farmland and bush has been ruined: "this lovely terrain has turned into a battlefield" (clip 8). The intimate connections of people and place have been broken by a vengeful Black government, and this calls for strong responses from those who still care for the fate of these hapless victims.

Declaring Independence

These solutions are proposed largely by the Afrikaner NGO and cultural groups who appear in the clips. Most prominent among these are the sibling organisations AfriForum and Solidarity Helping Hand (SHH), which both developed from the white Afrikaans trade union Solidarity (for a critical ethnography of AfriForum, see Boersema 2013). Representatives from these organisations are interviewed in clips 4, 5, 6, 8, 10, 11, 20 and 22, and it is not unlikely that their advocacy of this issue has influenced the framing of this story in other clips. Other Afrikaner intellectuals and organisations, such as the Vryheidsfront Plus (VF+) (e.g., clip 5) also make appearances. While there is some contestation of core values, most of the representatives of these various organisations work to reaffirm self-reliance as an Afrikaner value. Apartheid history is for example interpreted as a lesson in self-reliance by right-wing political analyst Harald Pakendorf, who says that under the National Party "it wasn't the Afrikaner government that elevated the Afrikaner, they did it themselves"[14] (clip 6). Dirk Herrmann of SHH explains that "the only complete answer to empowering people is to ensure that people in the shelters don't just stay there, but create a small economy that can help them become self-supporting"[15] (clip 4). He says that the point of SHH programmes is to "help them to help themselves"[16] (clip 6). In another clip, he offers a different interpretation of apartheid to that of Pakendorf: "the problem with the apartheid system was that it created a community that is actually dependent on the specific government" (clip 20) which meant that "when the government fell away, the whole support structure of the white community actually fell away." Dependence on the government is thus constructed as a problem by both Pakendorf and Herrmann, regardless of the particular race-group in power.

Importantly, these articulations are commensurable with neoliberalism. When the labour market fails to absorb people who want to work, it is because of distortions introduced into its efficient functioning by policies that drain time and capital from entrepreneurs, protect employment, or dole out state largesse. The solution is to remove distortions that interfere with the market's efficient functioning. Part of the classic liberal critique of apartheid is that it prevented industry from accessing the skills of the entire population, creating artificial restraints such as the colour bar that distorted the functioning of a market that would otherwise have tended towards greater efficiency, growth, and higher employment and prosperity for all. This post-apartheid critique of AA and BBBEE (which is also articulated on the intellectual right by think tanks such as the SAIRR and the Free Market Foundation) is built on broadly similar arguments, but only now on behalf of white people who feel they have been discriminated against.

It is in this space that Solidarity can present a racialized solution to what they have helped construct as a racialized problem: white people *themselves* must solve it, in a way that *specifically targets white people*. The host of the SABC *Fokus* programme is clearly speaking to this script when she introduces the *Gebroke land* documentary with the statement:

> One would expect that social assistance to whites would increase in proportion to the rise in white poverty. However, the opposite is true. Subsidies to welfare organisations that only support poor whites are being phased out . . .[17] (clip 6)

A right to pursue racially exclusive welfare projects with state funding is thus casually asserted by the national broadcaster. Even racist hiring practices can be proudly asserted: one employer boasts that he has "made a point of employing white people" (clip 3) as an act of charity. The manager of an old age home is not embarrassed to say "only elderly needy whites live here"[18] (clip 6). White poverty is even at one point framed by Dirk Hermann as a lack of access to "white housing"[19] as opposed to housing per se (clip 4).

In order to strengthen the appeal to a broader range of social demands than just those of Afrikaners, these charities also focus on showing the benefits to all social groups of Afrikaner self-sufficiency. Delivering these societal benefits is presented in a positive light, such as when Ernst Roets, erstwhile deputy CEO of AfriForum, is presented as an Afrikaans campaigner selflessly fighting for an independent judiciary (clip 8). Presenting Afrikaner self-determination as benefiting all South Africans has in fact been a key AfriForum strategy (Boersema 2013). The poor whites themselves that are active in programmes supported by these charities are pictured building a two-storey cottage and planting a lush and productive vegetable garden (clips 7 and 9); poor white homes are shown raising their own funds from woodwork by residents (clip 16) and feeding themselves using sophisticated plastic tunnel farming methods (clip 6). This return to racially specific programming is couched in the language of helping people help themselves, and fighting dependence on the government, which effectively articulates a powerful subject position valued both by the official discourse of the neoliberal state, and narrow, ethnic exclusive organisations such as Solidarity and AfriForum. These discursive moves also work to legitimise the institution of "enclave nationalism" described by van der Westhuizen (2016, 2) which "shifts the perspective from the nation state to smaller locales, targeted to be made 'homely' again." Close attention to the potential for Afrikaner solidarity and economic power akin to the *volkskapitalisme* of the twentieth century thus draws a parallel in this historical moment that makes space for ethnic exclusivity and racial purity in the present.

Counternarratives: Rainbows to the Rescue

Before concluding this chapter, it is worth noting that a small number of the clips framed the story of white people living in informal settlements differently. One of the films even draws attention to the repetitive tropes of white poverty that are seen in the other clips:

> Coronation Park . . . [is] an economically depressed shantytown . . . where the apartheid oppressor has become the economically oppressed, a place where the new Black superclass, affirmative action and, Black economic empowerment is to blame for all the residents' hardships—at least, that's the picture painted by international stories attempting to cover the complexities of South Africa's economic transformation through this filter. (clip 17)

The first half of this narration is more or less the picture that has been established so far, which pivots at the point the narrator says "at least." The actual story, one of many told about Irene van Niekerk and the people of Coronation Park, focuses on her resilience and not her victimhood. She coaches her athlete daughter, the talented "young" Irene. The family are portrayed as sharing lives of opportunity and hope, and their success as depending on their individual determination and ability to deal with adversity. In resisting the standard narrative, these filmmakers thus opt for a colour-blind market liberalism closely related to Rainbowism: there are chances for all South Africans and they just need to try harder if they want to escape poverty.

Clips that gave government officials and Black intellectuals the space to talk freely also offered a glimpse of a different story. Black consciousness scholar Xolela Mangcu for example clearly rejected the strangeness of white poverty, insisting that poverty is devastating across the board:

> When you see a white child who's five years old, who's homeless, it evokes in you the same feelings that it would evoke when you see a Black child. Because that's what our struggle was about—a response . . . a moral response to suffering and poverty and injustice. (clip 2)

In the very few cases where poor whites are depicted on camera receiving support from government, white gratitude and happiness are on display. "I am very happy that I've got this little house . . . and all my [Black] neighbours are very happy with me" says Harry Swanepoel (clip 16). In another clip, the move to Munsieville which appeared in clips 12 and 13 boding rape and death for the people of Coronation Park, is described as bringing people together into one big happy family again (clip 14). The possibility for mutual recognition and community to emerge between white and Black people living in poverty is briefly suggested by a poignant image of two elderly men, one Black and one white, who share a smile with each other from their separate tables, while eating their meals (Figure 4.4, clip 21).

That these moments of alternative articulations of the phenomenon of white poverty in post-apartheid South Africa are so rare in this corpus only underline the extent to which the choices that filmmakers and journalists tended towards reproducing a very specific myth. These exceptions are to a large extent reverting to the norm, the Rainbow Nation, which as we have seen elsewhere works as a discursive horizon to sediment the

Figure 4.4: A fleeting moment of mutual recognition (clip 21)

taken-for-grantedness of racial inequality, and the rationality of property under capitalism.

CONCLUSION: THE *VOLKSEIE* RESURGENT?

As a political discourse, apartheid was to a large extent primarily addressed not by dominant whites to subaltern Black people, but by subaltern Afrikaners to the culturally and politically dominant English whites (see van der Westhuizen 2018). Anthropological attention to "poor whites" has focused on their liminal racial status, and how they are involved in the perpetuation of white supremacy by constituting the boundaries of "white." But when these poor whites become pawns in a political game, as happened in the 1930s (Norval 1996; Willoughby-Herard 2015) and is again happening today, their function clearly is not at the boundaries, but at the very heart of whiteness.

Metonymically, the poor white experience rearticulates the lost Afrikaner community by standing in for the state of the *Afrikanervolk* as a whole. The suffering of individual poor white bodies is shown in stark relief: dark dirt on pale skin. Discomfort or disbelief at such an unnatural combination is affected. The *volk* is shown in bewilderment, confusion, and loss when confronted with a landscape they no longer recognise, surrounded by languages they no longer understand: their country is ruined; it has become a battlefield. The cause of this epidemic of pain and alienation is clearly the end of apartheid, which saw victims turn oppressors, and rich, callous, and unreliable Black people start to exact their revenge on their former masters. The graciously defeated whites, on the other hand, who "gave up" political power "altogether," bear their fates with stoicism. They are ready to do their part: to till the soil, to pick themselves up. All they need is the room for their *own* welfare programmes, their *own* jobs, their *own* language, and their *own* spaces to thrive: what they need is the *volkseie*. Instead of a society articulated around non-racialism, a society founded on the self-reliance of groups is advanced to vie for struggle for hegemony on the discursive battlefield.

Where the *volkseie* is not defended, the hegemony of Rainbowism is reinscribed: these are the only two shows in town. The appeal by Solidarity and its member organisations to the neoliberal discourse of self-reliance is very significant, as it clearly aspires to find space within a new hegemony, the counter-discourse to the robust policies of redistribution and social reengineering advocated by the few voices left on the left. They stand a real chance of being on the side of the winning team in the battle for civil society with this tactic, as they have the force of the business community, much of the media, and the economic mavens associated with ANC fiscal policy broadly on their side.

Solidarity and AfriForum articulate a myth similar to the *volkseie,* but also subtly different, in that its framework is a more libertarian dispensation abstracted from any specific claims about the destiny of the Afrikaner as connected to a specific territory. The territorial ambition here seems to be the spaces in between: to be left alone to pursue racially or ethnically exclusive projects, to operate economically unhindered by AA or BBBEE, and most importantly to not be challenged on the existing distribution of property and power, inside their ethnic enclaves (van der Westhuizen 2016). The poor whites are of course mere tokens in this game. The parading of their suffering bodies, and their articulation of a specific worldview, is indeed an affecting display of whiteness as misery. They are useful objects for consolidating sympathy both nationally, and globally through the investments in whiteness that animate the concerns of the Western media. As is true of all poor people in South Africa, they in fact have the least to gain from the advance of the neoliberal order orchestrated in their name.

NOTES

1. Original Afrikaans: "Ek sou vry gewees het van hierdie lewe . . . hierdie helse lewe. . . . "

2. Original Afrikaans: "'n kultuur op sy eie, sy eie dialek, sy eie norme, sy eie kwessies, en sy eie voorkoms."

3. Afrikaans: "Om na die skeilings te gaan is 'n ander . . . ander situasie." In the almost three-second pause the charity worker appears to be searching for a better word. The English translation offered in the subtitles is "To go to these shelters is a strange experience."

4. Original Afrikaans: "My kleintjie word baie siek hierso."

5. Original Afrikaans: ". . . het die Afrikanervolk op sy kniëe gedwing."

6. Original Afrikaans: "Skies, ek kry hulle net so vreeslik jammer."

7. Original Afrikaans: "Dis gevaarlik! Die mense verstaan nie hoe gevaarlik is dit daar vir ons mense nie! Hulle word nie gevloek nie, hulle word nie sleggessê hierso nie, hulle word nie uitgeskel nie—[. . .] 'white trash' . . . Hulle sal ons uitbrand—hulle wag vir ons om daar te kom—hulle gaan ons doodmaak".

8. Original Afrikaans: "Ek weier om te gaan want ek gaan . . . nie by swartes bly nie, en ek gaan nie ge-rape word daar nie."

9. Original Afrikaans: "Die rede daarvoor is eenvoudig omdat die president van die land, Thabo Mbeki, 'n intellektuele ruimte geskep het wat nie voorsiening maak vir iets soos wit armoede nie. Hy't gesê dat Suid-Afrika het twee nasies. Die een is arm en swart; die ander een is ryk en wit. So dit wil sê hy't eintlik nie voorsiening gemaak vir iets soos wit armoede nie."

10. In the original Afrikaans context: "Hulle het munsipaliteit toe gegaan—die vrou was woedend vir my . . . ons sê julle moet julle krag betaal".

11. Original Afrikaans: ". . . dit het natuurlik alles verdwyn."

12. Original Afrikaans: "Wit armoede in Suid-Afrika is 'n stille armoede - niemand sê iets daaroor nie. Dis byna polities nie korrek om daaroor iets te sê nie. Dis eintlik ironies, want ek dink dis die enigste vorm van armoede in die wêreld wat nie polities korrek is om oor te praat nie."

13. "Gebroke" can be rendered in English as "broken (down) (fig.); ruined; broken-hearted; rent; humbled or crushed; dispersed, routed; shattered in health, spirit or position" (Bosman, van der Merwe, and Hiemstra 1984).

14. Original Afrikaans: "Die belangrike ding is dat dit nie die regering was—die Afrikanerregering—wat die Afrikaner opgehef het: hulle het dit self gedoen."

15. Afrikaans: ". . . die antwoord vir armoede lê nie daarin om dit bloot makliker vir mense te maak om in armoede te bly nie: ons moet hulle daar uitlei. Jy begin eenvoudig deur die jongmense uit daai armoede sirkel uit te haal deur hulle op te lei sodat hulle uit die armoededsirkel kan breek. En daarom het ons besluit om met 'n reuse opleidingsprogram te begin. . . . Dis aan die einde van die dag die eingste volledige antwoord om die mense te bemagtig, deur seker te maak dat in die skuilings mense nie net daar bly nie, maar hulle 'n klein ekonomie daar skep waardeur hulle self-onderhoudend kan raak."

16. Original Afrikaans: ". . . hulle help om hulle self te help."

17. Original Afrikaans: "'n Mens sou verwag dat maatskaplike besteding op wittes geleidelik sal toeneem, na gelang wit armoede styg. Maar die teendeel is waar. Subsidies aan welsynsorganisasies wat net help aan witarmes verleen, word uitgefaseer. . . ."

18. Afrikaans: "Hier bly net blankes . . . helpsbehowende bejaardes."

19. The original Afrikaans text in context is: "Daar's 430,000 wit armes wat nie eers toegang het tot tradisionele . . . kom ons sê . . . wit behuising het nie . . . so, dit wil sê, wat in informele omgewings moet bly." The word "white" is however not translated into English in the subtitles of this clip.

Chapter 5

"When You Return the Land"

On 28 April 2016, the day after South Africa's "Freedom Day" holiday, which commemorates the 1994 democratic elections, a Facebook post authored by Rhodes Must Fall activist and University of Oxford postgraduate student Ntokozo Qwabe went viral. Qwabe had used the "feeling" function of the platform's post creation module to indicate that he was "elated" and had written: "LOL wow unable to stop smiling because something so black, wonderful & LIT just happened!" (Qwabe 2016a). He went on to explain that, after a meal at the Obz Café in an edgy Cape Town suburb with fellow activist Wandile Dlamini, instead of leaving a tip for the white waitress who had served them, Dlamini had written on the slip: "WE WILL GIVE TIP WHEN YOU RETURN THE LAND." The waitress became upset, and enlisted the support of a colleague, who confronted them about this act of "racism." The activists engaged briefly with the waitress and her colleague before returning to their own conversation, and then leaving the restaurant.

Qwabe's online description of the action—framed explicitly as political—unleashed an international traditional and social media "firestorm" (see Johnen, Jungblut, and Ziegele 2018). The internet was suddenly full of many morally outraged, and a few more measured, reactions to the Facebook post. In the commentary on Qwabe and Dlamini's statement that ensued on my own Facebook wall, most of the (Black and white) middle-class professionals and academics who commented, while broadly sympathetic to the aims of Rhodes Must Fall, were swift to express various levels of discomfort with what had happened. One commenter, however, was insistent that Qwabe's post was "hilarious."[1] He explained that: "it was like a candid camera and the waitress fell straight into the trap." The commenter was both confirming the textual markers of laughter that Qwabe had included in his post—such as "LOL"—and expanding on the setup of the scene as a kind of situational comedy. Very few others saw the story as in any way funny. Where was the humour the rest of us were missing?

There is clearly something LOL-worthy about Dlamini's asking a white woman picked more or less at random to give the land back. Significantly, an entire joke cycle about giving back the land was spawned on social media, plausibly at least partly inspired by the events in the Obz Café. The humour in their action, and the subsequent reactions to it, will be the focus of this chapter. In the first section, I lay out the chain of discursive actions and reactions that were initiated in Cape Town and reverberated around the country and in the United Kingdom, from (post)colonial periphery to imperial metropole. I then lay out a critical theory of humour, arguing that jokes have a particularly powerful role to play as hegemonic or counter-hegemonic articulations that re-literalize or sediment elements of discursive regimes. In the five subsections that follow I apply these theoretical perspectives to the joke cycle that the action spawned, before circling back to analysis of the situational comedy at the Obz Café itself. In the conclusion, I argue that Dlamini's action and Qwabe's narrative together constitute counter-hegemonic discursive acts that challenge the idea that no individual white person is responsible for racial inequality, and identify land as a key nodal point in the articulation of hegemonic whiteness. I also argue that the joke cycle is an ambiguous formation, both rebellious and disciplinary in its effects, working at cross-purposes both to repair and dislodge existing hegemonic orders.

ACTION AND REACTION

On Qwabe's account, after reading what Dlamini had written the white waitress, whose name is Ashleigh Schultz, had started shaking, before bursting "into typical white tears" (Qwabe 2016a). He clarified later that by "white tears" he meant not literal tears, but a negative emotional reaction from a white person who is "challenged to think about a question and they start getting uncomfortable" (Qwabe 2016b). The subsequent reaction, however, to a large extent revolved around these tears, whether real or not. Sihle Ngobese, a spokesperson for the Western Cape government which is controlled by the centre-right Democratic Alliance, returned to the restaurant the following day to give the "bullied" waitress a R50 ($3.40) tip, as part of an attempt to "show what kindness is" (Ngobese 2016). Ngobese subsequently promoted a national fundraising campaign to increase the tip that had been initiated by the hosts of the Renegade Report, a right-leaning "liberal" online radio station. Combined with extensive promotion on Twitter and Facebook of this and other fundraising efforts, Schultz's tip was increased to over R140,000 ($9,450) (Davis 2016). Evident in most of the media response to the action was a particular pattern: symbolic and material value was shifted away from Qwabe and towards Schultz, while Dlamini was typically ignored or erased.

Qwabe was temporarily suspended from Facebook, and his post removed for "violating Facebook's community standards" confirming the political bias of Facebook's "technological gaze" (Ibrahim 2017, 5–6). As the press uncovered Schultz's backstory—she is not from a wealthy family, and her mother was battling cancer—attention focused increasingly on the class dimensions of the incident. This was particularly evident in the British press. Candice Holdsworth, writing for the right-wing *Spectator*, asked

> Whatever happened to the old leftist notion of solidarity with the working class? That has clearly been abandoned in favour of fractious identity politics. Qwabe and his political ilk are so selfishly absorbed in their own self-declared "pain" that they feel justified lashing out at an entirely innocent person whose own hurt they are incapable of registering. (Holdsworth 2016)

The affective theme of Holdsworth's assertion—where a supposedly shared class position serves as a natural cohesive force that is broken by Qwabe's adhesion to a "fractious identity [i.e. racial] politics" that both comes from and causes pain—is common throughout the reaction. Her explicit discounting (using scare quotes and dismissive language) of the notion of Black pain—a concept that is often operationalized in the decolonial and Black activist tradition to centre Black experience (see K. D. Brown 2021 for a sympathetic critique)—attempts to close off the possibility of any historically inspired sympathy with Qwabe's own experience. Similar affective strategies are evident in other reportage. A headline in *The Sowetan* reported "Internet turns on activist who made waitress cry" (TMG Digital 2016) and websites that focus on good news stories about South Africa eagerly tracked growing donations to Schultz, with one proclaiming that "Kindness Wins!" (SAPeople 2016). Dlamini's note and Qwabe's post were constructed as mean and gratuitous actions against the waitress that needed to be healed by an outpouring of goodwill aimed at her, and concomitantly avenged through the bile directed at them. Qwabe was thus called an "international figure of hate" by British tabloid the *Daily Mail* (J. Robinson and Greenhill 2016), denounced for "borderline criminal behaviour" by ANC Western Cape spokesperson Yonela Diko (eNCA.com 2016), and even reprimanded by his own father, who told a newspaper: "I want to sit down with him, tell him that he is young and he needs to follow proper procedures when he is not happy about something" (Buthelezi 2016). News reportage repeatedly tied this particular action to the Rhodes Must Fall movement at the universities of Cape Town and Oxford. Viciously worded petitions were launched to strip Qwabe of his Rhodes scholarship and expel him from Oxford; he was threatened with increasing levels of violence, and with death (Qwabe 2016b).

In the context of near-unanimous media hostility (see Shandu 2016; and Xaba 2016 for exceptions) the most sophisticated and subtly theorised interpretation of the action and the ensuing media fracas, dubbed #TipGate, was written by Qwabe himself for the Daily Vox (Qwabe 2016b). In it, Qwabe addresses the erasure of Dlamini, defines what is meant by "white tears," and deconstructs the brazenly inaccurate and racist reporting of the Western and South African press. He lays out his response to people who considered Dlamini's action "racist" by observing that racism cannot be reduced to "exchanges of unkind words between people of varying melanin content" (ibid.). Qwabe explains how racism includes a variety of vicious, insidious, and exploitative social conditions that were absent from Schultz's experience of #TipGate. In this vein, far from denying the need for class solidarity, he goes on to outline the reasons for the insufficiency of a class analysis in the South African context, and the ways in which #TipGate proves Schultz is not a "vulnerable working-class person" (ibid.) at all—but a white working-class person, which gives her access to a completely different set of affordances and outcomes than those available to working-class Black people.

Qwabe's analysis is incisive and far-ranging, and I will not recapitulate it here. Instead, I will explore one aspect of #TipGate that is not addressed by Qwabe in his response, and analyse in a little more depth the links between two others that he touches on only briefly. Firstly, he does not discuss his thinking behind the "LOL" with which his post started. Much of Qwabe's writing brims with humour and irony. For example, he starts his analysis of why there was nothing racist about #TipGate with the statement: "Firstly, there's no way that I can be 'racist' as some of my best friends are white" (Qwabe 2016b). This deadpan imitation of a typical white response to being called racist—which he neither marks as funny nor explains to readers—predictably traps the first commenter on the article on the Daily Vox website, one "Cliff Smith," who attacks Qwabe for thinking this is a "get out jail free card" (ibid.). Qwabe's brand of humour seems to be especially effective at provoking displays of white fragility. The second and third aspects I want to link together—which Qwabe does mention—are on the one hand, the perceived asymmetries of power, and, on the other, the way they play out spatially. Qwabe articulates a distinction between the nastiness of the racialized structure of the social order, which is sedimented in powerful institutions, spaces, and processes, and the comparative niceness and powerlessness of Ashleigh Shultz working a shift in the Obz Café. On this issue, he writes:

> Often, we make ourselves "objects of political protest" because we wrongly personalise political acts that are directed at making structural critiques of the society we exist in. . . . Ashleigh was uncomfortable . . . because she made the whole affair about her when it wasn't. (ibid.)

Qwabe is here referring to a specific relation between the individual and the structural dynamics of social change that raises specific ethical issues for political action. This dynamic will be discussed in more detail below. On why the restaurant was an appropriate location for the action, Qwabe reminds readers of the work of Rhodes Must Fall in larger and more powerful institutions, before stating:

> We just believe that while we are at it [engaging large and powerful institutions] it is valuable to live our decolonial politics by taking the conversation to everyday public spaces—including our classrooms, communities, restaurants, shopping centres and all other sites of public presence. Tipgate therefore forms part of an ongoing deliberate attempt to re-politicise the public space and raise consciousness regarding how unjust the society we exist in is. (ibid.)

This work of "re-politicising" public space may include some of the discursive acts of "re-literalization" I discussed in chapter 1, laying bare the rhetorical and contingent meanings of identification and social meaning, in this case those of the sedimented spaces of racial and class belonging into which South Africa remains parcelled. The dynamics of how "appropriate" protest is delimited in specific spatial contexts will now be approached through a critical engagement with laughter and ridicule.

HUMOUR AND THE SOCIAL ORDER

Michael Billig's *Laughter and Ridicule* (2005) addresses a tendency in various scholarly traditions to approach humour with a mind-set he dubs "ideological positivism" (Billig, 2005, p. 5). This tradition emphasises the supposedly positive and healthy aspects of having a laugh, while those aspects of humour that are perceived as cruel or motivated by a desire to ridicule are either repressed, or defined as unfunny. In so doing, humour studies has laboured—and in certain circles continues to labour—under outdated or naïve theories of discourse. For example, in a monograph on digital humour, it is asserted that comedians may be smarter and more honest than most politicians, but that jokes themselves are politically inert, serving only to "make us feel better" (Chiaro 2017, 3). Humour "takes the temperature of a society at a given moment" (2017, p. 3). The idea that jokes are thermometers as opposed to thermostats is advanced by some scholars of humour who argue that "jokes are an extremely weak force in a world dominated by very strong social and political forces" (Davies 2017, 240). These strong forces include things such as the military invasions, tax laws, or the death penalty, against which jokes are constructed as more or less powerless. For critical humour scholars such as Abedinifard (2016, 248) however, who analyses homophobic joke cycles in Iran, jokes have powerful "heteronormalizing and disciplinary functions." Humour keeps the strong (religious, legal) forces strong through a process of constant affirmation. Jokes are key discursive acts that, like meaning-making in general, point to the ways in which "the microstructures of language are linked with and help to shape the macrostructures of society" (Mayr 2008, 9). Gendered humour is one example of a disciplinary technique that employs ridicule to deepen and renew hegemonic masculinity through producing "self-regulating social subjects" (Abedinifard 2016, 235).

What is found funny within a particular society thus often provides good clues as to the nature of the prevailing hegemonic order. The popular idea in traditional humour theory that jokes are a hopelessly weak force compared to the "strong" forces that actually change the world is clearly irreconcilable with theorisations of discursive hegemony that emphasise how the consent of social groups is secured for the political direction of social life. While "ideological positivism" cordons off the realm of the funny from the realm of what is "really" oppressive, critical humour studies follows the opposite path, showing how oppression, discipline, and social control lie at the very heart of humour. Billig distinguishes two ways in which ridicule interacts with the social order: it can be "disciplinary" when it enforces that order, or "rebellious" to the extent that the order itself is challenged (Billig 2005, 202). However, even when people think they are being rebellious, they may in fact be engaging in acts of disciplining. There is no guarantee that the psychological motivation of the person attempting humour, and the sociological effects that humour has, will match up (2005, p. 211). Agents "might claim to occupy the position of rebelliousness" when in fact "the consequences of such humour might be conformist rather than radical, disciplinary not rebellious" (ibid.). The social function of humour tends to be not unlike that of a parental authority figure training an infant's sense of humour to find ridiculous that which subverts the social order. These experiences happen throughout people's lives. When professsionals play a practical joke on an apprentice, the joke both "teaches the conventions and takes innocuous revenge against them" and is thus a "momentary release . . . from the enduring power of constraint" (2005, p. 211). While they enjoy seeing their joke undermine the social order, this undermining is only momentary, and its real effect is to teach the apprentice what the rules really are. These tendencies are visible in entire cultures, as Billlig gloomily observes. Far from the twenty-first century being a golden age of rebellious humour, "the world of late capitalism [promotes] the enjoyment of mass-marketed rebellious humour [that] directly aids the economic structures that have produced such enjoyment" (2005, p. 212). Not only does it fail to undermine repressive power structures, such joking serves also to clear the individual conscience of a sense of responsibility for perpetuating them, while at the same time not recognizing "that rebellion has thus become a joke" (2005, p. 213).

In Billig's account, seriousness and humour are symbiotically intertwined in the perpetuation of the social order. Embarrassment—the fear of being laughed at—works as "an internalized force to protect codes and ensure routine social compliance" (2005, p. 215). The fact that we enjoy laughing explains, in Billig's view, something that Freud explained only partially: why social life is able to continue despite the fact that it requires that we limit our own pleasure (2005, pp. 216–217). Human beings can actually enjoy the process of constraining our own freedom; we take pleasure (even "malicious pleasure" [2005, p. 228]) from the embarrassment of others, and even laugh at our previous embarrassment later (2005, p. 233). This pleasure may of course also have the dimension of being an enjoyment of seeing the social order subverted—through the "rebellious" aspect of humour. This therefore places a paradox at the heart of social life, that "the same mechanism that ensures social compliance also expresses pleasure at subversion" (2005, p. 234). But is subversion even possible? Humour's "vital, disciplinary role in the maintenance of social life" (2005, p. 238) seems to leave little room for social change, as even as we laugh at subversion, we seem to be again disciplining ourselves into compliance. It is as if the critical and traditional theories of humour have converged on the conclusion that "jokes will never change the world"—while at least the critical theory has established that jokes are important forces in keeping the world as it is. There is, however, no reason to dwell in this quagmire, which is a familiar one: that of the horizon of intelligibility, and the delimitation of what may be thought (or indeed laughed at) within reigning definitions of common sense.

Humour is clearly a socially powerful articulatory practice that disciplines social agents into appropriate subject roles, and may thus be involved in the renovation or erosion of existing hegemonic structures. When in 2013 the Turkish prime minister called protestors opposing his increasingly repressive regime "çapulcu" ["ruffians"], they responded by turning the word into a badge of pride, a revolutionary appellation that inverted the supposed meaning of the word, and united (albeit briefly) opposition to tyranny (Varol 2014). Humour and satire have indeed become hallmarks of organised protest around the world, and in the context of both Turkey and the Arab Spring the term "revolutionary humour" has gained currency (Helmy and Frerichs 2013; Mersal 2011; Varol 2014). Humour spreads very quickly on social media, affecting non-contiguous domestic and global discourses, influencing thinking and activism on specific reforms and demands, building solidarity around these demands, and "piercing the culture of fear prevalent in tyrannical regimes [. . . while depicting] an alternate, and more appealing, reality" (Varol 2014, 558). So, while always avoiding the tendency to focus on attempts to oversell the positive effects of humour that Billig so thoroughly discredits, we should also be clear that humour does not have a special place outside of discourse: it too is involved in the processes of contesting social vision. In the Gramscian account of the role of ideology, "organic intellectuals" are not produced in relations of corroboration with the traditional institutions of the reigning social group, and are thus able to think outside of this established consensus. The jokes they tell may thus play important roles in piercing established hegemonies and in showing up the contingency of sedimented articulations. Just being able to laugh in contexts of repression and dehumanisation is tied up with hegemonic orders. In a discussion of the French child on the train, Fanon offers some revealing remarks on his ability to laugh:

> "Mama, see the Negro! I'm frightened!" Frightened! Frightened! Now they were beginning to be afraid of me. I made up my mind to laugh myself to tears, but laughter had become impossible. I could no longer laugh, because I already knew that there were legends, stories, history, and above all historicity. (Fanon [1952] 2008, 84)

Being "battered down" into the racial epidermal schema (as was discussed in chapter 2) by the figure of the *négre* has the effect of making laughter impossible, as laughter speaks to communion between humans in relations of reciprocity in a social order. Fanon only recovers a sense of his humanity when he insults the woman who says "Look how handsome that Negro is!" by saying: "Kiss the handsome Negro's ass, madame!" ([1952] 2008, 86):

> Shame flooded her face. At last I was set free from my rumination. At the same time I accomplished two things: I identified my enemies and I made a scene. A grand slam. Now one would be able to laugh.

As we have seen, for Billig, embarrassment—or at least the fear of being ridiculed—lies at the very heart of the disciplinary power of humour. This subversion of the racial order—where the discursive construction speaks back to the white woman—temporarily frees Fanon from the epidermal schema, allowing him to laugh at her shame. I say "temporarily" in response to Fanon's own implied sense of a fleeting victory; he has "made a scene" now, but this is hardly a permanent reversal of fortunes. But it is important to note that, for however brief a moment, she is the one who is disciplined, with a particularly sexual reversal. Whereas her invocation of the "handsome Negro" reduces Fanon to a racial object, his ability to bring so vividly to her mind his human ass that she should kiss floods her with recognition of a desire that subverts the social order: sexual reciprocity between Black and white. Her shame uncovers the fact of Fanon's humanity, releasing him momentarily from the zone of nonbeing.

Dodds and Kirby (2013) argue that humour has a geopolitical dimension. Examining Stephen Colbert's highly ironic hosting of the White House Correspondents' Association Dinner in 2006, they observe that Colbert was considered unfunny in the room where President George W. Bush was both the guest of honour and the butt of the humour, but a huge success around the world on the internet (2013, 45–46). At the banquet, Colbert was met with what Billig (2005, p. 179) calls "unlaughter": the rhetorical performance by an audience of refusing to respond to a supposedly humorous situation with laughter. Unlaughter is a response to a joke's failure to correspond "to the appropriateness of the social occasion and circumstance in which it occurs" (Lockyer and Pickering 2008, 810). Colbert in Washington D.C. in 2006 and Dlamini/Qwabe in Cape Town in 2016 certainly show that a joke lands differently in different spaces and on different occasions. The "geographical mechanics of humour" may extend into space in other ways: a joke has "boundary-marking" effects, for it includes some and excludes others, producing some people as being in place, and others as being out of place (Dodds & Kirby, 2013, p. 48). Humour is entangled in national belonging, as Danish Muslims meeting the Jyllands Posten cartoons of the Prophet Mohammed with unlaughter realised (2013, p. 50). Danes are the people who were able to laugh at the cartoons; unlaughter, on the other hand, makes one un-Danish. As specific articulations sediment or reactivate hegemonic discursive formations, we are hailed into the subject roles of people who have the common (and commonsense) sense of humour. Counter-hegemonic humour, on the other hand, may be met with blank unlaughter. That is, unless the pattern is repeated, and a greater number of articulations start to challenge the assumptions of the old formation. Below, we will examine how this happened in the aftermath of #TipGate.

JOKING ABOUT THE LAND

Ntokozo Qwabe's post about Wandile Dlamini's "WE WILL GIVE TIP WHEN YOU RETURN THE LAND" joke fed into a genre of jokes circulated online, centring around the theme of white people "giving back the land." While Qwabe was certainly not the first activist to use the hashtag #IzweLethu ("#OurLand"[2]), it was frequently used in humorous contexts after April 2016. The jokes that will be presented here are not exhaustive of the genre, but present selected examples of five specific themes that emerged in a much larger corpus of jokes I collected.

"At Least You Still Have the Land"

The first key theme to note was the idea that having land makes up or compensates for other problems or absences that people may have in their lives.

(1a)	Tweet: Leatitia (@leatitiajvr) 14/08/2016	@MTNza really upset. *141# confirms I have airtime but I cannot make calls. Data and airtime disappears. No response from emails. . . .
(1b)	Reply: MTN South Africa (@MTNza) 14/08/2016	That's sad. At least you still have the land

In the first example, the official MTN account allegedly[3] responded to a customer (who appears to be a white woman in her profile picture) who complains about disappearing airtime. She is advised by one of South Africa's largest mobile telephony companies to cheer up as she "still" has the land. The humour here trades on subverting two dominant discourses: one, that in a capitalist society the customer is deferred to in order to retain them; and two, that the post-apartheid land détente made the question of colonial dispossession something for government to sort out (between landowning "willing seller" farmers and land claimant "willing buyer" communities). It does not matter whether @leatitiajvr actually owns land; what is ridiculed here is the caricature of her as an entitled white consumer who expects never to be called to account personally for historical injustices. The idea that a brand such as MTN would publicly mock their own customer, in a gentle but ironic tone, for belonging to a historically privileged group is at the core of the transgressive and thus "rebellious" nature of the joke. "Having" land can also compensate for national failings, as in the second example.

(2)	Tweet: Nqaba Matshazi (@nqabamatshazi) 15/03/2017	Air Zimbabwe is such a joke, but who cares, we've got the land

This tweet contains a screen grab of a Facebook post by a frustrated Air Zimbabwe customer who had tried to check into their flight to Harare at OR Tambo International Airport in Johannesburg, only to be told that the plane was not full enough for a takeoff to be considered economical, and that the flight had thus been cancelled without any alternative arrangements made by the airline. The humour in Matshazi's affected indifference to this diatribe rests on shared knowledge about Zimbabwean and South African politics. In newly independent African countries, the national airline has often stood in for the "gleaming future" (Msimang 2017, 31) and represented the possibility and hope of the postcolonial period. That their national pride, as wound up in the national carrier, is now a "joke" has to be compensated for by pride in something else, which in this case is articulated as the precipitous land reform process in Zimbabwe, which differs so starkly from the South African case. That the failure of the airline itself is not the important issue in the future of Zimbabwe, but that it is ownership of land that is, suggests that Black land control is a nodal point for narratives of national or ethnic success. This comparison is however simultaneously shot through with irony, and even pathos, as it can also be read as suggesting that Zimbabwe-style land reform may represent something of a Pyrrhic victory. The predicament of the Air Zimbabwe customer stranded at the airport is hardly something to be aspired to. These tensions are also apparent in example 1b, where lost airtime is a consumer issue that is a popular point of complaint across social divides in South Africa. It is thus possible that MTN's customer service is being laughed at—if indeed this meme was created using graphic design software and not actually tweeted by MTN (see footnote 36). The person behind the MTN account is reimagined as an incompetent agent who, unable to offer the customer a complete answer, deflects the conversation to a popular meme about land reform. So, while these jokes may be enjoyed for violating the norms of consumerism or a Rainbowist national commitment to forgetting about the spoils of colonialism, they may also have a disciplinary dimension in the construction of a hopeless customer service agent, clutching at straws to deal with an angry white woman, or the self-deluding Zimbabwean trying to cling to some sense of national pride.

Who Deserves the Land?

The second theme trades in jokes about who actually deserves to have the land. Here, a future where land is earned on the basis of what appears to be trivial behaviour is imagined. Ntokozo Qwabe himself participates in telling this kind of joke, as in examples 3 and 4. Having the good fashion sense not wear sunglasses at night, and being skilled at the i-vosho dance[4] are playfully proposed as qualifying criteria.

(3)	Facebook post: Ntokozo Qwabe 08/05/2017	When we take back the land, not even a single square meter must go to people who wear shades at night!

(4)	Facebook post: Ntokozo Qwabe 27/10/2017	We reject people who can't dance. Can we trust you with the land if you can't do i-vosho on it?

The allocation of land is thus constructed in almost absurdist terms. While these discursive moves may seem flippant, the history of South Africa is full of bizarre turns; the land was taken from under Black people's feet using all manner of trickery and deceit. Pointing to the absurdity of who gets the land thus at least partly constitutes the rebellious facet of the joke: the aspect of the social order rebelled against is the frequently articulated idea during the South African transition and since that property rights are "sacrosanct" (cf. Hart 2014). Qwabe is playing the fool around a topic that for many people has an almost religious seriousness about it.

At the same time, it is also hard to escape the sense that there is a disciplinary undercurrent to the fun, driven perhaps by an anxiety over never seeing the day of true land transformation come, or of not seeing it properly managed: the spectre of a tribunal that repeats past mistakes, excluding people from landownership for arbitrary reasons, surely reinforces the existing rather tighter and stricter rules of land title. A variation on this logic is suggested by the prominent editor and columnist Sipho Hlongwane in example 5. Here, he deals with linguistic authenticity. Balls of fried dough, which are eaten plain or with a sweet or savoury filling or sauce, are popular in many local cuisines, where they are typically referred to as *vetkoek* (Afrikaans) or *amagwinya* (isiZulu) in everyday spoken South African English. People who say "fat cakes" are lampooned for their supposed social pretention: in attempting to erase the traces of other languages from their linguistic performance, supposedly because they consider these languages to have a lower status than English, they go too far and erase words that have been borrowed into English. Hlongwane encourages multilingual speakers to take pride in their native languages and cuisines, and to use home-grown terms, while at the same time making the less rebellious point that "fat cakes" is in fact not correct South African English at all.

(5)	Facebook post: Sipho Hlongwane 16/07/2017	You people who call vetkoeks "fat cakes" are the reason we have not got back the land yet. [emoji: unhappy face]

Another Janus-faced disciplinary/rebellious facet of this joke is the implication that if Black people were less pretentious in taking on supposedly English affectations, they would get the land back. Agency is a double-edged sword, as if this is all Black people need to do to get back the land, it might also be their own fault for not having effectively done so. This joke can also be read as taking aim at a present cultural lapse, that will be surpassed when people have the land back, and try less eagerly to live up to the pseudo-white Englishness voiced in "fat cakes."

The final example in this theme is also about language, and is a joke with two layers. Popular South African author Khaya Dlanga has over 580,000 followers on Twitter and is generally considered an influential social media celebrity. When he quipped that a white woman who is fluent in an indigenous South African language, whose picture he screen-grabbed from an SABC broadcast and included, could "keep the land" his tweet was reframed in a quote tweet by a user with a significantly different interpretation.

(6a)	Tweet: Khaya Dlanga (@khayadlanga) 19/09/2017	She can keep the land [image of a white woman speaking an African language on SABC]
(6b)	Quote tweet: loki (@NotYetUhuru_) 19/09/2017	And what do we keep since we speak English and Afrikaans?

The equivalence that is drawn in these tweets between linguistic/cultural authenticity and the right to land—retraces the same structure Hlongwane appealed to in example 5. Loki's wry reframing of Dlanga's tweet articulates a complex argument. At one level, it is affirmed that learning a language is not equivalent to a claim for reparations based on historical dispossession. Dlanga, she implies, has missed the point: white people cannot erase historical injustices by learning a language any more than Black people were able to lay claim to South Africa by learning to speak Afrikaans, nor to England by speaking English. The jokes in this theme produce a particular subject role of the "authentic" future landowner in South Africa while at the same time poking fun at the institutions that would produce and police this "authenticity." The existing institution of an arbitrary and unjust end-state distribution protected by sacrosanct property rights is simultaneously undermined.

Exploiting White Vulnerability

The next theme can be read against Sihle Ngobese's assertion that his fundraising efforts for Ashleigh Schultz's tip were to "show what kindness is." In this theme, which was quite a common one, jokes are contextualised in intimate relationships between Black people and white people, where one might expect kindness to be on display. The first example shows a stylishly dressed Black man wearing sunglasses and a Panama hat cradling what looks like a white baby in a pink babygro while he teaches the baby to say the word "land" before promptly demanding it back (example 7).

(7) Tweet: Barry (@A_Young_Padawan) 02/09/2016
"Sayyyy Land. Lllllaaaaannnndddd. Yes, now give it back" [image of a Black man holding a white baby]

The next joke includes a picture of two attractive young people at what appears to be a party. A dark-skinned man is kissing a light-skinned woman with a comically wide-open mouth, which the author of the tweet says he is doing in order to swallow the land out of the woman (example 8).

Tweet: Axola Sirayi (@axolasirayi) 28/03/2017
Finally someone is standing up for us. . . . Swallow our land out buti [*buti* means "brother"; image of a Black man kissing a white woman with his mouth comically wide open]

Another example of this style of joke is tweeted by an EFF supporter, who tags the party's official account in her tweet making an in-group joke about the "ladies" of the EFF. In the meme attached to this tweet, a Black woman hugging a white man from behind as he orders a chicken takeaway is ventriloquised as saying "Baby I don't want chicken. I want land" (example 9).

(9) Tweet: Lelethu Williams (@Leskorate) 15/11/2016
Eff ladies be like this [4 emojis: crying laughing face] down with white monopoly **we want land** @EFFSouthAfrica [emphasis in original; image of a Black woman hugging a white man from behind while he orders from a Chicken Licken outlet, with the text "Baby I don't want chicken. I want land."].

After a call was made by a group of citizens perceived to be mostly middle-class and white for all citizens to wear black on Monday the 3rd of April 2017 in order to protest President Jacob Zuma's cabinet reshuffle of the previous week, a witty Twitter user says he is only wearing black to blend in, and will try to get the land back (example 10).

(10)	Tweet: Motheo (@Motheo_ie) 03/04/2017	Guys I'm wearing black because I am going under cover. I might come back with the land. Keep your fingers crossed.

In a final example, popular internet personality Esethu Hasane tweeted a picture of the popular athlete Caster Semenya after she had won a race, comforting Linsey Sharp, an runner who had been very negative about Semenya before the competition, and who lost her race badly at the IAAF World Athletics Championships in August 2017. Hasane resignifies what seemed like a moment of magnanimity on Semenya's behalf, by adding the statement: "I'm coming for the land."

(11)	Tweet: Esethu Hasane (@itsEsethu) 14/08/2017	"I'm coming for the land" [image of Caster Semenya touching Linsey Sharp's shoulder after she lost her race].

Getting back the land is done up close and personal, individual to individual, in all five of these jokes. What is remarkable here is the humorous play with everyday relationships where people become vulnerable to each other—holding a baby, becoming romantically involved, or even going to a protest together. Vulnerability plays an important role in the rebellious dimension of these jokes. One aspect of the social order being rebelled against is the idea that the South African national project, built on the compromises and negotiated settlements of Codesa and the acts of disclosure and absolution at the TRC, is incompatible with an ambitious programme of socioeconomic redress and reparation. White people are supposed to already be forgiven for apartheid and colonialism. The white people in these tweets are not in powerful positions, and yet land is demanded from them. What is being rebelled against at one level in these jokes is the way that a white power structure is able to remain obscured behind social norms that enforce the "kind" treatment of white people. At another level, it is the diffuseness of the power structure itself, where no individual white person can be held accountable for an historical pattern laid down over centuries. Whiteness is peculiarly a "collective without individuals" (Ahmed 2004a, n.p.) or what could be thought of in this context as a "structure without bodies." These jokes both make these individual bodies visible and ridicule the idea that they should be treated with kindness. This is not to say that there is not also a disciplinary dimension to these examples, which emerges from within the rebellion: you can't actually swallow land out of a white person, and the baby won't actually be able to give you the land back. So in a subtle but very limited way, the catch-all intended audience of the call to "give back the land" is being undermined, as landing in untargeted places at perhaps inopportune moments. Similarly, in example 10 the request by Motheo to his followers that they "keep your fingers crossed" has a self-defeating irony built in: he's only kidding, there is no real point in hoping.

Rejecting Locke

The debate over land restitution in South Africa is in dynamic tension with the debate over food security and rural livelihoods (see Kepe and Tessaro 2014). The complexities of the agricultural sector of the economy are regularly deployed in the public debate to counter militant calls for land reform. It is asserted that there are bigger issues than the distribution of land: people must eat, the highly capitalised and efficient South African agricultural economy cannot be allowed to founder due to imprudent, populist policies. A theme in the land joke cycle developed in response to this tactic is thus the assertion that "taking the land back" is not reducible to agriculture or the maintenance of food security. This irreducibility does not in every case mean that food production is devalued, but rather that it is put into its historical context. In a representative example of this discursive move, the hip-hop producer and radio personality Rashid Kay tweets an image of a Black man sitting smartly dressed in his suit and tie, seated on a carved wooden chair placed in a maize field, with the text "WHEN WE GET OUR LAND BACK."

(12)	Tweet: RASHID KAY™ (@rashid_kay) 10/06/2017	WHEN WE GET OUR LAND BACK bit.ly/2r5LsVR [*link broken*] #BringBackOurLand [picture of man sitting on an ornate chair in a maize field].

The image concisely articulates the overlapping space of landownership, agriculture, and dignity. The image is posed in a genre reminiscent of the official photograph—a CEO seated at a boardroom table, or a president seated in front of their cabinet—but also of old-fashioned portrait photography, where families would get dressed up in their Sunday best to go into town to have an official portrait taken, to be handed down across generations. What makes the tweet humorous is the incongruity between the business suit and ornate chair—which are usually associated with formal, inside activities—and the earthiness of the maize field. A business suit is not appropriate attire for agricultural work; the chair will get damaged and the man's shoes will get muddy. So while there is a quiet dignity in the man's posture and gaze, there is also an undercurrent of pathos, and even a slight element of the ridiculous. In this particular instance it might be argued that the ridiculous rebels against the social order, by showing the extent to which dignity can be grounded in apparently incongruous elements that supersede purely agricultural use of land. Land is linked to legacy, pride, and to personal agency. A tweet by the popular radio DJ Sibongile Mafu expands on this theme by showing Oprah Winfrey on the cover of *O Magazine* in various relationships to the land: reading books on it with a cocker spaniel against her breast, walking over it in a floral dress, feeding horses green apples, and contemplating what to "let go" of, while holding an ear of corn. This collage is offered as the rhetorical answer to a question Mafu poses in the voice of someone challenging her to explain what she is "even going to do with the land when you get it?." The tweet clearly rebels against the idea that any future landowner would have to justify to anybody what they are using the land for. The deployment of Oprah Winfrey is significant. Winfrey grew up poor and became a billionaire. Her particular lifestyle brand promotes a mix of social consciousness and self-actualisation, enabling consumption (in this case, of enjoyment of the land and an associated idealised rural lifestyle) without guilt. The tweet projects the carefree wealth of Oprah Winfrey onto future Black landownership in South Africa.

(12)	Tweet: Sibongile Mafu (@sboshmafu) 25/07/2017	'What are you even going to do with the land when you get it?' [collage of four Oprah magazine covers showing Oprah Winfrey in various poses enjoying country life].

A similar idea is articulated in another tweet, which works as a dialogue between two accounts:

(13a)	Tweet: Ditaru (@DitaruMusic) 05/10/2017	Many people can't take care of a pot plant but they want 8 ha land . . . bazawenzantoni?
(13b)	Quote tweet: Bonga Ntshingila (@thentshingila) 05/10/2017	Sizowubuka sibe siphulula imikhaba

This conversation takes place partly in isiZulu. "*Bazawenzantoni*" means "What are they going to do with it?." "8 ha" refers to eight hectares. @DitaruMusic expresses scepticism about the usefulness of transferring land to people who are demanding it back. Ntshingila's response is to say "*Sizowubuka sibe siphulula imikhaba*": "We will look at it while rubbing our tummies" which means, idiomatically, that we will look at it with admiration.

The land may thus be enjoyed for the purposes only of admiring it—it does not even need to be used productively. The claim to the land—that it must be given back by the legatees of colonial dispossession—is thus asserted as not depending on plans for its future use. Issues of justice and restitution are thus articulated as superordinate to instrumental concerns about farming. This theme to a certain extent closes the loop of establishing the land as the key value or nodal point of the discourse, as described in the first theme. Ultimately, the target of this humour is the idea of the dependence of land justice on plans for the productive use of land. This is a clear response to the lineage of argument in the liberal tradition that comes down from John Locke (discussed in the introduction) that says that people come to own land only by virtue of mixing their labour with it—an argument that, as has been shown, was used to justify colonial dispossession. This lineage is incredibly influential in thinking about land and landownership, and in this sense this tweet can be read as encapsulating an anti-Lockean position.

Yt msunery

White people feature in the next theme—not as friends, children, or intimate partners, but as deceivers, thieves, or aggressors. In an op-ed that supports Dlamini and Qwabe, the Black feminist activist and scholar Wanelisa Xaba concludes with the following statement:

> Lastly, imisunu yenu yazi 1652's. The white liberals. The white feminists. The white leftists. NONKE (Xaba, 2016).

"*Imisunu yenu yazi 1652's*" can be loosely translated as: "fuck you 1652s." *Imisunu yenu* is "your assholes" and "1652" is an appellation for a white person that indexes their shallow and nonindigenous roots in South Africa through a reference to the date that Jan van Riebeeck landed at the Cape to establish the first official European settlement. *NONKE* means "ALL OF YOU." The isiZulu insult *imisunu yenu* has been borrowed into English and grammaticalized as "msunery." I thus use the term "yt msunery" to categorise Black critique of white complicity and in maintaining hegemonic orders of property ownership and spatial control. Spelling white as "yt" is an occasional orthographic convention in the corpus, as can be seen in the following example.

(14) Tweet: Gladiator (@Khanyi_T) 11/11/2016

I see now
Black people: Give us land
Yts: Education?
BP: No, we want land
Yts: A new government?
BP: L.A.N.D.
Yts: What do these people want

In example 14, the author of the tweet dramatizes the unintelligibility to white people of Black claims for land. White people are presented as only being able to listen to Black people through the filters of their own prejudices: Black people must be in need of education, or they need to stop voting against their own interests for a corrupt and incompetent government. The first two white questions end in question marks, whereas the final one trails off without punctuation. This suggests exasperation at not getting the answer they want, or the abandonment of any pretence of listening to Black answers. The final sentence articulates the inscrutability of Black people's desires to white people, rather than forming an actual question. Black calls for land are constructed as outside of rational common sense, making them unintelligible as political claims. The rebellious humour of this tweet pierces the idea that "interracial" deliberation, debate, and compromise, the foundation stones of the "Rainbow Nation" myth, are even possible with white people when it comes to the land question.

That South African institutions are complicit in the production of a particular ideology about land is satirised in example 15, which includes a version of the "Confused Lady / Math Lady" meme.[5] This meme usually features complex mathematical formula superimposed on images of a blonde Brazilian telenovela actress, but in this version the blonde woman has been replaced by the Barbadian singer Rihanna. The meme is usually used to signify a slow and difficult process of working something out. In the final frame of the meme, Rihanna is shown covering her mouth in shock, as if she has just come to an important realisation. What exactly it is that she has realised is articulated in the text of the tweet.

(15) Tweet: smiley (@_MaZulu) 31/03/2017

Our primary school teachers had us growing beans from cotton pads because they knew good and well we'll never get the land to plant them in [meme of Rihanna as confused lady / math lady]

This moment of clarity, shared by the author of the tweet through Rihanna's reaction, is clearly the joke's punchline. The conclusion that growing beans in cotton wool is part of an elaborate conspiracy to alienate Black children from the land is clearly calculated to be parodic. In this joke, as in many others, both rebellious and disciplinary readings are possible. This is at one level a serious critique of how institutions such as schools are fundamental to the reproduction of hegemonic white ways of thinking that have lingered long after the end of apartheid. Here, the yt msunery is in their social engineering of a schooling system that perpetuates the immutable economic and moral laws that keep Black people landless. At another level, the silliness of the conclusion suggests a disciplinary undercurrent, as if to say that the whole discourse of getting the land back has taken on some of the wilder and less serious characteristics of conspiracy thinking.

The theme of yt msunery was also explored in a tweet that responded to one of its most vociferous champions, Western Cape premier and former leader of the DA, Helen Zille. Zille had unleashed a major controversy in March 2017 when she tweeted that colonialism had not only had bad consequences, but had actually benefited countries such as Singapore. This was not the first time that Zille had been publicly exposed for historical insensitivity, but it was arguably on many people's minds when she tweeted a photograph of Table Mountain in May 2017. The Cape Town City Bowl, Atlantic Sea Board and Southern Suburbs are among some of the most racially segregated areas of South Africa, and to a large extent the heart of the city has become synonymous with white property interests. Tweeter @Zee_Mbana's deadpan question in response to Zille's tweet in example 16 is made funnier by shared knowledge of this history.

(16a)	Tweet: Helen Zille (@helenzille) 29/05/2017	What a Cape Town Winter's evening! [image: Table Mountain under a clear blue sky]
(16b)	Quote tweet: Zethu Mbana (@Zee_Mbana) 29/05/2017	Mntase, when are we getting lanto back?

The author of the tweet uses a familiar and intimate form of address: "mntase"—short for "mntasekhaya"—usually used when speaking to a sibling or a family member, to address the premier, setting an ironic tone upfront. "Lanto" means "that thing"—i.e., Table Mountain—a natural feature that has become iconic both of the nation, and, through its colonial history, of the process of land dispossession. Her request for Table Mountain is framed as a friendly and polite one, as if between members of a family who had loaned something from each other. There is incongruous situational comedy in asking the direct question on Twitter, an open forum without official status, as a member of the public. This tweet can also be fruitfully contrasted to the images of Oprah discussed in example 12, above. Zille's enjoyment of the land as scenery, on a clear winter's evening, where the premier is living her "best life" guilt-free, must be interrupted by the reminder that she is enjoying land that was stolen from Indigenous people. The question of time lines for giving the land back is arguably prompted by Zille's ongoing defence of minimising the harms of historical colonial dispossession, and its long-lasting consequences in the present.

A different type of yt msunery is met with demands for land in example 17. In chapter 2, I discussed the extent to which cultures of automobility are racialised in South Africa. White motorists often consider themselves upholders of decent driving and the rules of the road, while Black minibus taxi drivers are typically constructed as bad and dangerous drivers, the ultimate villains of traffic etiquette. White people have attempted to associate themselves with rules with public order, and Black people with the breakdown of such rules, and this unruliness in turn rationalises discourses of spatial "neo-separatism" (Durrheim and Dixon 2001).

(16)	Tweet: I am An African (@Uncle_JayB) 03/08/2017	White man slows down to shout at the taxi driver for "bad driving" and half the passengers shouted "we want our land" lol we are close

The inverted commas around "bad driving" indicates that the tweeter does not accept the rules or interpretation of the driving appealed to by the white driver, but that a growing number of people have seen through the equivalence drawn between whiteness and adherence to the rules, and that the primordial rule that was broken—the theft of the land—is now being asserted against the claims of white people to be rule-abiding citizens. It is interesting that the tweeter both augments the amusing anecdote with a "lol," and makes the observation that "we are close," explicitly linking the growing sense of disjuncture, and the dislocation of sedimented social practices and discourses, with laughter. It is as if the old order is being ridiculed out of existence.

Another aspect of the white response to calls to give back the land is parodied in a tweet that uses a popular meme of actress Meryl Streep at the Oscars, her hands cupped around her mouth as she cheers. The context of the tweet is shifted to the singing of the South African national anthem, and Meryl Streep is deployed as iconic of white people.

(17) Tweet: Buhle Xulu (@boohley) 26/02/2017 — Everyone: let us live and strive for freedom, in South Africa. . . .
White people: OUR LAAAND!
[image of Meryl Streep cheering at the Oscars]

The tweet contains the last two lines of the South African national anthem, "Nkosi Sikel' iAfrika," which starts with a stanza in isiXhosa and isiZulu, then one in Sesotho, then one in Afrikaans, and a final stanza in English. White South Africans are known for making themselves ridiculous when they sing the anthem, mangling or mumbling the first two stanzas, while belting out the last two in patriotic fervour. This racist selectivity is enabled within the Rainbow Nation's articulation of the idea that everybody should be able to see themselves represented in national symbols, which has worked to protect the discursive space open to historically powerful groups, who drown out the voices of less powerful groups in the national conversation, while others do their best to "live and strive for freedom." What is lampooned here is that the real investment in these symbols of the nation is a possessive one to begin with, allowing for ongoing claims of ownership of the land, and latter-day entitlement to the spoils of historical colonialism and dispossession.

The final joke I want to discuss here feigns shock at the sacrilegious idea that God does not exist, using the reaction meme of the comically expressive Nigerian actor Odunlade Adekola.

(18) Tweet: Firi (@McfiriOD) 22/08/2017 — Bathi if heaven was real white people would've kept the bible to themselves like they do with the land . . . [emoji: shocked face and image of Odunlade Adekola looking shocked]

"Bathi" [isiZulu: "They say"] distances the author of the tweet from full agreement. The tweet echoes a popular anecdote, probably first spoken by Jomo Kenyatta but often attributed to Desmond Tutu:

> When the missionaries arrived, the Africans had the land and the missionaries had the Bible. They taught us how to pray with our eyes closed. When we opened them, they had the land and we had the Bible.

The anecdote and the tweet also allude to Marx's critique of the way that religion functions to make unjust social relations seem alien to the realm of human action, and therefore beyond human agency to rectify (Marx and Engels [1846] 1970). It is not just that there was a shady exchange of religion for land, it is also implied that religion serves a masking role that prevents the redressing of the situation. The joke's mock shock thus softens the blow of the claim that "heaven is not real"—while still offering the social critique of religion as an ideology, a false consciousness that consists in masking relations of domination, making them appear outside of our control to deal with. At the level of yt msunery, they are not only deceiving us about heaven: they are also deceiving us that the land is theirs.

THE CONTOURS OF HEGEMONY

These five themes work together to trace the contours of white land hegemony in South Africa. The notion of "at least you still have the land" anchors the counter-hegemonic discourse around "land" as a nodal point, an aspect of the discursive formation that is leveraged to critique and ultimately reject the Lockean notion of landownership relying on "efficient" use. Specific subject roles and institutions are proposed (and simultaneously critiqued) in the playful imagination of who deserves the land, and social norms that would generally favour kindness to (white) people who are vulnerable in their relationships with Black people are eroded as they are shown to support the perpetuation of an unkind structure. If whiteness is a structure without bodies, these bodies are re-literalized as individuals being confronted with the call for the land to be given back. The reference in the theme of yt msunery to an horizon of intelligibility that separates the Black call for land from a white "commonsense" approach to what they consider to be theirs is perhaps the clearest indicator of the existence of a hegemonic land discourse that is imbricated with the racial order. In this theme, the extent to which white interests have been inscribed in the social vision as the interests of all social groups is undermined through picking at national symbols, education, and religion. That these jokes all subtly undermine themselves, having both rebellious and disciplinary aspects, suggests ongoing discursive struggle. The dislocation of sedimented identities happens under conditions of affective activation, and the pleasure of a wryly subversive joke is heightened by some ironic distance from more straightforward revolutionary readings.

The structure of #TipGate as a joke now comes into clearer view. I will suggest here that it is a joke with three stages. The first stage is the initial provocation itself: Wandile Dlamini wrote "WE WILL GIVE TIP WHEN YOU RETURN THE LAND" where they were asked to write a gratuity amount. The action itself fits Billig's definition of rebellious humour in that it takes pleasure in seeing the social order subverted. The norm that individual white people should never be asked by individual Black people to account for historically produced inequalities, and that the unequal structure of society should not itself structure everyday social interactions, is a powerful pillar of the Rainbow Nation détente. Dlamini's action is bold and interesting in that they did not send their message out into the Twitter ether, but directly to a particular white person, in a particular space. Dlamini plays with the ethical conundrum intrinsic to this particular unequal social order. Responsibility for perpetuating inequality is distributed across many agents, with little concentration of responsibility in any particular person. The bad effects of the order—poverty, death, disease, etc. – are however concentrated in individual people further down the hierarchy. So while the benefits of apartheid are socialised for a whole group and not anybody's fault in particular, the costs of ongoing inequality and poverty are individualised in discourses that rationalise the justness of the liberal democratic order. Dlamini turns this conundrum on its head by arbitrarily insisting that one beneficiary of inequality—Schultz—bear some of the weight of historical debt caused by colonialism and white supremacy. The subversive humour of Dlamini's action relies on the situation where a negligible amount of money withheld from a white person ridicules norms of kindness and Rainbows. The joke seeks for a moment to imagine a social order where this dissipated responsibility for perpetual inequality could indeed be concentrated in everyday social interactions, where every person with any access to some kind of social power was held responsible for working together to "give back the land."

The second stage of the joke turns from Dlamini's wit, which is "created" and intentional, to the realm of the "comic" which is situational, and found (this is Freud's distinction, quoted in Billig, 2005, p. 232). Qwabe's Facebook post describes the events in Obz Café, and his use of "LOL" draws attention to the comic dynamics of the situation. The fact that the waitress and her colleague do not find Dlamini's joke funny—that they meet it with unlaughter, get upset, and indicate that they think it is racist—turns Schultz and her colleague for the first time into ridiculous figures. What is ridiculous about them is their "white tears." This concept is interesting to trace in its global development which was born online from a meme originating from the subversive animated American series Southpark (Shifman, Levy, and Thelwall 2014). In a 2001 episode, Cartman (who is comically mean) is shown licking the tears off an enemy's face, saying "Oh the tears of unfathomable sadness, mmm yummy, yummy!"[6] The idea that the tears of your enemy are delicious was taken up from about 2008, when feminist bloggers started to refer to "male tears" as delicious.[7] Male tears are not just any tears, of course: they are tears cried by men when they are challenged for sexist or otherwise patriarchal behaviour. The meme thus evolved to refer to a specific defence mechanism: claiming to be hurt, attacked, offended, under siege, etc., in defence of a system that itself causes disproportionately greater harm to others. Because the mantle of masculinity benefits all men, their investment in protecting patriarchal arrangements may not always be clear to them, and this meme is intended to disrupt that specific cultural script. What makes male tears so funny is precisely this insistence on valuing the comfort of men in a system that serves them, over the liberation of women. Rather than being tears that deserve sympathy, they are tears that deserve ridicule. Memes related to "white tears" took off with the #BlackLivesMatter movement in the United States from about 2013. In a similar symbolic structure to male tears, what makes white tears ridiculous is that they are shed as a defence mechanism to induce sympathy for an affective attachment to a particular harmful power structure over the liberation of people harmed by that structure. Though the whites who cry, and the people who are not white who rush to console them, may not realise why they are crying, their tears betray their affiliation to the power structure of whiteness. Instead of responding to these tears with sympathy, we are justified in responding to them instead with laughter. Dlamini's wit in the first step is to hold Schultz accountable for colonial land theft; the comic situation in the second step evolves from the white tears, which Qwabe reveals in his Facebook post in ways that work to discipline ridiculous social actors into a new social order in which racial power structures were dismantled instead of tearfully defended. The affective economy (Ahmed 2004b)—i.e., will her tears be traded for sympathy?—operative in this moment of disjuncture is that Schultz meets Dlamini's wit with unlaughter, and Qwabe and Dlamini in turn meet her "tears" with an assertion that they have no currency. Not only will she not get a tip, but she cannot trade her tears for sympathy. Indeed, empathy and ridicule are in competition with each other (Billig, 2005, p. 225): one cannot attach value to her tears and seek to discipline her into a new social order at the same time. Instead, Qwabe attempts to get the online space to laugh with him at the comedy of the ridiculous white tears.

The third step lays hegemony bare, as unlaughter breaks out across the world. The *Spectator* attacks Qwabe for being incapable of registering the pain of the waitress; the *Daily Mail* calls him an international figure of hate; fundraisers for Schultz claim that "Kindness Wins!" His refusal to exchange his empathy for her white tears, the "most valuable currency" (Davis 2016), places Qwabe outside of the realm of the "normal" social human being. He is like Fanon stuck in two dimensions by the white gaze: he cannot laugh until he is able to insult. The hundreds of thousands of rands raised for Schultz, and the attempts to get Qwabe expelled from Oxford, only prove Dlamini and Qwabe's point about the order they are critiquing: that the weight of white supremacy is felt in all racialised bodies, but that responsibility for it seems to exist in no particular white body. Trying to hold one white body to account results in attempts to obliterate the Black person. As already alluded to, Sara Ahmed has noted a similar structure in institutional attempts to implement anti-racism programmes, where "the transformation of the collective into an individual (a collective without individuals) might allow individual actors to refuse responsibility for collective forms of racism" (Ahmed 2004a, n.p.). A collective performance of vulnerability thus has the confounding effect of producing invulnerability.

CONCLUSION: THINKING ABOUT THE PUNCHLINE

In Qwabe's disciplinary ridicule of Ashleigh Schultz, we can read an attempt to corral not only her, but broader online publics into a new social order, an order most white people have yet to wrap their heads around. This analysis has revealed some ways in which post-Marxist theories of discourse may account for the role of humour in social change. Humour and irony often trade on polysemy, ambiguity, and plays of meaning; they are thus tools well suited to the reactivation or re-literalization of seemingly "fixed" meanings and relations of particular discursive identities, which have become sedimented over time. So, for example, the ambiguities around whether or not having the land is fair trade for having a "joke" of an airline like Air Zimbabwe (example 2) or whether demanding land back from an infant is a revolutionary act (example 7) draw attention to the contingency of the identities in a particular articulation, and the fixedness of the nodal points around which they are articulated. They create a sense of uncertainty and flux around concepts like ownership, responsibility, efficient land use, or national identity. In so doing, humour can be seen to be a key tactic in discursive struggle, introducing ambiguity and affective "heat" around joints in the social imaginary that had seemed solid, cold, and immovable before.

That one should find #TipGate "hilarious" while others find it egregious or unnerving is not surprising, as our particular subjectivities are produced by existing hegemonic orders, as articulated by traditional intellectuals, while organic intellectuals such as Dlamini and Qwabe seek to interpellate social agents into new ones. Between these groups, "common sense" overlaps also with a "sense of humour." And it is in allowing ourselves to be hailed into new myths and social imaginaries that we can learn to laugh again. These new myths directly address the space-making and boundary-marking functions of colonial assumptions about where white people and Black people could feel as if they belonged in South Africa. Dlamini and Qwabe prioritised taking their decolonial struggle to everyday spaces. The joke cycle that they sparked seeks to dislocate easy white assumptions about unbounded land control, re-literalizing key terms in hegemonic property relations. As was noted in many instances, there is often a disciplinary dynamic at play that seems to puncture some of the dislocatory ambition of the joke. It remains to be seen whether new ways of thinking about land, race, and ownership in

South Africa will prevail in inscribing themselves onto a future South African social imaginary.

NOTES

1. Post by Tommaso M. Milani, Friday, 29 April 2016 at 7.26pm.

2. All translations from isiZulu are by Nonhlanhla Ntuli.

3. This tweet and reply was shared as a screenshot on Twitter and Facebook. The tweet by @leatitiajvr is archived at Twitter at twitter.com/leatitiajvr/status/764731326259929088. The reply however is not, suggesting either that it was tweeted and then deleted, or that the response itself was a fabrication created by somebody else as a joke.

4. This is a "dance style where you bend your knees for the bum to move towards the ground, and return to your upright position swiftly and rhythmically without losing balance" (Nonhlanhla Ntuli, personal communication).

5. See knowyourmeme.com/memes/math-lady-confused-lady last accessed 14 August 2021.

6. See knowyourmeme.com/memes/your-tears-are-delicious (accessed 21 August 2021).

7. See knowyourmeme.com/memes/male-tears (accessed 21 August 2021).

Conclusion

The Future of White Belongings

This book has shown how the property rights and sense of belonging of South Africa's white minority are interwoven in a discourse regime I have called "white belongings." While elements of this symbolic order were articulated in the justificatory myths that historically sanctified European dispossession and displacement of Indigenous people from their ancestral lands, it has endured through momentous political changes by articulating new elements of reigning hegemonic orders as internal to itself. Non-racialism could thus serve as a guiding principle in white post-apartheid social vision not as a promise of material equality between the former apartheid "population groups" but as a guarantee that equality for whites meant the right to start off in the New South Africa with a clean moral slate, and with no concomitant duty to sacrifice the material benefits of generations of land theft and racial oppression. Much like the colourful arc it was meant to resemble, the Rainbow Nation was held together by a trick of the light, and always out of reach; a floating signifier par excellence. ANC concessions to the dictates of economic orthodoxy in the 1990s further cemented a social compact in which white dominance in agricultural, commercial, and prime residential landholding could remain unchallenged. Vast swaths of countryside and wilderness were then and largely still are available as territorial screens onto which white belonging might be projected without obstruction.

Aileen Moreton-Robinson (2015, 113) has analysed the logics of "white possession" as a socio-discursive regime that "ontologically shaped the formation of white subjectivity." For Moreton-Robinson, "possession" can be achieved with or without legal ownership; it is related to the notion of self-possession, a sense of control over one's own mind and body that historically worked to produce the European imperialist and his desires as the source of rational social ordering. "White belongings" in turn refers to how these subjectivities become interwoven with an imagined countryside or ethnoscape, rootedness within which becomes a fundamental part of white settler identity. The entitlement to possess the land—whether this means accessing, owning, or enjoying it, or consuming space in a commodified form—is culturally elaborated around a sense of its being the coloniser's rightful home. Landscapes reflect their identity back to subjects, whose social roles and institutions are also elaborated in relation to possession of the land. In this concluding chapter, I will distil the analysis of the analytical chapters into a discourse map that shows how discourses, subject roles, and institutions are connected in white belongings. I will then locate this specific version of the regime in the period "after Madiba" and connect it to current events in South Africa and elsewhere, probing its relations to other critical work on whiteness, and exploring what might be said about its future prospects. Before I turn to either of these tasks, however, I will review the argument up to this point.

FROM RHODES'S SOUL TO #IZWELETHU

South African apartheid involved the "enforced coincidence of racial and spatial relations" (Cohen 1988, 8). In this respect it was both heir to European imperial projects which established racial capitalism around the world, and progenitor to a new social order which continued to produce inequality and spatial segregation after 1994. The Rudyard Kipling elegy for Cecil John Rhodes with which I started this book proclaimed that the imperialist's soul would live on in the land long after his death. For centuries, South Africa was imagined as a white man's land; a place of hunts and adventures and pastoral or mercantile toil, a place in which those who were bold enough (and white enough) could make their fortunes, and where the Black dispossession and labour that enabled this prosperity was occluded, discounted, and systematically cheapened. It has been a key premise of the analysis presented here that these imaginings matter profoundly for socio-spatial relations. Distinctions between poacher and hunter, squire and squatter emerged in concert with expanding juridical orders of ownership that favoured white settlers as uniquely entitled to exclude the common rights of (racialised) others. As white supremacist law expanded, Black people were reduced to the state of pariahs and vagabonds, while settlers rationalized and legitimated their entitlement to occupation both legally and culturally, producing their own strong sense of place and of belonging.

This combination of untroubled belonging and secure entitlement to property constituted a form of racial privilege that, as Biko ([1978] 2006, 29) observed, had a homogenising effect on white people across the political spectrum. After the fall of apartheid, whites who had expressed anti-Nationalist views were happy to take credit for the liberation struggle, claiming their position on the right side of history and bristling at the merest critique. This social group was prominently involved in framing the transition to multiparty, multiracial democracy as the triumph of colour-blind economic liberalism over the market distortions of racial engineering. In this respect, white liberals in politics, in the academy and media, in the private sector, and in government found themselves in broad alignment with the neoliberal accommodations of ANC policy. This was no less true of the land question. The national land reform and redistribution programme was conceived and executed on principles of economic liberalism, and it was within these constraints that it failed. The supposed "fable" of colonial dispossession was answered by the fables of historical legal title and of rational market actors maximising productivity in order that land not go to waste. Failed project after failed project established land reform as a Black problem, confirming the historical pattern of "racial liberalism" (Mills 2008).

Protecting entitlements to benefit from the legacies of historical dispossession and oppression turns whiteness itself into an inalienable kind of property under economic liberalism (Harris 1993). At least part of the reason for the endurance of whiteness as property in South Africa through a period of immense political change is the successful inscription of white interests onto the social horizon as if they were the interests of all social groups. This inscription has, crucially, included the cultural production of the land and who rightfully owns it. It is thus to the hegemonic nature of discourses of land, race, space and place that more critical attention ought to be directed. "Hegemony" in the Gramscian sense involves securing the spontaneous consent of the masses to the political direction of social life, on the insight that it is not possible to use brute force to dominate all of the people all of the time. Part of what secured the hegemony of apartheid was the promise that all ethnic groups could have their "own" identity in parallel with the Afrikaner *volkseie*: their own territory, their own language, their own space for cultural expression. It was this gambit for a stable hegemonic order that Biko feared might lead Black people to abandon the broader struggle for South Africa while seeking political rights in "Bantustan" areas (Biko [1978] 2006, 40). After apartheid, the hegemony of non-racialism was secured through a negotiated transition in the 1990s. Its long-term success as a social imaginary would however be determined by the extent to which the new order was able to deliver on the elimination of material inequalities, while sustaining relations of difference between social groups that did not descend into zero-sum antagonism (Norval 1996, 305). While lip service to eradicating inequality is the bread and butter of the contemporary South African political scene, its realisation seems to slip further and further from reach with every passing year. The maintenance of agonistic differences between social groups, on the other hand, has some life left in it. The post-apartheid order has arguably endured not because of any inherent stability, but rather because there has been no clear successor to the discourse of non-racialism that seems capable of hegemonizing social relations.

The task of postfoundational discourse analysis in this context of disequilibrium and discursive struggle is to reconstruct articulatory formations from individual textual fragments, or acts of articulation (see Figure 1.1) which reveal how specific regimes are inscribed on the social horizon as hegemonic, or gradually dissolved in counter-hegemonic praxis. It can thus provide a partial, but indicative picture of the ongoing flow of meaning within social life. Acts of articulation can work to confirm or sediment existing hegemonic chains of signification; they can also reactivate or re-literalize taken-for-granted discursive relations, drawing attention to the ultimately arbitrary and contingent nature of all signification, and thus all identification. In this theorisation of social and political change, material conditions enter into social life structured by a discursive field; and while the "real" is causally impactful in a conjunctural sense, change is never reducible to a purely material cause. Articulation "pierces the entire material density" of the world (Laclau and Mouffe [1985] 2014, 95) and is the fundamental political practice.

To get to the heart of the articulatory practices of contemporary white South Africans in relation to land and space, popular media campaigns and everyday conversations on social media are rich and revealing sites for investigation. The country's middle class, to which nearly all whites belong, is very much online, and participates extensively in social networking sites (Bosch 2021). Analysis of the causes and campaigns to which middle-class whites devote considerable energy and attention reveals important dynamics of their daily sense-making at scales not efficiently accessed through other ethnographic methods. While there is a plethora of crises that spur whites into forms of online or offline participation, nature conservation and environmental protection are treasured, ostensibly apolitical, and historically unifying causes that a broad base of activists across social groups have rallied behind. And there are specific currents in mainstream environmental activism that have had a noticeable predominance of white involvement. Among these are the campaigns to address the ongoing rhino poaching crisis, and to scupper plans to implement hydraulic fracturing for natural gas in South Africa's vast central semidesert region, the Karoo. Two other discursive phenomena that starkly reveal discursive struggle in action are the supposed "crisis" of white people living in poverty, and the formation of a contrasting, progressive affective public of commentators who are critical of white land domination on social media around hashtags such as #IzweLethu and #LandBack. These formations have developed more-or-less contemporaneously in the decade since 2011.

As I showed in chapter 2, the poaching of South Africa's white and black rhinoceroses evokes strong emotions in nature lovers, as well as offering an outlet for "more general feelings of rage and violence" (Büscher and Ramutsindela 2016, 19) pent up in the white minority. While the problem of green militarization and violence is a global one, in South Africa the extrajudicial killing and torture of poachers is legitimated through the construction of specific actor-fictions that interweave discourses of race, gender, and sexuality; what in Frantz Fanon's ([1952] 2008) psychosexual account of the sedimentation of colonial racism in the cultural unconscious are called "imagos." A triad of masculine imagos represented in anti-poaching materials constitute three such actor-fictions. The first is the unassimilable Other onto whom the illicit sexual desires of the white man are projected: the "Black satyr," a penis symbol and the master of rape, whose rightful punishment is castration. The Black satyr appears in anti-poaching texts both as the rapacious HIV-positive Black man ready to murder poachers so that he might turn their testicles into *umuthi*, and as the poacher himself, the cutting off of whose nose or penis is a warning to others of the inviolability of the rhino's phallic horn. The second is the feminized Asian consumer, whose "striking absence down there" (Fung 1996, 183) must be compensated for by ingesting masculinity that is bought in the form of rhino horn purchased in the markets of Vietnam and China. The only figure among the three who can be trusted is the central one: the White Father, who in the cultural unconscious is "charged with maintaining order . . . as a garrison controls a conquered city" (Fanon [1952] 2008, 112). The White Father appears in the anti-poaching texts at the confluence of discourses of patriotic authenticity and authority as a celebrity sportsman wearing khaki, the axis around which the white heteropatriarchal family turns. While the non-racial nation is powerfully reaffirmed in the imaginaries of South Africa's preeminence in sports, wildlife protection, and patterns of middle-class consumption, the prismatic rainbow is produced as best focused through the leadership of a white man. The White Father has neither too much masculinity (like the Black poacher) nor too little (like the Asian consumer) and can therefore be trusted as the steward of the rhino, and by extension of the land itself. The White Father symbolically coordinates the construction of the cordon between animals and people, ensuring security for South Africa's enigmatic wildlife in treasured protected areas. And thus, in an ironic twist, are the contemporary beneficiaries of racial fictions that enabled the historical decimation of African fauna and flora resignified as the ecosystem's last hope for protection from barbarian hordes.

Resistance to gazetted plans to explore the viability of extracting shale gas from the Karoo basin on a mostly white Facebook group, as I detailed in chapter 3, coalesced around three key discursive frontiers which separated "us" from "them." It was adherence to specific ethical principles or values, which in postfoundational discourse analysis are referred to as nodal points, that guided the drawing of these lines. Along the frontier of Rainbow Consumerism, non-racialism is made equivalent with an individualistic and ahistorical market liberalism that reframes attempts at Black Economic Empowerment and Affirmative Action as racist interference in the functioning of an otherwise fair economic system. The rights of poor people to welfare and prosperity are constructed as threatening the entitlements of current property holders, whose activism in response is represented in consumerist terms as "voting" with their wallets. The second frontier hinged on rootedness in the Karoo. The land itself is a nodal point, connection to which determines insider/outsider status. This connection however complicates the scope of white settler identification, and introduces into the campaign an anxiety about indigeneity which is resolved through a one-sided rhetorical alliance with the ghostly presence of Khoisan people. Speaking on behalf of the Khoisan gives the anti-frackers scope both to align their own subjectivity with the trope of noble indigenes who are close to the land, and erase the settler acts of dispossession and genocide that created modern South Africa. A third frontier was articulated around rationality. High levels of agency and logical thinking were consistently attributed to scientists, politicians, and businesspeople who were white. Africa and Blackness on the other hand were broadly associated with superstition, corruption, and subhuman degeneration. The anti-frackers thus construct themselves as the protectors of rainbows, roots, and reason. These nodes are also visible in how the Karoo is constructed as a "heartland." Affective bonds to the land are understood as strengthened by scientific knowledge of it, where connecting to the Karoo in geological time conveniently avoids engagement with more recent history. Their place on the land is further anchored through the production of an ethnoscape, a poetic space wound up in the myths that serve as "vital 'evidence' for territorial 'title-deeds'" (Smith 1999, 69). This space is constructed as an agricultural idyll that is both pristine and ordained by God. White connection to the land is naturalised, and mythically sanctified, absolving its current occupiers of any connection to the violence of its original conquest.

The actor fictions of the anti-poaching materials and the ethnoscape of the anti-frackers are mythical articulations of entitlement to the land; the right to dream it, to control access to it, to manage its use, and to determine its future. This entitlement is however vulnerable to the demands of other social groups who have their own aspirations and claims on sharing equally in the riches of South Africa. Discourses of entitlement and belonging thus need to be supplemented by discourses of injury and victimization, which represent the white minority as already on the back foot, and already routed from the security of their former statutorily enforced supremacy. The existence of an ostensible white poverty "crisis" in South Africa works alongside other media panics such as white flight and farm murders (see Deumert 2019) to make race-based redistribution in South Africa seem cruel and unjust. As I showed in chapter 4, the documentation on film of white suffering is a powerful spectacle that offers visual proof of the brokenness of white power in South Africa. While poverty is articulated as unbearable and unfitting for whites, it is produced as completely normal for Black people. In the mythical world that is spun in white poverty discourse, the struggle for Black liberation was definitively won, resulting in orgies of consumption for the victors, who now treat a defeated race with derision and spite. The existence of a non-racial social net in the post-apartheid order is at times concealed, and at times dismissed as unfit for whites. International and local journalists from respected channels collaborate with ethnocentric NGOs to dramatically inflate the numbers of white people living in poverty and informal housing. The "crisis" is confected from a small group of poor whites whose story is told and retold. Potential conflicts between the confabulations of the filmmakers and the official statistical picture are explained away in advance as a matter of bravely revealing what a vengeful Black government is trying to conceal, and as working against the dictates of political correctness. Importantly, post-1994 urban and rural spaces are represented as disordered or unrecognisable, or even as "killing grounds," for white people. Whites are represented as if they are out of place, or what I have called dis-located, on a new landscape ruined by a Black government. A consistent theme of these clips is the importance of NGOs and charities which focus on whites only as vital lifelines out of this crisis. The work of organisations such as AfriForum and Solidarity Helping Hand is presented as the ideal way to unlock the internal, natural self-determination and resilience of the Afrikaner, who can once again show the societal value of developing *volkseie* institutions, in their "own" areas. While it is not clear whether this discourse provides any lasting, structural improvement in the living standards of people living in actual poverty, it certainly provides a powerful legitimation for the ongoing development of "enclave nationalism" (van der Westhuizen 2016) to the benefit, mostly, of middle-class Afrikaners. In this respect, it is yet another marketing coup by AfriForum, an organisation whose coffers swell when Afrikaners make the news as a uniquely persecuted minority (Holmes 2020).

The shape of the discourse regime of white belongings is thrown into stark relief by satirical social commentators who seek to turn it into an object of ridicule. The joke cycle analysed in chapter 5 which developed on social media in the wake of the #TipGate saga is evidence of how the organic intellectuals of the Fallist movements and Black Twitter seek to undermine the persisting fundamental principles of colonial material-symbolic racial orders. In the "white tears" of a slighted waitress, the discourse of injury and victimization is pitilessly lampooned as nothing more than defensive camouflage. The very act of laughing at white pain is enjoyed for its liberatory, transgressional, and cathartic effects. In a parallel mode to the role of the Karoo in chapter 3 as a guiding value for the anti-fracking movement, the land is here reclaimed as a nodal point for parodic resistance. Having the land compensates for other misfortunes or failures; it is the imagined base for future linguistic and cultural authenticity. Social intimacy between Black and white South Africans is transformed into a site of struggle where individual, vulnerable whites are singled out from a structure without bodies, and instructed directly to give back the land. Lockean notions of the connection between landownership and productivity are teased apart, and their iron necessities comprehensively rejected. The jokes resignify the cultural power of white people to maintain the discourse regime of white belongings, from being connected to rationality and expressions of citizenship into forms of white trickery, or *msunery*. It is recognition of the commonsense nature of white belongings that sustains the humour of the joke cycle, and in subjecting conformity to the hegemony of this discourse to ridicule, counter-hegemonic work is done. At the same time, however, for every rebellious reading of these jokes there was also a disciplinary dimension, which finds pleasure in the relief from the stifling nature of the existing order, while also subtly reproducing it as inevitable. The emergence of truly revolutionary humour from that which is merely rebellious is thus foreshadowed in this joke cycle, if incompletely realised.

"WHITE BELONGINGS" AS A DISCOURSE REGIME

In order to tease out the logics of each of the data sets, I developed a conceptual apparatus that borrows key ideas from, respectively, Fanon ([1952] 2008), Smith (1999), Norval (1996) and Billig (2005). This unpicking revealed patterned acts of articulation working to sediment, repair, or reactivate the relations between elements of a discourse regime. The model of how these discursive processes work that I presented in chapter 1 (Figure 1.1) operationalizes (post)-Marxist theorizations of institutions as sedimented discourses, and discourses as material practices producing subjects. To map white belongings as a discourse regime, it is thus important to make clear (i) how institutions and subject roles are motivated and rationalized in specific discursive formations; (ii) how these formations in turn are validated and materialized in institutions and subject roles; and (iii) how subject roles work to corroborate institutions, and institutions in turn to subjectivate social agents. I argue that while nature conservation and environmentalist discourses are implicated mostly in *sedimentation*, articulating white poverty is an attempt at discursive *repair*, while humour about giving back the land is made up of acts that seek to *reactivate*—or re-literalize—discursive relations that have been naturalized as common sense. Each of these processes opens a useful window onto the structure of white belongings as a discourse regime.

Sedimentation: Ecological Indigeneity

Threats of poaching or fracking serve as important motivations for the sanctity of private property and the necessity of securitization. In the "locked gates and loaded shotguns" of the Karoo landowners, and the armed rangers and shoot-to-kill trigger-happiness of the anti-poaching campaign, private property is produced as the right to exclude strangers from land on pain of death. As was revealed in the analysis of the SANParks Honorary Rangers Facebook page, even the extrajudicial execution of an unarmed man is cause for celebration. These institutionally sanctioned entitlements to defend land and wildlife are articulated around the value of "nature." The beautiful and supposedly pristine (agricultural) Karoo is produced as a heartland, as soul country, while the enigmatic, majestic rhino is embraced as a member of the Rainbow Nation. Erasures of historical enclosures, exclusions, and genocides mystify racialised landholding patterns, producing innocent white ecological subjects whose production of the land as an ethnoscape naturalises their history as indigenous to the land. White dominance in conservation and environmentalism is further rationalized by a supposed innate readiness to lead these efforts, and an intrinsically rational approach to the history and future of the land. The role of the white conservationist is to confirm and protect the borders of securitized ecological property, while the existence of these spaces necessitates the presence of these paragon stewards of the land in the first place. In environmental stewardship, white liberal subjectivity after apartheid has thus found its own justification for continued land domination. While many continuities with historical colonial and Bantustan discourses are in evidence, this articulation is at home in the post-1994 order. It does not appeal to explicitly racist values, but to the protection of nature, the inviolability of property, the truth of science, and to whites having a deep-rooted claim to belong on the land. To the extent that it corroborates liberal institutions, and reproduces the structural arrangements of the post-apartheid order, the discourse of ecological indigeneity thus works to sediment the form of liberal non-racialism that became hegemonic after 1994.

Repair: Enclave Entrepreneurialism

The hegemony of non-racialism in the post-apartheid order required a balancing act between the maintenance of agonistic differences (such as political or religious views, cultural and linguistic practices, or other dimensions of difference that in some cases trace historical racially delineated "population groups") and "affirmative" policy making to tackle material inequality that required naming the terms of historical racial exclusion and oppression. In essence, this demanded a confrontation with whiteness as a structure of power and privilege under the banner of non-racialism. The dislocation that the end of the master-narrative of *baasskap* (Steyn 2001b) occasioned for whites opened up a gap between the category "white" and what it was supposed to signify; defining whiteness thus became a terrain of struggle where social agents attempted to fix the meaning of discursive elements into moments of a new discourse. Two decades after the end of apartheid, a cluster of news and documentary film representations of poor white Afrikaners shared online reveals an attempt to replicate the key historical role played by white poverty in legitimating the organising principle of apartheid, the *volkseie* (Norval 1996), but with some key changes. Repairs to the myth of the *volkseie* take place in the context of a new hegemonic order, where the state cannot be counted on to maintain 87 percent of the landmass of South Africa as a white paradise. The emergence of Afrikaner enclave nationalism was enabled by patterns of middle-class consumption in a liberal market order that allowed a domestic and suburban horizon for Afrikaner political subjectivity to emerge (van der Westhuizen 2016). In the resurgence of white poverty discourse, these enclaves are further rationalized and their institutional scope is motivated and expanded. Ethnocentric rights organisations such as AfriForum and Solidarity are able to consolidate projects that exclusively benefit whites as appropriate in the context of government Affirmative Action and Black Economic Empowerment. It is arguably in the liberal triumph of the 1990s that the connections were loosened between affirmative policy making and specific historical injustices (as opposed to abstract calculations) allowing for the development of relations of equivalence and alongsidedness (Ahmed 2004a) between groups to be asserted by ideological entrepreneurs who framed white people as the new victims of a "reverse racist" dispensation. The subject role of the Afrikaner rights campaigner, and the institutions of whites-only charity and lawfare work, thus corroborate and confirm each other. These institutions and roles supplement and consolidate the neoliberal backbone of Afrikaner enclaves, which, far from bringing about structural change that might benefit people living in poverty, are established centres of middle-class consumption and privilege. The actor fiction of the Afrikaner as being naturally entrepreneurial and independent furthermore makes a positive argument for a symbiotic relationship between the enclaves and the rest of the Rainbow Nation, both as the lifting of a welfare burden and a contribution to the national economy. In the elaboration of this myth into a powerful social imaginary, Afrikaner rights organisations have been extensively abetted by local and international news media, whose largely uncritical reporting on a supposed reversal in racial fortunes is eagerly circulated as proof of the global need to protect white identity from degeneration and eventual extinction.

Reactivation: Rational Market Liberals

In the introduction, I observed that commonsense discourses of the land in South Africa seemed to reflect an ongoing struggle to make white dispossession *unthinkable* within a stable social order. This struggle is especially visible in the lampooning of white landownership in progressive online spaces. Here, organic intellectuals seek to exploit the inherent instability of signification in all social orders by drawing attention to the contingent, historical, and unnecessary nature of specific discursive relations. An important dynamic revealed in the situation comedy of #TipGate and the ensuing joke cycle was how white comfort and prosperity is produced as a structure without bodies. This practice of abstraction works to protect individual whites from uncomfortable accountability, and to frame any exploitation of their vulnerability to reproach or restitution as cruel and unjustified. That an unequal share of the land and its riches is the fault of no single white person, and should cause them no discomfort, is reactivated as a site of discursive struggle in humour that rebels against its obviousness, its naturalness, its taken-for-grantedness in the liberal order. Reactivation involves re-literalization, where the metaphorical and rhetorical underpinnings of race and of inequality are retrieved from abstractions, and once again made real in the bodies of individual people. The shape of white possession as a mode of rationality is thus revealed in the photographic negatives contained in the jokes. Private landownership and its associated institutions are rationalized by subjects such as farmers and businesspeople, while radical decolonial redistribution would cause famine and economic collapse. This commonsense script is reproduced by the media, schools, churches, and politicians. Anxiety in the jokes about how redistribution would be equitably managed, and whether the social and economic effects would ultimately be worth such a process, reveals the extent to which competing myths of a social order after the liberalism of the Rainbow Nation have not yet succeeded in articulating them as imaginaries that can secure the affective affinity of a large enough social bloc. Struggle between competing visions of how to expand #IzweLethu into a social imaginary capable of hegemonizing social relations is set to characterize the near future of South African politics, and the odds are uncertain.

WHITE BELONGINGS AFTER MADIBA

The argument of *White Belongings* deployed the concept of hegemony to explain the endurance of whiteness as a power structure in South Africa through momentous political changes. It sought to provide an account of how the racial order is replicated that extends beyond the racist acts or intentions of various factions of an elite minority at various times in history, to instead probe the conditions of possibility of whiteness as "ownership of the earth forever and ever, Amen!" (Du Bois 1920). In focusing on the stability and endurance of hegemonic discursive regimes, there is always a tension between what changes, and what stays the same. And a lot clearly has changed. In this section, I will sketch some suggestions for a periodization of whiteness in South Africa, at the same time as connecting the argument of *White Belongings* back to key works by critical scholars.

At the outset of the book, I presented Steve Biko's ([1978] 2006, 19) observation that security and material comfort have a homogenizing effect on white South Africans as a social group. The alignment of their racial and class interests does however paper over deep internal divisions and diversity. While tens of thousands of Black people died during the 1899–1902 South African War, it was largely seen as a "white man's war" where the territorial aggression of the British and the humiliation and deaths of Boer women and children in concentration camps drew a hostile frontier between Afrikaans- and English-speaking whites. As I discussed in chapter 1, many Afrikaners in the 1930s sympathised far more with German Nazism than the liberal pretentions of the British Empire, and South Africa's entry into the Second World War in 1939 was a key precipitating factor in the eventual triumph of the Nationalists in 1948 which heralded the onset of statutory apartheid. The supposed liberalism of English-speaking whites during the apartheid period was however never thoroughly anti-racist, and except for the very few who joined the ranks of Afrikaner allies of the liberation struggle, they ended up throwing in their lot with apartheid (see Southall 2022). English speakers fabricated for themselves a closer-to-civilized European whiteness in contradistinction to the earthiness of the Afrikaner (van der Westhuizen 2018). The apartheid order was relatively short-lived; it entered into a series of crises caused by inflation and resistance movements in the 1970s, which deepened in the 1980s through successive waves of labour action, the effective organisation of economic sanctions by the ANC in exile, and the organisation of local progressive movements into the United Democratic Front (UDF). While the apartheid government implemented desperate repairs to the hegemonic order in constitutional changes and States of Emergency, the sense that the "end of whiteness" was imminent grew. Related moral panics between the mid-1980s and mid-1990s centring on real and imagined acts of domestic degeneration in the form of Afrikaner patriarchs murdering their families, and white children becoming Satanists, were stoked by the media. As Nicky Falkof (2015) has comprehensively demonstrated, these panics were the "morbid symptoms" of a Gramscian "interregnum" between hegemonic orders, occasioning a crisis where the "old is dying and the new cannot be born" (Gramsci 1971, 276). In the decade before the first democratic elections, the precariousness of minority rule in South Africa as an accident of history contingent on repression and violence became clearer, and novel myths of social dis/ordering multiplied in everyday discourse.

A new order was however born in 1994; one which was able to secure the consent of the masses to the political direction of social life. Critical work on whiteness in the period immediately after the transition focused on how whites constructed narratives of authenticity, innocence, and belonging that made sense of their place in a New South Africa. Floating discursive elements were available for articulation as moments in novel narratives which implied acceptable social roles (Steyn 2001b, 152). Across the political spectrum, white South Africans accommodated themselves to this new discourse regime, learning "New South Africa Speak" in order to produce themselves as decent members of a modern society (Steyn and Foster 2008), enabled by revisionist histories of ignorance and innocence which sought to cleanse the white conscience of implication in historical atrocities (Steyn 2012). Whites who had to various extents supported progressive movements were as resistant as dyed-in-the-wool racists to suggestions that they should be the targets of redistribution. In their understanding of history it was their brave defence of liberal values which had won out in the end, and enabled the transition to democracy (Conway 2017). In the first term of the ANC, significant resistance to the "Africanisation" of higher education was already being shown by liberal academics (Statman and Ansell 2000). It is a noteworthy finding in Melissa Steyn's early work that, among the senses of loss experienced by whites that she documents—loss of the sense of a familiar home country, the loss of a sense of autonomy and control, loss of relevance, legitimacy, and face (Steyn 2001b, 157)—the loss of material privilege was not felt, though perhaps it was feared. The fieldwork for that study was conducted in 1996 and, as I documented in the introduction, white poverty in fact decreased during the first fifteen years of democracy, while white households continued to be far wealthier on average than Black ones, disproportionately reaping the benefits of newly accessible global markets for their skills, goods and services.

Something fundamental has undoubtedly shifted in the twenty years since then. Arguably, the awakening Steyn (2001b, 156) describes, of whites who "for several centuries [believed] they were feudal lords [and] woke up to find they had actually been squatters all along" was never a decisive one. White daydreaming, organised around an insistence on not being "woke," has come to dominate the official opposition's political discourse (see, e.g., Zille 2021). The shift in white identity projects, from broad accommodation with a hegemonic order to a resurgent and implacable racial hubris (van der Westhuizen 2018, 211) does not have a decisive inflection point, though there a number of key dates to consider. One of these is 2006, the year that both AfriForum and the far-right ethnonationalist "prepper" group *Suidlanders*[1] were launched. Pop star Bok van Blerk also released the hit single *De La Rey* in 2006. The song, which hails an anti-imperialist Boer general and hero of the South African War, marked an important development in Afrikaans popular culture, where young people could sing along to a pop anthem confidently reasserting an injured identity that had been tainted by "feelings of guilt and shame" (van der Waal and Robins 2011, 778). It is similarly not uncommon for English-speaking whites to irascibly reject the idea of any personal implication in racial inequality. A key period to consider in this respect is what is popularly known as the "nine wasted years" between 2009 and 2018 during which President Jacob Zuma hollowed out the capacity of the state, awarding billions of Rands worth of sinecures, gifts, and contracts to friends, family, and creditors. The blatant corruption of this period was grist for the mill of stereotypical narratives of African postcolonial decline. Zuma's contempt for liberal institutions made him a useful foil for an increasingly strident opposition from the right, while his nepotistic demagoguery was also relentlessly targeted by populists on the left. The DA enjoyed its best ever election performance in 2014, and the EFF catapulted themselves into Parliament as the third-largest party; the ANC's majority was at this time reduced by fifteen seats. Five years later, the ANC lost a further nineteen national Members of Parliament, while the EFF gained nineteen and the DA lost five. The politics of this period has hinged almost entirely on how a "radical" economic transformation ought to be achieved, and on the centrality to this project of land reform, restitution and redistribution. On this point, the EFF has consistently gained ground on making promises to expropriate and redistribute land, while the DA has gained to the extent that it has managed to convince voters that it will protect their property interests and social positions (Southall 2022).

If identifying a specific inflection point from this tumultuous period is ultimately an arbitrary exercise, then the 5th of December 2013, the day Nelson Mandela died, is as good a date as any. Mandela had in many respects come to embody the Rainbow Nation, and an avuncular willingness to let bygones be bygones had been projected onto the superhuman figure of a forgiving "Madiba," especially by whites. While for many the South African dream had already come to a horrific end with the massacre of thirty-four striking miners at Marikana in August 2012, the interests of white property holders and the small multiracial elite were more closely aligned with the success of the mining company Lonmin than they were with the impoverished workers who died. In the wake of this and other traumatic events, the passing of Madiba was a last hurrah for the New South Africa as a global symbol of hope. The Obamas were there, as was Angela Merkel; a trio of Windsors came, as did Kofi Annan, Bono, and Oprah Winfrey. After the period of mourning was over, there were few good South African stories to tell. When Sisonke Msimang (2015) declared the end of the Rainbow Nation myth in an op-ed for the *New York Times*, she cited the hardened attitudes of young white South Africans who claim that "talking about racism is itself racist." This is a line that has been followed obsessively by a white political leadership that has embroiled itself in culture wars they have waged, while claiming to be "liberals" in the sense used in other parts of the English-speaking world, on terms that mirror exactly those waged by Republicans in the United States and Conservatives in the United Kingdom. It is as if they have decided that for whiteness to persist after Madiba, the best defence is offence.

And yet, as Steven Friedman (2021) has recently argued, it is as true to point to the immense upheavals and flux of South African society as proof that everything has changed, as it is to point to its continuities, and conclude that nothing has really changed. After a period of relatively stable equilibrium between 1994 and 2013, we are now living through a renewed period of the multiplication of social differences and identities similar to that identified by Falkof (2015). This time, the morbid symptoms have arisen from the end of the hegemony of non-racialism—at least in its Rainbowist iteration. There are strong parallels between the moral panics towards the end of apartheid and the imported (but locally elaborated) furore about "wokeness" in youth culture and the academy, as well as the "crisis" of white poverty analysed in chapter 4. And yet the discourses deployed by white South Africans are the same old stories we have been telling ourselves since colonialism: that this land belongs to us, and that we belong in this land. The contribution of this book, arising from its focus on the years between 2013 and 2018, has been to show how everyday white discourse works to sediment and repair the discourse regime of white belongings, even in the context of attempts to challenge its hegemony. This historical shift is of course not in a strong sense dependent on the agency or political will of white South Africans, but on the failure of the post-apartheid order to deliver on its promise of a better life for all.

CONCLUSION

There is still plenty of room to echo the hope expressed by van der Westhuizen (2018, 211) that white identity might draw on "uncertainty, humility and self-reflection to remake itself." And yet "remaking" whiteness *qua* whiteness as an identity will necessarily never go far enough if it is understood as voluntary self-critique and disconnected from its material conditions of privilege and prosperity. What I have attempted to do in this book is to move discourse analysis of South African whiteness beyond a preoccupation with how white identities have shifted in the post-apartheid order, and into an analysis of how these identities are materialised in the institutions and subject roles that protect white belongings. In environmental and conservation movements, I have shown how white property rights are shrouded in the sanctifying mantle of green activism, extending its roots deep into the landscape as the rightful possession and heartland of ecological indigenes. I have also shown how in the discourse of white poverty the ideological entrepreneurs of AfriForum and other organisations have rationalized novel institutional backbones for enclave nationalism using narratives of a much older vintage. And finally, I have shown how in the rebellious humour of progressive online spaces, the rationality of the edifice of the liberal post-apartheid order is lampooned, while at the same time being subtly and insidiously reproduced as inescapable.

South Africa today is in the midst of an especially severe economic crisis compounded by the COVID-19 pandemic, which has left nearly two-thirds of people between the age of fifteen and twenty-four unemployed (Mlatsheni and Graham 2021). These young people are ambitious, talented, energetic, and increasingly impatient for change. The restructuring that is required for all South Africans to share in the riches of the country are so extensive that it is uncertain whether they could be implemented without a new revolution to correct the mistakes of the previous one. White South Africans who seek to participate fully in this revolution and in this future must surrender our strong property entitlements and affective attachments to cherished institutions and ethnoscapes. We will need to abandon our imagined centrality as experts and voices of reason. And we will need to recognise, that while this process is not possible without pain, it is the only way to justice.

NOTE

1. Afrikaans: Southlanders

Bibliography

Abedinifard, Mostafa. 2016. "Ridicule, Gender Hegemony, and the Disciplinary Function of Mainstream Gender Humour." *Social Semiotics* 26 (3): 234–49. https://doi.org/10.1080/10350330.2015.1134817.

Abidin, Crystal, Dan Brockington, Michael K. Goodman, Mary Mostafanezhad, and Lisa Ann Richey. 2020. "The Tropes of Celebrity Environmentalism." *Annual Review of Environment and Resources* 45 (1): 387–410. https://doi.org/10.1146/annurev-environ-012320-081703.

Adhikari, Mohamed. 2011. *The Anatomy of a South African Genocide: The Extermination of the Cape San Peoples*. Athens: Ohio University Press.

AgriSA. 2017. "Land Audit: A Transactions Approach." Pretoria: AgriSA. https://www.agrisa.co.za/wp-content/uploads/2017/11/AgriSA_Land-Audit_November-2017.pdf.

Ahmed, Sara. 2004a. "Declarations of Whiteness: The Non-Performativity of Anti-Racism." *Borderlands E-Journal* 3 (2). http://www.borderlands.net.au/vol3no2_2004/ahmed_declarations.htm.

———. 2004b. "Affective Economies." *Social Text* 22 (2 (79)): 117–39. https://doi.org/10.1215/01642472-22-2_79-117.

———. 2007. "A Phenomenology of Whiteness." *Feminist Theory* 8 (2): 149–68. https://doi.org/10.1177/1464700107078139.

Akinola, Adeoye O. 2020. "Land Reform in South Africa: Interrogating the Securitisation of Land Expropriation Without Compensation." *Politikon* 47 (2): 215–32. https://doi.org/10.1080/02589346.2020.1715178.

Alim, H. Samy, Quentin E. Williams, Adam Haupt, and Emile Jansen. 2021. "'Kom Khoi San, Kry Trug Jou Land': Disrupting White Settler Colonial Logics of Language, Race, and Land with Afrikaaps." *Journal of Linguistic Anthropology* 31 (2): 194–217. https://doi.org/10.1111/jola.12308.

Althusser, Louis. 1967. "Contradiction and Overdetermination." *New Left Review* 41: 15–35.

———. 1971. *Lenin and Philosophy, and Other Essays*. London: New Left Books.

Appadurai, Arjun. 1990. "Disjuncture and Difference in the Global Cultural Economy." *Theory, Culture & Society* 7 (2–3): 295–310. https://doi.org/10.1177/026327690007002017.

Atkinson, Doreen. 2016. "Is South Africa's Great Karoo Region Becoming a Tourism Destination?" *Journal of Arid Environments* 127 (April): 199–210. https://doi.org/10.1016/j.jaridenv.2015.12.006.

Baldwin, Andrew. 2012. "Whiteness and Futurity: Towards a Research Agenda." *Progress in Human Geography* 36 (2): 172–87. https://doi.org/10.1177/0309132511414603.

Ballard, Richard. 2004. "Assimilation, Emigration, Semigration, and Integration: 'white' Peoples' Strategies for Finding a Comfort Zone in Post-Apartheid South Africa." In *Under Construction: "Race" and Identity in South Africa Today*, edited by Melissa E. Steyn and Natasha Distiller, 51–66. Johannesburg: Heinemann.

———. 2005. "When in Rome: Claiming the Right to Define Neighbourhood Character in South Africa's Suburbs." *Transformation: Critical Perspectives on Southern Africa* 57 (1): 64–87.

———. 2010. "'Slaughter in the Suburbs': Livestock Slaughter and Race in Post-Apartheid Cities." *Ethnic & Racial Studies* 33 (6): 1069–87. https://doi.org/10.1080/01419870903477320.

Ballard, Richard, and Gareth A. Jones. 2011. "Natural Neighbors: Indigenous Landscapes and Eco-Estates in Durban, South Africa." *Annals of the Association of American Geographers* 101 (1): 131–48. https://doi.org/10.1080/00045608.2010.520224.

Barrett, Michèle. 1991. "History, Discourse, 'Truth' and Power: Foucault's Critique of Ideology." In *The Politics of Truth: From Marx to Foucault*, 123–56. Cambridge: Polity Press.

Beavon, Keith S. O. 2000. "Northern Johannesburg: Part of the 'rainbow' or Neo-Apartheid City in the Making?" *Mots Pluriels*, no. 13. http://motspluriels.arts.uwa.edu.au/MP1300kb.html.

Bhandar, Brenna. 2018. *Colonial Lives of Property: Law, Land, and Racial Regimes of Ownership*. Durham: Duke University Press.

Biko, Steve. (1978) 2006. *Steve Biko "I Write What I like": A Selection of His Writings*. Johannesburg: Picador Africa.

Billig, Michael. 1997. "The Dialogic Unconscious: Psychoanalysis, Discursive Psychology and the Nature of Repression." *British Journal of Social Psychology* 36 (2): 139–59. https://doi.org/10.1111/j.2044-8309.1997.tb01124.x.

———. 2005. *Laughter and Ridicule: Towards a Social Critique of Humour*. Theory, Culture & Society. London; Thousand Oaks: Sage.

Bishop, Kristina Monroe. 2012. "Anglo American Media Representations, Traditional Medicine, and HIV/AIDS in South Africa: From Muti Killings to Garlic Cures." *GeoJournal* 77 (4): 571–81. https://doi.org/10.1007/s10708-010-9352-z.

Bloch, L-R. 2000. "Mobile Discourse: Political Bumper Stickers as a Communication Event in Israel." *Journal of Communication* 50 (2): 48–76. https://doi.org/10.1111/j.1460-2466.2000.tb02841.x.

Blommaert, Jan, Mary Bock, and Kay McCormick. 2006. "Narrative Inequality in the TRC Hearings: On the Hearability of Hidden Transcripts." *Journal of Language and Politics* 5 (1): 37–70. https://doi.org/10.1075/jlp.5.1.04blo.

Boersema, Jacob R. 2013. "Afrikaner, Nevertheless." PhD thesis, University of Amsterdam. http://dare.uva.nl/document/2/124517.

Bolsmann, Chris, and Andrew Parker. 2007. "Soccer, South Africa and Celebrity Status: Mark Fish, Popular Culture and the Post-Apartheid State." *Soccer & Society* 8 (1): 109–24. https://doi.org/10.1080/14660970600989442.

Bond, Patrick. 1998. *Elite Transition: Globalisation & the Rise of Economic Fundamentalism in South Africa*. London: Pluto.

Bonilla-Silva, Eduardo. 2006. *Racism without Racists: Color-Blind Racism and the Persistence of Racial Inequality in the United States*. Lanham: Rowman & Littlefield.

Bosch, Tanja E. 2021. *Social Media and Everyday Life in South Africa*. London: Routledge. https://doi.org/10.4324/9780429316524.

Bosman, D. B., I. W. van der Merwe, and L.W. Hiemstra. 1984. *Tweetalige Woordeboek - Bilingual Dictionary*. Edited by P. A. Joubert and J. J. Spies. 8th ed. Cape Town: Tafelberg.

Bosworth, Kai. 2021. "'They're Treating Us like Indians!': Political Ecologies of Property and Race in North American Pipeline Populism." *Antipode* 53 (3): 665–85. https://doi.org/10.1111/anti.12426.

Brockington, Dan, and Katherine Scholfield. 2010. "The Conservationist Mode of Production and Conservation NGOs in Sub-Saharan Africa." *Antipode* 42 (3): 551–75. https://doi.org/10.1111/j.1467-8330.2010.00763.x.

Brodie, Nechama. 2013. "Are SA Whites Really Being Killed 'like Flies'? Why Steve Hofmeyr Is Wrong." Africa Check. 24 June 2013. http://africacheck.org/fact-checks/reports/are-sa-whites-really-being-killed-flies-why-steve-hofmeyr-wrong.

Brown, Justin, and Ana Deumert. 2017. "'My Tribe Is the Hessequa. I'm Khoisan. I'm African': Language, Desire and Performance among Cape Town's Khoisan Language Activists." *Multilingua* 36 (5): 571–94. https://doi.org/10.1515/multi-2017-3046.

Brown, Keffrelyn D. 2021. "The Limits of Justice-Informed Research and Teaching in the Presence of Antiblackness and Black Suffering: Surplus of Transformation or (Un)Just Traumatic Returns?" *Qualitative Inquiry*, July, 107780042110269. https://doi.org/10.1177/10778004211026903.

Brown, Wendy. 2017. *Undoing the Demos: Neoliberalism's Stealth Revolution*. New York: Zone Books.

Bryman, Alan. 2016. *Social Research Methods*. 5th ed. Oxford: Oxford University Press.

Burnett, Scott. 2022. "'Without White People, the Animals Will Go': Covid-19 and the Struggle for the Future of South African Conservation." *Environment and Planning E: Nature and Space*. Online First. https://doi.org/10.1177/25148486211069884.

Büscher, Bram. 2016. "'Rhino Poaching Is Out of Control!' Violence, Race and the Politics of Hysteria in Online Conservation." *Environment and Planning A* 48 (5): 979–98. https://doi.org/10.1177/0308518X16630988.

———. 2020. *The Truth about Nature: Environmentalism in the Era of Post-Truth Politics and Platform Capitalism*. Oakland: University of California Press.

Büscher, Bram, and Robert Fletcher. 2015. "Accumulation by Conservation." *New Political Economy* 20 (2): 273–98. https://doi.org/10.1080/13563467.2014.923824.

Büscher, Bram, and Maano Ramutsindela. 2016. "Green Violence: Rhino Poaching and the War to Save Southern Africa's Peace Parks." *African Affairs* 115 (458): 1–22. https://doi.org/10.1093/afraf/adv058.

Buthelezi, Siphelele. 2016. "It's Not Right, Says Qwabe's Dad." *Independent Online*, 8 May 2016. https://www.iol.co.za/news/south-africa/kwazulu-natal/its-not-right-says-qwabes-dad-2018864.

Carruthers, Jane. 1995. *The Kruger National Park: A Social and Political History*. Pietermaritzburg: University of Natal Press.

Case, Charles E. 1992. "Bumper Stickers and Car Signs Ideology and Identity." *The Journal of Popular Culture* 26 (3): 107–19. https://doi.org/10.1111/j.0022-3840.1992.2603_107.x.

CEE. 2021. "21st Commission for Employment Equity (CEE) Annual Report (2020–2021)." Annual Report RP180/2021. Commission for Employment Equity. Pretoria: Department of Labour.

Chiaro, Delia. 2017. *The Language of Jokes in the Digital Age: Viral Humour*. London and New York, NY: Routledge.

Chigumadzi, Panashe. 2016. "Hair and Land Issues Woven Together in South Africa." *African Independent*, 2 September 2016, Online edition. https://www.africanindy.com/news/hair-and-land-issues-woven-together-in-south-africa-5547924.

Chiluwa, Innocent. 2008. "Religious Vehicle Stickers in Nigeria: A Discourse of Identity, Faith and Social Vision." *Discourse & Communication* 2 (4): 371–87. https://doi.org/10.1177/1750481308091909.

Cock, Jacklyn, and David Fig. 2001. "The Impact of Globalisation on Environmental Politics in South Africa, 1990–2002." *African Sociological Review* 5 (2): 15–35.

Coetzee, J. M. 1980. "Triangular Structures of Desire in Advertising." *Critical Arts* 1 (2): 34–41. https://doi.org/10.1080/02560048008559034.

———. 1988. *White Writing: On the Culture of Letters in South Africa*. New Haven: Yale University Press.

Cohen, Robin. 1988. *Endgame in South Africa?: The Changing Structures & Ideology of Apartheid*. Trenton: Africa World Press.

Collins, Anthony. 2013. "Bullies, Sissies and Crybabies: Dangerous Common Sense in Educating Boys for Violence." *Agenda* 27 (1): 71–83. https://doi.org/10.1080/10130950.2013.796074.

Collins, Patricia Hill. 1986. "Learning from the Outsider Within: The Sociological Significance of Black Feminist Thought." *Social Problems* 33 (6): S14–32. https://doi.org/10.2307/800672.

———. 2000. "What's Going On? Black Feminist Thought and the Politics of Postmodernism." In *Working the Ruins: Feminist Poststructural Theory and Methods in Education*, edited by Elizabeth St. Pierre and Wanda Pillow, 41–73. New York and London: Routledge.

Connell, Raewyn. 2007. *Southern Theory: The Global Dynamics of Knowledge in Social Science*. Cambridge: Polity.

Conway, Daniel. 2017. "Shades of White Complicity: The End Conscription Campaign and the Politics of White Liberal Ignorance in South Africa." In *Exploring Complicity: Concept, Cases and Critique*, edited by Afxentis Afxentiou, Robin Dunford, and Michael Neu, 119–42. London: Rowman & Littlefield.

Conway, Daniel, and Pauline Leonard. 2014. *Migration, Space and Transnational Identities: The British in South Africa*. London: Palgrave Macmillan.

Cronje, Frans. 2013. "W(h)Ither the Whites?" *News24*, 19 May 2013. https://www.news24.com/Archives/City-Press/Whither-the-whites-20150429.

Culler, Jonathan D. 1982. *On Deconstruction: Theory and Criticism after Structuralism*. Ithaca: Cornell University Press.

Davies, Christie. 2017. "Reply to Abedinifard." *HUMOR* 30 (2): 239–46. https://doi.org/10.1515/humor-2017-0006.

Davis, Rebecca. 2016. "White Tears: The Most Valuable Currency." *The M&G Online*, 6 May 2016. https://mg.co.za/article/2016-05-04-white-tears-the-most-valuable-currency/.

Death, Carl. 2010. *Governing Sustainable Development: Partnerships, Protests and Power at the World Summit*. New York: Routledge.

Debord, Guy. (1967) 2014. *The Society of the Spectacle*. Translated by Ken Knabb. Berkeley: Bureau of Public Secrets.

Deumert, Ana. 2019. "Sensational Signs, Authority and the Public Sphere: Settler Colonial Rhetoric in Times of Change." *Journal of Sociolinguistics* 23 (5): 467–84. https://doi.org/10.1111/josl.12377.

Dixon, J. A., D. H. Foster, K. Durrheim, and L. Wilbraham. 1994. "Discourse and the Politics of Space in South Africa: The 'Squatter Crisis.'" *Discourse & Society* 5 (3): 277–96. https://doi.org/10.1177/0957926594005003002.

Dlakavu, Simamkele, Sandile Ndelu, and Mbali Matandela. 2017. "Writing and Rioting: Black Womxn in the Time of Fallism." *Agenda* 31 (3–4): 105–9. https://doi.org/10.1080/10130950.2017.1392163.

Dlamini, Jacob S. T. 2020. *Safari Nation: A Social History of the Kruger National Park*. Athens: Ohio University Press.

Dodds, Klaus, and Philip Kirby. 2013. "It's Not a Laughing Matter: Critical Geopolitics, Humour and Unlaughter." *Geopolitics* 18 (1): 45–59. https://doi.org/10.1080/14650045.2012.668723.

Doyle, Kylie, and Kieran Tranter. 2015. "Automobility and 'My Family' Stickers." *Continuum* 29 (1): 70–83. https://doi.org/10.1080/10304312.2014.968524.

Du Bois, W. E. B. 1920. *Darkwater: Voices from within the Veil*. New York: Harcourt, Brace and Company.

Du Toit, Julienne. 2013. "A Shell Game Falters: Fracking Update November 2013.' *Karoo Space* (blog). 2 November 2013. http://karoospace.co.za/shell-game/.

Duffy, Rosaleen. 2014. "Waging a War to Save Biodiversity: The Rise of Militarized Conservation." *International Affairs* 90 (4): 819–34. https://doi.org/10.1111/1468-2346.12142.

Durrheim, Kevin, and John Dixon. 2001. "The Role of Place and Metaphor in Racial Exclusion: South Africa's Beaches as Sites of Shifting Racialization." *Ethnic and Racial Studies* 24 (3): 433–50. https://doi.org/10.1080/01419870020036738.

Dyer, Richard. 1997. *White*. London; New York: Routledge.

Edwards, Megan, and Tommaso M. Milani. 2014. "The Everyday Life of Sexual Politics: A Feminist Critical Discourse Analysis of Herbalist Pamphlets in Johannesburg." *Southern African Linguistics and Applied Language Studies* 32 (4): 461–81. https://doi.org/10.2989/16073614.2014.999991.

eNCA.com. 2016. "ANC Condemns 'Foolish' Rhodes Must Fall Bully." *ENCA.Com*, 2 May 2016, Online edition. http://www.enca.com/south-africa/social-media-weighs-in-after-rhodesmustfall-leader-no-land-no-tip.

Eng, David L. 2001. *Racial Castration: Managing Masculinity in Asian America*. Durham: Duke University Press.

Epstein, Helen, and Rachel Jewkes. 2009. "The Myth of the Virgin Rape Myth." *The Lancet* 374 (9699): 1419.

Fairclough, Norman. 1992. *Discourse and Social Change*. Cambridge: Polity Press.

Falkof, Nicky. 2015. *Satanism and Family Murder in Late Apartheid South Africa: Imagining the End of Whiteness*. London: Palgrave Macmillan.

———. 2016. "Out the Back: Race and Reinvention in Johannesburg's Garden Cottages." *International Journal of Cultural Studies* 19 (6): 627–42. https://doi.org/10.1177/1367877915581856.

Fanon, Frantz. 1968. *The Wretched of the Earth*. New York: Grove Press.

———. (1952) 2008. *Black Skin, White Masks*. London: Pluto Books.

Fig, David. 2013. "Hydraulic Fracturing in South Africa: Correcting the Democratic Deficits." In *New South African Review 3: The Second Phase—Tragedy or Farce?*, edited by John Daniel, Prishani Naidoo, Devan Pillay, and Roger Southall, 173–94. Johannesburg: Wits University Press.

Fletcher, Robert. 2013. "How I Learned to Stop Worrying and Love the Market: Virtualism, Disavowal, and Public Secrecy in Neoliberal Environmental Conservation." *Environment and Planning D: Society and Space* 31 (5): 796–812. https://doi.org/10.1068/d11712.

Fletcher, Robert, Jan Breitling, and Valerie Puleo. 2014. "Barbarian Hordes: The Overpopulation Scapegoat in International Development Discourse." *Third World Quarterly* 35 (7): 1195–1215. https://doi.org/10.1080/01436597.2014.926110.

Fogel, Benjamin. 2012. "Renouncing the Rhino." *Africa Is a Country* (blog). 12 December 2012. http://africasacountry.com/2012/12/renouncing-the-rhino/.

Foster, Jeremy A. 2008. *Washed with Sun: Landscape and the Making of White South Africa*. Pittsburgh: University of Pittsburgh Press.

Fraser, Nancy. 1995. "From Redistribution to Recognition? Dilemmas of Justice in a 'Post-Socialist' Age." *New Left Review*, no. I/212 (August): 68–93.

Friedman, Steven. 2021. *Prisoners of the Past: South African Democracy and the Legacy of Minority Rule*. Johannesburg: Wits University Press.

Fuchs, Christian. 2017. *Social Media: A Critical Introduction*. 2nd edition. London: SAGE.

Fung, Richard. 1996. "Looking for My Penis: The Eroticized Asian in Gay Video Porn." In *Asian American Sexualities: Dimensions of the Gay and Lesbian Experience*, edited by Russell Leong, 181–98. London: Routledge.

Geertsema, Johan. 2006. "White Natives? Dan Roodt, Afrikaner Identity and the Politics of the Sublime." *The Journal of Commonwealth Literature* 41 (3): 103–20. https://doi.org/10.1177/0021989406068737.

Georgalou, Mariza. 2016. "'I Make the Rules on My Wall': Privacy and Identity Management Practices on Facebook." *Discourse & Communication* 10 (1): 40–64.

Gilmore, Ruth Wilson. 1999. "Globalisation and US Prison Growth: From Military Keynesianism to Post-Keynesian Militarism." *Race & Class* 40 (2–3): 171–88. https://doi.org/10.1177/030639689904000212.

———. 2002. "Fatal Couplings of Power and Difference: Notes on Racism and Geography." *Professional Geographer* 54 (1): 15.

———. 2007. *Golden Gulag: Prisons, Surplus, Crisis, and Opposition in Globalizing California*. Berkeley and Los Angeles: University of California Press.

Goldberg, David Theo. 1993. "Modernity, Race, and Morality." *Cultural Critique*, no. 24: 193–227. https://doi.org/10.2307/1354133.

———. 2006. "Racial Europeanization." *Ethnic and Racial Studies* 29 (2): 331–64. https://doi.org/10.1080/01419870500465611.

Goldhaber, Michael. 2006. "The Value of Openness in an Attention Economy." *First Monday*, June. https://doi.org/10.5210/fm.v11i6.1334.

Gordon, Lewis R. 2015. *What Fanon Said: A Philosophical Introduction to His Life and Thought*. Johannesburg: Wits University Press.

Gorlier, Claudio. 2002. "Post-Marxism in an African Context: The Usability of Antonio Gramsci." *Research in African Literatures* 33 (3): 97–103.

Gosine, Andil. 2005. "Dying Planet, Deadly People: 'Race'-Sex Anxieties and Alternative Globalizations." *Social Justice* 32 (4): 69–86.

Goyanes, Cristina. 2017. "This All-Female Anti-Poaching Unit in South Africa Is Saving Rhinos and Wildlife." *National Geographic Onlne*, 12 October 2017. https://www.nationalgeographic.com/adventure/article/black-mambas-anti-poaching-wildlife-rhino-team.

Gqola, Pumla D. 2001. "Defining People: Analysing Power, Language and Representation in Metaphors of the New South Africa." *TRANSFORMATION* 47: 94–106.

Graham, James. 2007. "Exploding Johannesburg: Driving in a Worldly City." *Transtext(e)s Transcultures 跨文本跨文化*, no. 3 (September): 67–83. https://doi.org/10.4000/transtexts.140.

Gramsci, Antonio. 1971. *Selections from the Prison Notebooks of Antonio Gramsci*. Edited and translated by Quintin Hoare and Geoffrey Nowell-Smith. London: Lawrence and Wishart.

Gressier, Catie. 2015. *At Home in the Okavango: White Batswana Narratives of Emplacement and Belonging*. New York: Berghahn Books.

Hall, Stuart. 2001. "The Spectacle of the Other." In *Discourse Theory and Practice: A Reader*, edited by Margaret Wetherell, Stephanie Taylor, and Simeon J. Yates, 324–44. London: SAGE.

———. 2021. *Selected Writings on Race and Difference*. Edited by Paul Gilroy and Ruth Wilson Gilmore. Stuart Hall: Selected Writings. Durham: Duke University Press.

Harris, Cheryl I. 1993. "Whiteness as Property." *Harvard Law Review* 106 (8): 1707–91.

Hart, Gillian P. 2002. *Disabling Globalization: Places of Power in Post-Apartheid South Africa*. Berkeley: University of California Press.

———. 2014. *Rethinking the South African Crisis: Nationalism, Populism, Hegemony*. Athens: University of Georgia Press.

Hartigan, John. 2005. *Odd Tribes: Toward a Cultural Analysis of White People*. Durham: Duke University Press.

Helmy, Mohamed M., and Sabine Frerichs. 2013. "Stripping the Boss: The Powerful Role of Humor in the Egyptian Revolution 2011." *Integrative Psychological and Behavioral Science* 47 (4): 450–81. https://doi.org/10.1007/s12124-013-9239-x.

Hickel, Jason. 2021. "The Anti-Colonial Politics of Degrowth." *Political Geography*, 102404. https://doi.org/10.1016/j.polgeo.2021.102404.

Hill, Jane H. 2008. *The Everyday Language of White Racism*. Malden: Wiley-Blackwell.

Hiramoto, Mie, and Phoebe Pua. 2019. "Racializing Heterosexuality: Non-Normativity and East Asian Characters in James Bond Films." *Language in Society* 48 (4): 541–63. https://doi.org/10.1017/S0047404519000381.

Hoang, Nguyen Tan. 2004. "The Resurrection of Brandon Lee: The Making of a Gay Asian American Porn Star." In *Porn Studies*, edited by Linda Williams, 223–70. Durham: Duke University Press.

Holdsworth, Candice. 2016. "Rhodes Must Fall Activists Have Become the Very Thing They Hate." *The Spectator Blog* (blog). 30 April 2016. https://blogs.spectator.co.uk/2016/04/rhodes-must-fall-activists-have-become-the-very-thing-they-hate/.

Holmes, Carolyn E. 2020. "Victimhood Gone Viral: Portrayals of Extra-Lethal Violence and the Solidarity of Victims in the Case of South African Farm Violence Activists." *Politics, Groups, and Identities*, November, 1–21. https://doi.org/10.1080/21565503.2020.1838303.

Holtmann, Barbara. 2008. "Why Law Enforcement Is Not Enough: Lessons from the Central Karoo on Breaking the Cycle of Crime and Violence." *South African Crime Quarterly*, no. 23 (March): 13–20. https://doi.org/10.17159/2413-3108/2008/v0i23a959.

Hook, Derek. 2011. "Retrieving Biko: A Black Consciousness Critique of Whiteness." *African Identities* 9 (1): 19–32. https://doi.org/10.1080/14725843.2011.530442.

Hoops, Björn. 2019. "Expropriation without Compensation: A Yawning Gap in the Justification of Expropriation?: Research." *South African Law Journal* 136 (2): 261–302.

Howarth, David R. 2013. *Poststructuralism and After: Structure, Subjectivity and Power*. Basingstoke: Palgrave Macmillan.

Hübinette, Tobias, and Catrin Lundström. 2014. "Three Phases of Hegemonic Whiteness: Understanding Racial Temporalities in Sweden." *Social Identities* 20 (6): 423–37. https://doi.org/10.1080/13504630.2015.1004827.

Hughes, David McDermott. 2005. "Third Nature: Making Space and Time in the Great Limpopo Conservation Area." *Cultural Anthropology* 20 (2): 157–84.

———. 2010. *Whiteness in Zimbabwe: Race, Landscape, and the Problem of Belonging*. New York: Palgrave Macmillan.

Humphreys, Jasper, and M. L. R. Smith. 2014. "The 'rhinofication' of South African Security." *International Affairs* 90 (4): 795–818. https://doi.org/10.1111/1468-2346.12141.

Hurt, R. Douglas. 2002. *American Agriculture: A Brief History*. West Lafayette: Purdue University Press.

Ibrahim, Yasmin. 2017. "Facebook and the Napalm Girl: Reframing the Iconic as Pornographic." *Social Media + Society* 3 (4): 1–10. https://doi.org/10.1177/2056305117743140.

Ingle, Mark. 2010. "Making the Most of 'Nothing': Astro-Tourism, the Sublime, and the Karoo as a 'Space Destination.'" *Transformation: Critical Perspectives on Southern Africa* 74 (1): 87–111. https://doi.org/10.1353/trn.2010.0013.

Jankielsohn, R., and A. Duvenhage. 2017. "Radical Land Reform in South Africa—a Comparative Perspective?" *Journal for Contemporary History* 42 (2): 1–23. https://doi.org/10.18820/24150509/JCH42.v2.1.

Johnen, Marius, Marc Jungblut, and Marc Ziegele. 2018. "The Digital Outcry: What Incites Participation Behavior in an Online Firestorm?" *New Media & Society* 20 (9): 3140–60. https://doi.org/10.1177/1461444817741883.

Jørgensen, Marianne, and Louise J. Phillips. 2002. *Discourse Analysis as Theory and Method*. London: SAGE.

Kalogeropoulos, Antonis, Federica Cherubini, and Nic Newman. 2016. "The Future of Online News Video." Digital News Project. Oxford, U.K.: Reuters Institute for the Study of Journalism. https://ssrn.com/abstract=2882465.

Keegan, Timothy J. 1997. *Colonial South Africa and the Origins of the Racial Order*. London: Leicester University Press.

Kepe, Thembela. 2009. "Shaped by Race: Why 'Race' Still Matters in the Challenges Facing Biodiversity Conservation in Africa." *Local Environment* 14 (9): 871–78. https://doi.org/10.1080/13549830903164185.

Kepe, Thembela, and Danielle Tessaro. 2014. "Trading-off: Rural Food Security and Land Rights in South Africa." *Land Use Policy* 36 (Supplement C): 267–74. https://doi.org/10.1016/j.landusepol.2013.08.013.

Khan, Farieda. 2000. "Environmentalism in South Africa: A Sociopolitical Perspective." *Macalester International* 9 (1): 11.

KhosraviNik, Majid, and Johann W. Unger. 2016. "Critical Discourse Studies and Social Media: Power, Resistance, and Critique in Changing Media Ecologies." In *Methods of Critical Discourse Studies*, edited by Ruth Wodak and Michael Meyer, 3rd ed., 205–33. Los Angeles: SAGE.

Kipfer, Stefan. 2007. "Fanon and Space: Colonization, Urbanization, and Liberation from the Colonial to the Global City." *Environment and Planning D: Society and Space* 25 (4): 701–26. https://doi.org/10.1068/dkipfer.

Kitis, E. Dimitris, Tommaso M Milani, and Erez Levon. 2018. "'Black Diamonds,' 'Clever Blacks' and Other Metaphors: Constructing the Black Middle Class in Contemporary South African Print Media." *Discourse & Communication* 12 (2): 149–70. https://doi.org/10.1177/1750481317745750.

Kress, Gunther, and Theo Van Leeuwen. 2006. *Reading Images: The Grammar of Visual Design*. Abingdon: Routledge.

Kruger, Christi. 2016. "(Dis)Empowered Whiteness: Un-Whitely Spaces and the Production of the Good White Home." *Anthropology Southern Africa* 39 (1): 46–57. https://doi.org/10.1080/23323256.2016.1157026.

Laband, John. 2020. *The Land Wars: The Dispossession of the Khoisan and AmaXhosa in the Cape Colony*. Cape Town: Penguin Random House.

Laclau, Ernesto. 1990. "New reflections on the revolution of our time." In *New reflections on the revolution of our time*, 3–85. London: Verso.

———. 2014. *The Rhetorical Foundations of Society*. London: Verso.

Laclau, Ernesto, and Chantal Mouffe. (1985) 2014. *Hegemony and Socialist Strategy: Towards a Radical Democratic Politics*. 2nd edition. London: Verso.

Lenggenhager, Luregn. 2015. "Nature, War and Development: South Africa's Caprivi Strip, 1960–1980." *Journal of Southern African Studies* 41 (3): 467–83. https://doi.org/10.1080/03057070.2015.1025337.

Lentin, Alana. 2020. *Why Race Still Matters*. Cambridge: Polity.

Lewis, Amanda E. 2004. "'What Group?' Studying Whites and Whiteness in the Era of 'Color-Blindness.'" *Sociological Theory* 22 (4): 623–46.

Locke, John. (1690) 1960. *Two Treatises of Government*. Edited by Peter Laslett. Cambridge: Cambridge University Press.

Lockyer, Sharon, and Michael Pickering. 2008. "You Must Be Joking: The Sociological Critique of Humour and Comic Media." *Sociology Compass* 2 (3): 808–20. https://doi.org/10.1111/j.1751-9020.2008.00108.x.

Lorde, Audre. (1984) 2007. *Sister Outsider: Essays and Speeches*. Berkeley: Crossing Press.

Lunstrum, Elizabeth. 2014. "Green Militarization: Anti-Poaching Efforts and the Spatial Contours of Kruger National Park." *Annals of the Association of American Geographers* 104 (4): 816–32. https://doi.org/10.1080/00045608.2014.912545.

———. 2017. "Feed Them to the Lions: Conservation Violence Goes Online." *Geoforum* 79 (February): 134–43. https://doi.org/10.1016/j.geoforum.2016.04.009.

Machin, David, and Andrea Mayr. 2012. *How to Do Critical Discourse Analysis: A Multimodal Introduction*. London: SAGE.

MacKenzie, Alison, and Ibrar Bhatt. 2020. "Opposing the Power of Lies, Bullshit and Fake News: The Value of Truth." *Postdigital Science and Education* 2 (1): 217–32. https://doi.org/10.1007/s42438-019-00087-2.

Mager, Anne. 2005. "'One Beer, One Goal, One Nation, One Soul': South African Breweries, Heritage, Masculinity and Nationalism 1960–1999." *Past & Present* 188 (1): 163–94. https://doi.org/10.1093/pastj/gti021.

Makiwane, M., and E. Udjo. 2006. "Is the Child Support Grant Associated with an Increase in Teenage Fertility in South Africa?: Evidence from National Surveys and Administrative Data." Pretoria: HSRC Press.

Marttila, Tomas. 2016. *Post-Foundational Discourse Analysis: From Political Difference to Empirical Research*. New York: Palgrave Macmillan.

Marx, Karl, and Friedrich Engels. (1846) 1970. *The German Ideology*. Edited by C. J. Arthur. London: Lawrence & Wishart.

Mayr, Andrea. 2008. *Language and Power: An Introduction to Institutional Discourse*. London: Continuum International Publishing Group.

Mazur, Allan. 2016. "How Did the Fracking Controversy Emerge in the Period 2010–2012?" *Public Understanding of Science* 25 (2): 207–22. https://doi.org/10.1177/0963662514545311.

Mbeki, Thabo. 1998. "Statement of Deputy President Thabo Mbeki at the Opening of the Debate in the National Assembly, on 'Reconciliation and National Building.'" University of South Africa Online Archive. 19 May 1998. http://www.unisa.ac.za/contents/colleges/docs/1998/tm1998/sp980529.pdf.

Mbembe, Achille. 2017. *Critique of Black Reason*. Translated by Laurent Dubois. Durham: Duke University Press.

McCay-Peet, Lori, and Anabel Quan-Haase. 2017. "What Is Social Media and What Questions Can Social Media Research Help Us Answer?" In *The SAGE Handbook of Social Media Research Methods*, edited by Luke Sloan and Anabel Quan-Haase, 13–26. London: SAGE.

McDonald, David A. 2002. *Environmental Justice in South Africa*. Cape Town: University of Cape Town Press.

McEwen, Haley, and Melissa Steyn. 2013. "Hegemonic Epistemologies in the Context of Transformation: Race, Space, and Power in One Post-Apartheid South African Town." *Critical Race and Whiteness Studies* 9 (1). http://www.acrawsa.org.au/files/ejournalfiles/194McEwenSteyn20131.pdf.

McKaiser, Eusebius. 2012. *A Bantu in My Bathroom!: Debating Race, Sexuality and Other Uncomfortable South African Topics*. Johannesburg: Pan Macmillan.

Mersal, Iman. 2011. "Revolutionary Humor." *Globalizations* 8 (5): 669–74. https://doi.org/10.1080/14747731.2011.629030.

Milani, Tommaso M. 2014. "White Skin—Black Ghosts: Language and the Racialization of Desire in Post-Apartheid South Africa." Unpublished conference paper presented at the meeting of the *Association Internationale de Linguistique Appliquée* (International Association of Applied Linguistics) AILA in Brisbane, Australia, August 2014.

Milani, Tommaso M., and Mooniq Shaikjee. 2013. "A New South African Man? Beer, Masculinity, and Social Change." In *Gender and Language in Sub-Saharan Africa: Tradition, Struggle and Change*, edited by Lilian Lem Atanga, Sibonile Edith Ellece, Lia Litosseliti, and Jane Sunderland, 131–48. Amsterdam: John Benjamins Publishing.

Mill, John Stuart. (1859) 1997. *Mill: The Spirit of the Age, On Liberty, The Subjection of Women*. Edited by Alan Ryan. New York: W.W. Norton.

Mills, Charles W. 2005. "Kant's 'Untermenschen.'" In *Race and Racism in Modern Philosophy*, edited by Andrew Valls, 169–93. Ithaca: Cornell University Press.

———. 2007. "White Ignorance." In *Race and Epistemologies of Ignorance*, edited by Shannon Sullivan and Nancy Tuana, 11–38. Albany: State University of New York Press.

———. 2008. "Racial Liberalism." *PMLA* 123 (5): 1380–97.

Mlatsheni, Cecil, and Lauren Graham. 2021. "Young People and Women Bear the Brunt of South Africa's Worrying Jobless Rate." The Conversation. 9 September 2021. http://theconversation.com/young-people-and-women-bear-the-brunt-of-south-africas-worrying-jobless-rate-167003.

Mohamed, Ashfak. 2017. "No Thanks, KP, the Proteas Don't Need You." *Independent Online*, 20 July 2017, sec. Sports. https://www.iol.co.za/sport/cricket/proteas/no-thanks-kp-the-proteas-dont-need-you-10381757.

Moreton-Robinson, Aileen. 2006. "Towards a New Research Agenda?: Foucault, Whiteness and Indigenous Sovereignty." *Journal of Sociology* 42 (4): 383–95. https://doi.org/10.1177/1440783306069995.

———. 2015. *The White Possessive: Property, Power, and Indigenous Sovereignty*. Minneapolis: University of Minnesota Press.

Mouffe, Chantal, ed. 1979. "Hegemony and Ideology in Gramsci." In *Gramsci and Marxist Theory*, 168–204. London: Routledge & Kegan Paul.

———. 2018. *For a Left Populism*. London & New York: Verso.

Mpofu-Walsh, Sizwe. 2017. *Democracy and Delusion: 10 Myths in South African Politics*. First. Cape Town: Tafelberg.

———. 2021. *The New Apartheid*. Cape Town: Tafelberg.

Msimang, Sisonke. 2015. "The End of the Rainbow Nation Myth." *New York Times*, 12 April 2015. http://www.nytimes.com/2015/04/13/opinion/the-end-of-the-rainbow-nation-myth.html.

———. 2017. *Always Another Country: A Memoir of Exile and Home*. Cape Town and Johannesburg: Jonathan Ball Publishers.

National Planning Commission. 2012. "National Development Plan 2030: Our Future - Make It Work." Pretoria: National Planning Commission. https://www.gov.za/documents/national-development-plan-2030-our-future-make-it-work.

Ndelu, Sandy, Simamkele Dlakavu, and Barbara Boswell. 2017. "Womxn's and Nonbinary Activists' Contribution to the RhodesMustFall and FeesMustFall Student Movements: 2015 and 2016." *Agenda* 31 (3–4): 1–4. https://doi.org/10.1080/10130950.2017.1394693.

Ndlovu-Gatsheni, Sabelo J., ed. 2018. "Rhodes Must Fall." In *Epistemic Freedom in Africa: Deprovincialization and Decolonization*, 221–42. Rethinking Development. London: Routledge.

Neumann, Roderick P. 2004. 'Moral and Discursive Geographies in the War for Biodiversity in Africa.' *Political Geography*, 23 (7): 813–37. https://doi.org/10.1016/j.polgeo.2004.05.011.

Newhagen, John E., and Michael Ancell. 1995. "The Expression of Emotion and Social Status in the Language of Bumper Stickers." *Journal of Language and Social Psychology* 14 (3): 312–23. https://doi.org/10.1177/0261927X95143004.

Newitz, Annalee, and Matt Wray. 1997. *White Trash: Race and Class in America*. New York: Routledge.

Ngcukaitobi, Tembeka. 2018. *The Land Is Ours: Black Lawyers and the Birth of Constitutionalism in South Africa*. Cape Town: Penguin Random House.

Ngobese, Sihle. 2016. "I Found @Obz_Cafe & Spoke to Waitress Who Was Bullied by #RhodesMustFall Doucherbags. Let's Show What Kindness Is! Pic.Twitter.Com/KLNG1cE6MN." Tweet. *@SihleDLK*. 11 April 2016. https://twitter.com/SihleDLK/status/726110365612908545.

Norval, Aletta J. 1990. "Letter to Ernesto." In *New Reflections on The Revolution of Our Time*, edited by Ernesto Laclau, 135–58. Phronesis. London: Verso.

———. 1996. *Deconstructing Apartheid Discourse*. New York: Verso.

Nteta, Chris. 1987. "Revolutionary Self-Consciousness as an Objective Force within the Process of Liberation: Biko and Gramsci." *Radical America* 21 (5): 55–61.

Papacharissi, Zizi. 2015. *Affective Publics: Sentiment, Technology, and Politics*. Oxford: Oxford University Press.

Plaatje, Solomon Tsekisho. (1916) 1982. *Native Life in South Africa*. Johannesburg: Ravan Press.

Posel, Deborah. 2010. "Races to Consume: Revisiting South Africa's History of Race, Consumption and the Struggle for Freedom." *Ethnic & Racial Studies* 33 (2): 157–75. https://doi.org/10.1080/01419870903428505.

Qwabe, Ntokozo. 2016a. "Ntokozo Qwabe:D Feeling Elated at OBZ Café." Status Update. Facebook.Com.

———. 2016b. "The Final Word on #TipGate and the Bullied White Waitress by Ntokozo Qwabe." *The Daily Vox*, 28 May 2016. http://www.thedailyvox.co.za/final-word-tipgate-ntokozo-qwabe/.

Rademeyer, Julian. 2013. "Do 400,000 Whites Live in Squatter Camps in South Africa? No." Fact Checking. Africa Check. 22 May 2013. https://africacheck.org/reports/do-400-000-whites-live-in-squatter-camps-in-south-africa-the-answer-is-no/.

Ramaphosa, Cyril. 2018. "State of the Nation Address 2018." Parliamentary Monitoring Group. https://pmg.org.za/briefing/25807/.

Ranuga, Thomas K. 1986. "Frantz Fanon and Black Consciousness in Azania (South Africa)." *Phylon* 47 (3): 182. https://doi.org/10.2307/274985.

Rhodes, Cecil John. 1877. "Confession of Faith." https://pages.uoregon.edu/kimball/Rhodes-Confession.htm.

Rieder, Bernhard. 2013. "Studying Facebook via Data Extraction: The Netvizz Application." In *Proceedings of the 5th Annual ACM Web Science Conference*, 346–55. ACM. http://dl.acm.org/citation.cfm?id=2464475.

Ritchie, Gemma. 2018. "Why Google Is Showing You White South African Squatters." *Mail & Guardian*, 14 June 2018, Online edition. https://mg.co.za/article/2018-06-14-why-google-is-showing-you-white-south-african-squatters/.

Robinson, Cedric J. (1983) 2021. *Black Marxism: The Making of the Black Radical Tradition*. London: Penguin Books.

Robinson, Julian, and Sam Greenhill. 2016. "Black Oxford Student Will Not Speak to 'White Media' over Cafe Tip Row." *Mail Online*, 4 May 2016, Online and Newspaper edition. http://www.dailymail.co.uk/news/article-3573220/Racist-black-Oxford-student-international-hate-figure-refusing-tip-Caucasian-waitress-refuses-defend-actions-white-media.html.

Rothberg, Michael. 2020. *The Implicated Subject: Beyond Victims and Perpetrators*. Stanford: Stanford University Press.

Said, Edward W. (1994) 2014. *Culture and Imperialism*. London: Vintage.

Salter, Phia, and Glenn Adams. 2013. "Toward a Critical Race Psychology." *Social and Personality Psychology Compass* 7 (11): 781–93. https://doi.org/10.1111/spc3.12068.

SANParks. 2020. "South African National Parks Annual Report 2019/20." Pretoria: South African National Parks. https://www.sanparks.org/assets/docs/general/annual-report-2020.pdf.

SANParks Honorary Rangers. 2016. 'Two Poaching Suspects Fatally Wounded Following Tourist Sighting.' Status Update. Facebook. 14 January 2016. https://www.facebook.com/SANParksHonoraryRangers/posts/1211608032188070

SAPeople. 2016. "Kindness Wins After Waitress Bullied by #RhodesMustFall Activist in South Africa." Good News. *SAPeople—Your Worldwide South African Community* (blog). 1 May 2016. https://www.sapeople.com/2016/05/01/kindness-wins-waitress-bullied-rhodesmustfall-activist-south-africa/.

Satgar, Vishwas. 2016. "Bringing Class Back In: Against Outsourcing During #FeesMustFall at Wits." In *Fees Must Fall: Student Revolt, Decolonisation and Governance in South Africa*, edited by Susan Booysen. Johannesburg: Wits University Press. https://doi.org/10.18772/22016109858.

Sayre, Gordon M. 1997. *Les Sauvages Américains: Representations of Native Americans in French and English Colonial Literature*. Chapel Hill: University of North Carolina Press.

Sekyi-Otu, Ato. 1996. *Fanon's Dialectic of Experience*. Cambridge: Harvard University Press.

Shandu, Jackie. 2016. "Qwabe's Tipping Point: What WE and YOU Really Mean | Daily Maverick." News. *The Daily Maverick* (blog). 3 May 2016. https://www.dailymaverick.co.za/opinionista/2016-05-03-qwabes-tipping-point-what-we-and-you-really-mean/.

Shaw, Mark, and Julian Rademeyer. 2016. "A Flawed War: Rethinking 'Green Militarisation' in the Kruger National Park." *Politikon*, June, 1–20. https://doi.org/10.1080/02589346.2016.1201379.

Shifman, Limor, Hadar Levy, and Mike Thelwall. 2014. "Internet Jokes: The Secret Agents of Globalization?" *Journal of Computer-Mediated Communication* 19 (4): 727–43. https://doi.org/10.1111/jcc4.12082.

Sibanda, Octavia. 2012. "'Social Pain and Social Death': Poor White Stigma in Post-Apartheid South Africa, a Case of West Bank in East London." *Anthropology Southern Africa* 35 (3–4): 81–90. https://doi.org/10.1080/23323256.2012.11500027.

———. 2014. "White Poverty in Post-Apartheid South Africa: The Case of West Bank in East London." PhD Thesis, University of Fort Hare. http://libdspace.ufh.ac.za/handle/20.500.11837/521.

Simbayi, L.C., K. Zuma, N. Zungu, S. Moyo, E Marinda, S. Jooste, M. Mabaso, et al. 2019. "South African National HIV Prevalence, Incidence, Behaviour and Communication Survey, 2017." V. SABSSM. Cape Town: Human Sciences Research Council. http://www.hsrc.ac.za/uploads/pageContent/10779/SABSSM%20V.pdf.

Simpson, John. 2013. "Reactions to BBC South Africa Report." *BBC*, 29 May 2013. http://www.bbc.com/news/magazine-22708507.

Smith, Anthony D. 1999. *Myths and Memories of the Nation*. Oxford: Oxford University Press.

Southall, Roger. 2022. *Whites and Democracy in South Africa*. London: Boydell & Brewer.

Statman, James M., and Amy E. Ansell. 2000. "Rise and Fall of the Makgoba a Case Study of Symbolic." *Politikon* 27 (2): 277–95. https://doi.org/10.1080/713692337.

Stats SA. 2012. "Statistical Release (Revised): Census 2011." P0301.4. Pretoria: Statistics South Africa. http://www.statssa.gov.za/publications/P03014/P030142011.pdf.

———. 2019. "Inequality Trends in South Africa: A Multidimensional Diagnostic of Inequality." 03–10–19. Pretoria: Statistics South Africa. http://www.statssa.gov.za/publications/Report-03-10-19/Report-03-10-192017.pdf.

———. 2020a. "Gross Domestic Product 2020 Q1." Statistical Release P0441. Pretoria: Statistics South Africa. http://www.statssa.gov.za/publications/P0441/GDP%202020%20Q1%20(Media%20presentation).pdf.

———. 2020b. "Mid-Year Population Estimates 2020." Statistical Release P0302. Mid-Year Population Estimates. Pretoria: Statistics South Africa. http://www.statssa.gov.za/publications/P0302/P03022020.pdf.

Steenveld, Lynette, and Larry Strelitz. 1998. "The 1995 Rugby World Cup and the Politics of Nation-Building in South Africa." *Media, Culture & Society* 20 (4): 609–29. https://doi.org/10.1177/016344398020004006.

Steyn, Melissa E. 2001a. "Whiteness in the Rainbow: Experiencing the Loss of Privilege in the New South Africa." In *Beyond Racism: Race and Inequality in Brazil, South Africa, and the United States*, edited by Charles V. Hamilton, Lynn Huntley, Neville Alexander, Antonio Sérgio Alfredo Guimarães, and Wilmot James, 85–104. Boulder: Lynne Rienner Publishers.

———. 2001b. *Whiteness Just Isn't What It Used To Be: White Identity in a Changing South Africa*. Albany: State University of New York Press.

———. 2005. "'White Talk': White South Africans and the Management of Diasporic Whiteness." In *Postcolonial Whiteness: A Critical Reader on Race and Empire*, edited by Alfred J. Lopez, 119–36. Albany: State University of New York Press.

———. 2012. "The Ignorance Contract: Recollections of Apartheid Childhoods and the Construction of Epistemologies of Ignorance." *Identities* 19 (1): 8–25. https://doi.org/10.1080/1070289X.2012.672840.

Steyn, Melissa E., and Don Foster. 2008. "Repertoires for Talking White: Resistant Whiteness in Post-Apartheid South Africa." *Ethnic & Racial Studies* 31 (1): 25–51. https://doi.org/10.1080/01419870701538851.

Suzuki, Yuka. 2017. *The Nature of Whiteness: Race, Animals, and Nation in Zimbabwe*. Seattle: University of Washington Press.

Taylor, Dorceta E. 1997. "American Environmentalism: The Role of Race, Class and Gender in Shaping Activism 1820–1995." *Race, Gender & Class* 5 (1): 16–62.

Taylor, Paul C. 2004. "Silence and Sympathy: Dewey's Whiteness." In *What White Looks Like: African-American Philosophers on the Whiteness Question*, edited by George Yancy, 227–42. Abingdon: Psychology Press.

Teppo, Annika Björnsdotter. 2004. *The Making of a Good White: A Historical Ethnography of the Rehabilitation of Poor Whites in a Suburb of Cape Town*. Helsinki: Helsinki University Press.

TMG Digital. 2016. "Internet Turns on Activist Who Made Waitress Cry." *SowetanLIVE*, 30 April 2016. http://www.sowetanlive.co.za/news/2016/04/30/internet-turns-on-activist-who-made-waitress-cry?ref=yfp.

Tracey, Ciaran. 2019. "Kevin Pietersen: Beast Of Man." BBC Radio 5. https://www.bbc.co.uk/programmes/articles/8mb5BLnX0qMpTrPjQJ9zhP/the-people-saving-the-rhino.

Tromble, Rebekah. 2021. "Where Have All the Data Gone? A Critical Reflection on Academic Digital Research in the Post-API Age." *Social Media + Society* 7 (1): 2056305121988929. https://doi.org/10.1177/2056305121988929.

Tuck, Eve, and K Wayne Yang. 2012. "Decolonization Is Not a Metaphor." *Decolonization: Indigeneity, Education & Society* 1 (1): 1–40.

Turner, Lou. 1996. "On the Difference between the Hegelian and Fanonian Dialectic of Lordship and Bondage." In *Fanon: A Critical Reader*, edited by Lewis R. Gordon, T. Denean Sharpley-Whiting, and Renée T. White, 134–54. Oxford: Blackwell.

Twine, France Winddance, and Charles Gallagher. 2008. "The Future of Whiteness: A Map of the 'Third Wave.'" *Ethnic & Racial Studies* 31 (1): 4–24. https://doi.org/10.1080/01419870701538836.

Urry, John. 2004. "The 'System' of Automobility." *Theory, Culture & Society* 21 (4–5): 25–39. https://doi.org/10.1177/0263276404046059.

van der Merwe, Lawrence. 2015. "The Anti-Frackers: An Ethnographic Account of the South African Fracking Debate." Masters Thesis, University of Cape Town. https://open.uct.ac.za/handle/11427/20108.

van der Westhuizen, Christi. 2007. *White Power & the Rise and Fall of the National Party*. Cape Town: Zebra Press.———. 2016. "Afrikaners in Post-Apartheid South Africa: Inward Migration and Enclave Nationalism." *HTS Teologiese Studies / Theological Studies* 72 (4): 9. https://doi.org/10.4102/hts.v72i4.3351.———. 2018. *Sitting Pretty: White Afrikaans Women in Postapartheid South Africa*. Pietermaritzburg: University of KwaZulu-Natal Press.

van Es, Karin, Daniela van Geenen, and Thomas Boeschoten. 2014. "Mediating the Black Pete Discussion on Facebook: Slacktivism, Flaming Wars, and Deliberation." *First Monday* 19 (12). http://firstmonday.org/ojs/index.php/fm/article/view/5570.

van Wyk Smith, Malvern. 1990. *Grounds of Contest: A Survey of South African English Literature*. Johannesburg: Juta.

Varol, Ozan O. 2014. "Revolutionary Humor." *Southern California Interdisciplinary Law Journal* 23 (1): 555–94.

Vincent, Louise. 2008. "New Magic for New Times: Muti Murder in Democratic South Africa." *Tribes and Tribals Special* 2: 43–53.

Waal, Kees van der, and Steven Robins. 2011. "'De La Rey' and the Revival of 'Boer Heritage': Nostalgia in the Post-Apartheid Afrikaner Culture Industry." *Journal of Southern African Studies* 37 (4): 763–79. https://doi.org/10.1080/03057070.2011.617219.

Wainaina, Binyavanga. 2005. "How to Write About Africa." Literary. *Granta* (blog). 2005. https://granta.com/how-to-write-about-africa/.

Walker, Cherryl. 2008. *Landmarked: Land Claims and Land Restitution in South Africa*. Johannesburg: Jacana Media.

Wet, Phillip de. 2021. "Govt Just Published New Draft Rules on Fracking with 5km Exclusion Zones for Springs and Towns." News. Business Insider South Africa. 7 May 2021. https://www.businessinsider.co.za/fracking-water-draft-rules-for-south-africa-with-gasification-and-radioactives-disposal-2021-5.

Wiegman, Robyn. 1999. "Whiteness Studies and the Paradox of Particularity." *Boundary 2* 26 (3): 115–50.

Wilkinson, Kate. 2016. "Mail Online's Claim of 400,000+ Poor Whites in South Africa Incorrect." Fact Checking. Africa Check. 19 April 2016. https://africacheck.org/reports/mail-onlines-claim-of-400000-poor-whites-in-south-africa-incorrect/.

Williams, Apryl. 2020. "Black Memes Matter: #LivingWhileBlack With Becky and Karen." *Social Media + Society* 6 (4): 2056305120981047. https://doi.org/10.1177/2056305120981047.

Williams, Vivienne Linda, and Martin John Whiting. 2016. "A Picture of Health? Animal Use and the Faraday Traditional Medicine Market, South Africa." *Journal of Ethnopharmacology* 179 (February): 265–73. https://doi.org/10.1016/j.jep.2015.12.024.

Willoughby-Herard, Tiffany. 2007. "South Africa's Poor Whites and Whiteness Studies: Afrikaner Ethnicity, Scientific Racism, and White Misery." *New Political Science* 29 (4): 479–500. https://doi.org/10.1080/07393140701688339.

———. 2015. *Waste of a White Skin: The Carnegie Corporation and the Racial Logic of White Vulnerability*. Oakland: University of California Press.

World Wildlife Federation. 2014. "Novel Chi Campaign Launched in Viet Nam on World Rhino Day Aims to Reduce Demand for Rhino Horn." 14 September 2014. http://www.wwf.org.za/?12061/Chi-campaign-launch.

Wray, Matt. 2006. *Not Quite White: White Trash and the Boundaries of Whiteness*. Durham: Duke University Press.

Xaba, Wanelisa. 2016. "The Waitress That Qwabe Refused to Tip Highlights Her Privilege in Facebook Response." *The Daily Vox* (blog). 5 May 2016. http://www.thedailyvox.co.za/waitresstip-ntokozo-qwabe-ashleigh-schultz/.

Yunupingu, Galarrwuy. 1997. *Our Land Is Our Life: Land Rights: Past, Present and Future*. St. Lucia: University of Queensland Press.

Yuval-Davis, Nira. 2006. "Belonging and the Politics of Belonging." *Patterns of Prejudice* 40 (3): 197–214. https://doi.org/10.1080/00313220600769331.

Zevin, Alexander. 2019. *Liberalism at Large: The World According to the Economist*. London: Verso.

Zille, Helen. 2021. *#StayWoke: Go Broke: Why South Africa Won't Survive America's Culture Wars (and What You Can Do about It)*. Obsidian Worlds Publishing.

Zuboff, Shoshana. 2019. *The Age of Surveillance Capitalism: The Fight for a Human Future at the New Frontier of Power*. London: Profile Books.

Zuckerman, Gregory. 2014. *The Frackers: The Outrageous Inside Story of the New Billionaire Wildcatters*. London: Penguin.

Appendix A: Anti-Fracking Facebook Corpus

POST	DATE	REAC-TIONS	COM-MENTS	SHARES	PERMALINK
1	14-Feb-13	17	60	0	www.facebook.com/groups/chaseshelloutofthekaroo/permalink/529895247034044
2	25-Apr-13	63	16	0	www.facebook.com/groups/chaseshelloutofthekaroo/permalink/557150407641861
3	31-May-13	19	45	0	www.facebook.com/groups/chaseshelloutofthekaroo/permalink/571243229565912
4	04-Jun-13	102	38	236	www.facebook.com/groups/chaseshelloutofthekaroo/permalink/573209542702614
5	14-Jun-13	84	28	30	www.facebook.com/groups/chaseshelloutofthekaroo/permalink/577495442274024
6	17-Aug-13	37	19	62	www.facebook.com/groups/chaseshelloutofthekaroo/permalink/605947522762149
7	27-Aug-13	26	40	1	www.facebook.com/groups/chaseshelloutofthekaroo/permalink/610241345666100
8	23-Sep-13	36	8	21	www.facebook.com/groups/chaseshelloutofthekaroo/permalink/621939001163001
9	07-Oct-13	15	40	0	www.facebook.com/groups/chaseshelloutofthekaroo/permalink/628056623884572
10	10-Oct-13	6	51	0	www.facebook.com/groups/chaseshelloutofthekaroo/permalink/629704313719803

POST	DATE	REACTIONS	COMMENTS	SHARES	PERMALINK
11	13-Oct-13	5	72	0	www.facebook.com/groups/chaseshelloutofthekaroo/permalink/631174870239414
12	15-Oct-13	10	49	2	www.facebook.com/groups/chaseshelloutofthekaroo/permalink/632305696792998
13	16-Oct-13	20	2	34	www.facebook.com/groups/chaseshelloutofthekaroo/permalink/632981150058786
14	16-Oct-13	31	1	49	www.facebook.com/groups/chaseshelloutofthekaroo/permalink/633139803376254
15	26-Oct-13	69	53	197	www.facebook.com/groups/chaseshelloutofthekaroo/permalink/637712116252356
16	28-Oct-13	12	6	39	www.facebook.com/groups/chaseshelloutofthekaroo/permalink/639249252765309
17	29-Oct-13	41	59	4	www.facebook.com/groups/chaseshelloutofthekaroo/permalink/640025929354308
18	02-Nov-13	76	24	0	www.facebook.com/groups/chaseshelloutofthekaroo/permalink/641679492522285
19	03-Nov-13	0	67	0	www.facebook.com/groups/chaseshelloutofthekaroo/permalink/642271949129706
20	05-Nov-13	19	44	0	www.facebook.com/groups/chaseshelloutofthekaroo/permalink/643371222353112
21	19-Nov-13	30	45	0	www.facebook.com/groups/chaseshelloutofthekaroo/permalink/651307868226114
22	23-Nov-13	10	50	0	www.facebook.com/groups/chaseshelloutofthekaroo/permalink/653026061387628
23	02-Dec-13	32	28	0	www.facebook.com/groups/chaseshelloutofthekaroo/permalink/657881317568769
24	04-Dec-13	57	23	0	www.facebook.com/groups/chaseshelloutofthekaroo/permalink/658475837509317
25	05-Dec-13	63	8	120	www.facebook.com/groups/chaseshelloutofthekaroo/permalink/658884267468474

POST	DATE	REAC-TIONS	COM-MENTS	SHARES	PERMALINK
26	21-Jan-14	56	32	97	www.facebook.com/groups/chaseshelloutofthekaroo/permalink/682422265114674
27	14-Feb-14	97	52	131	www.facebook.com/groups/chaseshelloutofthekaroo/permalink/696852417004992
28	14-Mar-14	7	78	0	www.facebook.com/groups/chaseshelloutofthekaroo/permalink/711130345577199
29	10-Apr-14	34	16	82	www.facebook.com/groups/chaseshelloutofthekaroo/permalink/724361924254041
30	19-Apr-14	72	9	34	www.facebook.com/groups/chaseshelloutofthekaroo/permalink/728864233803810
31	28-Apr-14	37	12	79	www.facebook.com/groups/chaseshelloutofthekaroo/permalink/733572896666277
32	13-May-14	25	65	0	www.facebook.com/groups/chaseshelloutofthekaroo/permalink/741089285914638
33	15-May-14	85	33	0	www.facebook.com/groups/chaseshelloutofthekaroo/permalink/741808719176028
34	21-Jun-14	46	5	42	www.facebook.com/groups/chaseshelloutofthekaroo/permalink/762667813756785
35	10-Jul-14	98	5	0	www.facebook.com/groups/chaseshelloutofthekaroo/permalink/774250989265134
36	19-Aug-14	82	7	0	www.facebook.com/groups/chaseshelloutofthekaroo/permalink/794649360558630
37	20-Aug-14	75	18	0	www.facebook.com/groups/chaseshelloutofthekaroo/permalink/794954807194752
38	21-Sep-14	21	62	2	www.facebook.com/groups/chaseshelloutofthekaroo/permalink/810199482336951
39	12-Oct-14	8	106	0	www.facebook.com/groups/chaseshelloutofthekaroo/permalink/821269431229956
40	31-Oct-14	76	5	138	www.facebook.com/groups/chaseshelloutofthekaroo/permalink/830817620275137

POST	*DATE*	*REAC-TIONS*	*COM-MENTS*	*SHARES*	*PERMALINK*
41	31-Oct-14	175	19	310	www.facebook.com/groups/chaseshelloutofthekaroo/permalink/830819170274982
42	21-Nov-14	76	3	78	www.facebook.com/groups/chaseshelloutofthekaroo/permalink/842141002476132
43	25-Nov-14	75	32	0	www.facebook.com/groups/chaseshelloutofthekaroo/permalink/844318022258430
44	27-Nov-14	75	14	0	www.facebook.com/groups/chaseshelloutofthekaroo/permalink/845284342161798
45	01-Dec-14	81	69	58	www.facebook.com/groups/chaseshelloutofthekaroo/permalink/847353605288205
46	07-Dec-14	90	23	0	www.facebook.com/groups/chaseshelloutofthekaroo/permalink/850217381668494
47	15-Dec-14	83	16	0	www.facebook.com/groups/chaseshelloutofthekaroo/permalink/854866781203554
48	18-Dec-14	50	1	35	www.facebook.com/groups/chaseshelloutofthekaroo/permalink/856497734373792
49	25-Dec-14	68	42	0	www.facebook.com/groups/chaseshelloutofthekaroo/permalink/859655567391342
50	28-Dec-14	86	5	0	www.facebook.com/groups/chaseshelloutofthekaroo/permalink/861874313836134
51	10-Feb-15	167	55	0	www.facebook.com/groups/chaseshelloutofthekaroo/permalink/887348614622037
52	22-Feb-15	141	12	0	www.facebook.com/groups/chaseshelloutofthekaroo/permalink/893284244028474
53	28-Feb-15	164	33	0	www.facebook.com/groups/chaseshelloutofthekaroo/permalink/895813203775578
54	09-Mar-15	139	71	0	www.facebook.com/groups/chaseshelloutofthekaroo/permalink/900445026645729
55	15-Mar-15	220	66	0	www.facebook.com/groups/chaseshelloutofthekaroo/permalink/904028006287431

POST	DATE	REAC-TIONS	COM-MENTS	SHARES	PERMALINK
56	15-Mar-15	306	38	4	www.facebook.com/groups/chaseshelloutofthekaroo/permalink/904199672936931
57	17-Mar-15	101	47	0	www.facebook.com/groups/chaseshelloutofthekaroo/permalink/905500109473554
58	18-Mar-15	180	4	0	www.facebook.com/groups/chaseshelloutofthekaroo/permalink/905925262764372
59	22-Mar-15	189	6	0	www.facebook.com/groups/chaseshelloutofthekaroo/permalink/907800262576872
60	28-Mar-15	518	45	1	www.facebook.com/groups/chaseshelloutofthekaroo/permalink/910859202270978
61	08-Apr-15	64	107	33	www.facebook.com/groups/chaseshelloutofthekaroo/permalink/916644198359145
62	15-Apr-15	56	183	0	www.facebook.com/groups/chaseshelloutofthekaroo/permalink/920135754676656
63	22-Apr-15	110	16	36	www.facebook.com/groups/chaseshelloutofthekaroo/permalink/923490694341162
64	15-May-15	156	41	22	www.facebook.com/groups/chaseshelloutofthekaroo/permalink/934242613265970
65	20-May-15	57	89	0	www.facebook.com/groups/chaseshelloutofthekaroo/permalink/937097216313843
66	20-May-15	32	114	0	www.facebook.com/groups/chaseshelloutofthekaroo/permalink/937369772953254
67	19-Jun-15	169	12	0	www.facebook.com/groups/chaseshelloutofthekaroo/permalink/952612381428993
68	25-Jun-15	130	13	80	www.facebook.com/groups/chaseshelloutofthekaroo/permalink/955904094433155
69	25-Jun-15	96	52	0	www.facebook.com/groups/chaseshelloutofthekaroo/permalink/956143887742509
70	28-Jun-15	106	8	34	www.facebook.com/groups/chaseshelloutofthekaroo/permalink/957425417614356

POST	DATE	REAC-TIONS	COM-MENTS	SHARES	PERMALINK
71	17-Jul-15	100	2	44	www.facebook.com/groups/chaseshelloutofthekaroo/permalink/967791483244416
72	07-Aug-15	148	20	0	www.facebook.com/groups/chaseshelloutofthekaroo/permalink/980299551993609
73	27-Aug-15	163	19	0	www.facebook.com/groups/chaseshelloutofthekaroo/permalink/992535684103329
74	23-Sep-15	239	16	488	www.facebook.com/groups/chaseshelloutofthekaroo/permalink/1006779456012285
75	13-Oct-15	33	12	199	www.facebook.com/groups/chaseshelloutofthekaroo/permalink/1015139205176310
76	04-Jan-16	22	7	99	www.facebook.com/groups/chaseshelloutofthekaroo/permalink/1055093857847511
77	07-Jan-16	152	11	0	www.facebook.com/groups/chaseshelloutofthekaroo/permalink/1056373804386183
78	10-Jan-16	119	11	1	www.facebook.com/groups/chaseshelloutofthekaroo/permalink/1058165687540328
79	25-Jan-16	107	18	0	www.facebook.com/groups/chaseshelloutofthekaroo/permalink/1065716030118627
80	27-Jan-16	136	9	0	www.facebook.com/groups/chaseshelloutofthekaroo/permalink/1066475503376013
81	16-Feb-16	169	9	305	www.facebook.com/groups/chaseshelloutofthekaroo/permalink/1077248522298711
82	17-Feb-16	97	80	0	www.facebook.com/groups/chaseshelloutofthekaroo/permalink/1077936315563265
83	26-Feb-16	140	14	0	www.facebook.com/groups/chaseshelloutofthekaroo/permalink/1082960528394177
84	09-Mar-16	207	23	0	www.facebook.com/groups/chaseshelloutofthekaroo/permalink/1090012627688967

POST	DATE	REAC-TIONS	COM-MENTS	SHARES	PERMALINK
85	13-Mar-16	87	19	485	www.facebook.com/groups/chaseshelloutofthekaroo/permalink/1092624987427731
86	19-Mar-16	109	14	0	www.facebook.com/groups/chaseshelloutofthekaroo/permalink/1096685963688300
87	23-Mar-16	144	4	65	www.facebook.com/groups/chaseshelloutofthekaroo/permalink/1099867510036812
88	06-Apr-16	150	12	0	www.facebook.com/groups/chaseshelloutofthekaroo/permalink/1112357595454470
89	24-Apr-16	258	16	0	www.facebook.com/groups/chaseshelloutofthekaroo/permalink/1123112444378985
90	27-Apr-16	197	12	0	www.facebook.com/groups/chaseshelloutofthekaroo/permalink/1125595504130679
91	03-May-16	146	8	0	www.facebook.com/groups/chaseshelloutofthekaroo/permalink/1128751650481731
92	23-May-16	31	26	148	www.facebook.com/groups/chaseshelloutofthekaroo/permalink/1141184889238407
93	05-Jun-16	125	8	0	www.facebook.com/groups/chaseshelloutofthekaroo/permalink/1148785571811672
94	05-Jun-16	130	10	0	www.facebook.com/groups/chaseshelloutofthekaroo/permalink/1148789615144601
95	06-Jun-16	155	7	0	www.facebook.com/groups/chaseshelloutofthekaroo/permalink/1149587591731470
96	07-Jun-16	245	8	0	www.facebook.com/groups/chaseshelloutofthekaroo/permalink/1149823675041195
97	25-Jun-16	346	15	0	www.facebook.com/groups/chaseshelloutofthekaroo/permalink/1160753503948212

POST	DATE	REAC-TIONS	COM-MENTS	SHARES	PERMALINK
98	19-Jul-16	154	23	0	www.facebook.com/groups/chaseshelloutofthekaroo/permalink/1177732992250263
99	31-Oct-16	106	1	19	www.facebook.com/groups/chaseshelloutofthekaroo/permalink/1266269273396634
100	02-Nov-16	143	13	24	www.facebook.com/groups/chaseshelloutofthekaroo/permalink/1267970903226471

Appendix B: Poor White Video Clips

Video 1: Australian Broadcast Corporation (Journeyman Pictures). 2007. "Are Poor White South Africans Being Left Behind?": 00.15.44; broadcast date ~2007; uploaded 16 Aug 2007; retrieved from www.youtube.com/watch?v=pFj0HdW2iDs

Video 2: World Focus (Martin Seemungal). 2009. "Poor white South Africans blame reverse discrimination": 00.05.29; broadcast date ~2009; uploaded 26 Feb 2009; retrieved from www.youtube.com/watch?v=jj84Sw1x2po

Video 3: Vlaamse Radio-en Televisieomroeporganisatie (Journeyman Pictures). 2009. "South Africa—Poor Whites/Rich Blacks": 00.06.08; broadcast date ~2009; uploaded 30 Apr 2009; retrieved from www.youtube.com/watch?v=e5jJSjpztmA

Video 4: Solidariteit Helpende Hand. 2010. "White Poverty in SA": 00.04.43; broadcast date 2010; uploaded 05 May 2010; retrieved from www.youtube.com/watch?v=fEkEF0phqDA&t=4s

Video 5: Russia Today. 2012. "Falling Through Cracks: Anti-white discrimination on rise in South Africa": 00.09.13; broadcast date 3 Aug 2012; uploaded 03 Aug 2012; retrieved from www.youtube.com/watch?v=WMrPQJoxaFE

Video 6: South African Broadcasting Corporation. 2010. "Gebroke land": 00.03.38; broadcast date before 2010; uploaded 29 Jun 2010; retrieved from www.youtube.com/watch?v=W2ddJLKpioY

Video 7: Beeld TV. 2013. "Kroningspark: 'Dis maar oraait hierso.'": 00.01.27; broadcast date 2013; uploaded 10 May 2013; retrieved from www.youtube.com/watch?v=3V2ug2ihv7A

Video 8: British Broadcasting Corporation. 2013. "Do white people have a future in South Africa?": 00.06.22; broadcast date 2013; uploaded 20 May 2013; retrieved from http://www.bbc.com/news/magazine-22554709

Video 9: Saskia Vredenveld. 2013. "White Poverty (in the New South Africa)": 00.06.21; broadcast date 2013; uploaded 27 Jul 2013; retrieved from www.youtube.com/watch?v=oWWzAdb2wbU

Video 10: euronews. 2013. "'Reverse apartheid': South Africa's white slums": 00.01.23; broadcast date 2013; uploaded 08 Dec 2013; retrieved from www.youtube.com/watch?v=_C2R12Xqdde

Video 11: British Broadcasting Corporation (Reggie Yates). 2014. Extreme South Africa s01e01 "The White Slums": 00.56.55; broadcast date 2014; uploaded 20 Feb 2014; retrieved from www.dailymotion.com/video/x2vzujs

Video 12: eNews Channel Africa (ENCA). 2014. "Dis te gevaarlik in Munsieville" / "It's too dangerous in Munsieville": 00.02.36; broadcast date 2014; uploaded 08 Aug 2014; retrieved from www.youtube.com/watch?v=FJ1zxgoJLUs

Video 13: Krugersdorp News. 2014. "Krugersdorp se wit plakkers moet hervestig": 00.01.23; broadcast date 2014; uploaded 20 Aug 2014; retrieved from www.youtube.com/watch?v=64LFQmrcVMk

Video 14: eNews Channel Africa (ENCA). 2014. "Verskuiwing voortydig" / "We can't live like this": 00.02.28; broadcast date 2014; uploaded 12 Nov 2014; retrieved from www.youtube.com/watch?v=La8vndD7VKQ

Video 15: Associated Press. 2015. "SOUTH AFRICA: UNEMPLOYED & HOMELESS PROBLEMS": 00.02.39; broadcast date 1999; uploaded 21 Jul 2015; retrieved from www.youtube.com/watch?v=HTGH49j98Zg

Video 16: Associated Press. 2015. "SOUTH AFRICA: LOW COST HOUSING FOR WHITE FAMILY": 00.03.35; broadcast date ~1994–1999; uploaded 21 Jul 2015; retrieved from www.youtube.com/watch?v=kuaa1YyCsnE

Video 17: Mirror Mountain Media. 2015. "Coronation Park": 00.11.22; broadcast date 2014; uploaded 27 Aug 2015; retrieved from www.youtube.com/watch?v=plNClN-GC0k

Video 18: UnionMag.co.uk. 2016. SOUTH AFRICAN White Squatter Camps: 00.04.48; broadcast date 2016; uploaded 12 Feb 2016; retrieved from www.youtube.com/watch?time_continue=5&v=Yvv7sNPx5Ts

Video 19: Reuters/Daily Mail. 2016. The "white squatter camps" of South Africa: 00.01.49; broadcast date before 2016; uploaded 24 Feb 2016; retrieved from http://www.dailymail.co.uk/news/article-3462336/The-white-squatter-camps-South-Africa-home-hundreds-families-enduring-terrible-poverty-blame-fall-Apartheid.html

Video 20: South African Broadcasting Corporation (Special Assignment). 2016. "25% Of White South Africans Are Now Living In Poverty": 00.22.53; broadcast date March 2006; uploaded 18 May 2016; retrieved from www.youtube.com/watch?v=y7q4p2bpBCo

Video 21: Saskia Vredenveld. 2017. "White Poverty in South Africa (trailer)": 00.01.41; broadcast date 2013; uploaded 27 Feb 2017; retrieved from www.youtube.com/watch?v=L3lfd5gsbh8

Video 22: ITV (Trevor McDonald). 2018. "Trevor McDonald: Return to South Africa—White Poverty After the Apartheid": 00.04.30; broadcast date 21 Jun 2018; uploaded 21 Jun 2018; retrieved from www.youtube.com/watch?v=YM4BE14pAgo&t=2s

Table: Numbers of views per video in 2018 and in 2021

Views 2018	*Views 2021*	*Growth*	*Video*
1,471,790	1,600,354	9%	1
520,970	1,798,276	246%	2
985,055	1,378,142	40%	3
2,354	2,616	11%	4
n/a	*56,993*	*n/a*	*5*
2,949	4,362	48%	6
6,076	9,590	58%	7
No count	*No count*	*No count*	*8*
95,552	221,312	132%	9
193,790	746,587	285%	10
No count	*No count*	*No count*	*11*
4,967	8,454	70%	12
1,448	12,475	762%	13
677	3,728	451%	14
2,032	15,430	659%	15
1,591	9,591	503%	16
5,668	33,072	483%	17
113,693	518,379	356%	18
No count	*No count*	*No count*	*19*
224,747	690,674	207%	20
3,215	44,377	1280%	21
n/a	*767,468*	*n/a*	*22*

Index

Note: Page references for figures are italicized; numbers containing n indicate notes.

About the Author

Scott Burnett is a discourse analyst focused on the intersections between race, gender, sexuality, and the social construction of space/place. He researches whiteness in the South African context, and masculinist and far-right movements in online toxic technocultures. He is currently a tenure-track assistant professor in communications in the department of applied information technology at the University of Gothenburg in Sweden.

www.ingramcontent.com/pod-product-compliance
Ingram Content Group UK Ltd.
Pitfield, Milton Keynes, MK11 3LW, UK
UKHW041838031026
15587UKWH00002B/846

9 781793 654946